Code Ahead

by Yegor Bugayenko

Volume 1

Copyright © 2017-2020 by Yegor Bugayenko

All rights reserved. No part of the contents of this book may be reproduced or transmitted in any form or by any means without the written permission of the publisher.

Printed and bound in the United States of America.

Version: 1.2
Git hash: 25ed1c3
Date: September 9, 2020
Words: 69381
Vocabulary: 8278

ISBN: 978-1982063740
Place: Palo Alto, California, USA
Size: 235 pages
Recommended price: $40,96
Web: http://www.yegor256.com/code-ahead.html

✉ book@yegor256.com 🐦 in ⌘ ⊙ f yegor256

Published by CreateSpace, an Amazon company.

"Most software today is very much like an Egyptian pyramid with millions of bricks piled on top of each other, with no structural integrity, but just done by brute force and thousands of slaves."[1]

Alan Kay
A Conversation with Alan Kay
ACM Queue, Volume 2, Issue 9, December 2004

---

[1] I'm not sure this is how Egyptian pyramids were actually built though.

Contents

Acknowledgements 9

Preface 11

How to Read It 13

Chapter 1: Adrian 15

Carriers and non-carriers 16

Deceitful formalities – How soon can you start? – Wrap everything up in one week – Coding for them or for myself? – I am not really lazy – Interview the interviewer – Three things I pay attention to – The more they pay, the better – Too small and too big are no good – Politics – Division of labor – Desor's rats experiment – Theft is not a sin – Equity theory – Look like a carrier, be paid like a non-carrier

The second interview 24

Impress and think vs. steal and dominate – Why Chris is here? – When are you going to hire me? – Quality is critical, but it's not Tony's fault – I'm selling myself high – Am I going to abandon my open source projects? – Responsibility – Loyalty – Agile – Dictators vs Managers – The more love they expect, the weaker they are – My biggest career mistakes – How I was fired for publishing my CV – True professionals are never loyal – The fake story about me being arrogant – Pocket mistakes for job interviews – Respect vs. management – My questions – My poker with Tony for the place in the hierarchy

Open source 38

$140,000 a year – Report and control – Obey the boss – Fear us, despise the enemy – Discipline – Fear of discipline – Pollock for $140 million – I'm too weak to steal, that's why I work – Open source is a new territory – How I started to open my code

Morning stand-ups 49

The usual round in a standing circle – Why do I waste my time? – Guilt – Empathy and exclusion anxiety – Survival instinct – Parents and teachers – Mother figure – Greed

Task tracking chaos 56

Silicon Valley – Political correctness – Inverse bullying – The more loyal they look, the easier they betray – Positive thinking – My first coding task – Does being hired by Facebook make one a good developer? – Bao is bullying me – Where are the requirements? – Experts don't need transparency – Experts vs. order – The flow of information must be obvious – I just need another scapegoat – I suggest task tracking formalities – Does Agile mean chaos?

Chapter 2: Dennis   69

Automated testing   70

What are unit tests for? – TDD – Merging the garbage – Branching – Code reviews – Merging script – Test coverage – Safety net

Rewards and punishments   78

Nobody writes unit tests – Quality must be enforced in order to happen – The business doesn't need quality – We must do what the business says – How can they punish us? – $100 for each ticket closed – Don't judge people, judge their results – Punishment without a logic – How to punish a kid right

Vague requirements and laziness   86

Who is guilty? – Lesson learned – She doesn't know what she wants – Punishment hurts when the scope is vague – Definition of Done – It's our responsibility – Product owners are always vague – A programmer is just a tool – Time machine example – Refining the requirements – Prototyping – We must kill weak ideas – Profit

Egoism and altruism   92

Be lazy, don't waste time – Transactional and transformational leadership – Equity theory – Egoists – Altruists – Balance – Why are altruists worse than egoists? – Loving wife example – Fail fast – Fail Safe – We must encourage egoism – "One can only lean on what resists" – Decomposition of complexity – "You have to become an egoist" – Rewards and punishment – Carrots and sticks – People are "fickle, hypocritical, and greedy of gain" – $20 per closed ticket – "It is not for us" – To fix the system, we have to fix its people – Surrender

Conflicts   103

The situation manages us, not the other way around – RESTful API conflict – Conflicts are progress catalysts – Conflict resolution techniques – Win-lose – Lose-lose – Win-win – Compromises are evil – Are there any conflict resolution procedures? – Technical leader – Lack of the architect role – Responsibility and authority – Democratic voting – Hierarchical team decision making – Discipline is stressful – Effective architect

Manual testing   110

Testing, testing, and testing – How many bugs do you find per week? – What is the goal of testing? – No bugs philosophy – Test scripts –

Testers must prove that the software is broken – Testing is a sadistic process – Failed vs passed – A test is successful when the product is broken – xUnit frameworks – Quality Assurance doesn't mean testing – ISO 9001 – Fake job titles – Testers and coders are equally important – The gate keeper misconception – Unlimited amount of bugs – Testing is not discrete – Inverted motivation – Testing and coding as parallel processes – Testing deliverables – Does testing have deliverables? – We need bugs! – We may pay for the bugs – Focus on bugs only – Testing metrics – Priorities

Equality and slavery   126

Two bosses – "Just lie, it's not so difficult" – The finger – The slavery paradigm – Modern instruments of enslavement – Doing the right thing – Do the right thing – "Always be helpful" lie – Stop working for the boss, work for yourself – Different roles vs. emotional equality – Guilt is the modern stick – Don't let them fire you, keep it under control – Greed – Inner motivation – Overtime – The project is your boss – Who do you work for? – Coercion is all they know – Methods of punishment – Innate desire to have a master – Forget the managers

Software architect   134

Logic and plans vs emotions and power – Management by force – Meritocracy – Employees are robots – Manageable data – Who is a project manager? – PMBOK and Rita's book – Management is important – Strawberries – Golf, Bentley, and prostate exams – Sadness of life – Fool the system! – Modern slaves – The architect configures the product – Configuring a product – The rules – A strong architect is always hated – Quality wall – Constantly working with the rules – Quality rules examples – We have no architect – Hysterical architects – A movie director allegory – Technical dictator – Making enemies – Meetings and white boards – Firing the architect

Losers and winners   147

Money is the fuel, not the goal – Why is life miserable? – Winner's gene – "The world is mine" – "Me and you are losers" – Billionaires are normal people – You already lost when you were born – Talent and intelligence vs. success – Re-distribute all money in the world – Fairness vs. profitability – Money is not the goal, power is – Ethics – "He who keeps his words doesn't deserve to be a king"

Hackers and designers   153

Modern education is flawed – Algorithms vs. people – The era of hackers – Cheap computers vs. expensive programmers – Open source dominates – The population of programmers is growing – Programming is easier – Remote work – Salaries are skyrocketing – Maintainability is king – Working code vs. software product – Software ecosystem – The era of designers – Job security – Replaceability is a merit – We should code ahead

Chapter 3: Tony   161

Performance metrics   162

Comfort vs. metrics – Paychecks as metrics – Coarse grained metrics – Lines of code – Agile – Rules of the game – Can we work only through tickets? – Racing horses – Rationality is scary – Emotions are attractive – "Our work is not that discrete" – Clarity, transparency and discipline – Story points as a local currency – Cryptocurrency

Experts and knowledge sharing   173

The "How does Google do it?" argument – Structure first, fun next – Stress and distress – Responsibility – Guilt – Partial refunds – Business knowledge – Business rules – Documentation – Remote work – People vs. documents – Tickets – Bus factor – Subject matter experts

Static analysis   183

Code formatting – Underwear metaphor – Good programmers – Force – We are greedy, selfish, and lazy – XY Theory – German shepherds allegory – A software is just a small piece of a software product – FindBugs – Auto-formatting – Educational aspect – Industry-adopted style guide – The stricter, the better – Pre-flight builder – Can we start in an existing project? – Speed of delivery is the most important metric – Boxing metaphor – Motivational conflict

Speed and quality   194

Humiliation of being a tester – Testing is more important than coding – Whose fault was it? – Bug-free code is a flawed objective – Delivery pipeline – Sieve – Weak testing – Product quality is not the concern of programmers – Speed first – Quality first – The truth in the middle

Delivery pipeline   202

Blame is counter effective – Fear – Eustress and distress – Depression – Individualism – Feature branches – $20 for a merged branch – Money doesn't motivate – Money does motivate – The best motivator is clear rules of the game – ABC players – Git flow and release branch – Unlimited number of bugs – Test to break – Down merging – Stabilizing the product – Abandoned branches – Obstacles – Acceptable vs. perfect quality

Epilogue   219

Index   221

Acknowledgements

MANY thanks to these kind people, who reviewed the book and helped me make it better and cleaner (in alphabetic order): Timur Ametov, Anton Babenko, Anaël Chardan, Benjamin Cisneros, Pavel Drankov, Filipe Freire, Guseyn Ismayylov, Jithin John, Vahid Keykhaey, Erik J. Larson, Valera Mironov, Martin Morlog, Enrique Pablo Molinari, John Page, Pablo Da Costa Porto, Silas Reinagel, Ivan Scherbak, SB Swae, Ziyavuddin Vakhobov, Sergii Zhuk, Evgeny Zislis, Vytautas Žurauskas.

Want to see your name in this list in the next edition? Just send your thoughts to `book@yegor256.com`. I reply to all emails.

And, of course, thanks to Andreea Mironiuc for the mushroom on the cover.

Preface

SOFTWARE development is not a code-writing discipline anymore. It's not about algorithms, formulas, bytes, files, or protocols. It's not about instructions, operators, unit tests, user interfaces, or deployment scripts. It's not about performance, scalability, resilience, or robustness. Even though all those ingredients are important, they are not what make one programmer more effective than another or one software team more successful than its competitors. It is something else that plays the crucial role in the modern world of software and hardware: It's not computers, it's people.

The success of a software project depends on people, who are very often lazy, ignorant, selfish, frustrated, and simply unhappy. It depends on people who very often don't know how to communicate, how to share knowledge, how to manage and lead, how to obey and follow. It depends on our ability to form teams, stay in them, and contribute to their activities. It depends on our social skills much more than on technical ones.

In the following few hundred pages you will stay together with a small group of programmers, architects, and managers who are paid to write software. They will face problems, go through conflicts, and discuss the philosophy of team work. I hope that their dialogues and monologues will help you understand the importance of the social aspect of software development and become a better engineer or a manager.

How to Read It

First of all, this is a work of fiction. It has a plot, a protagonist, a few characters, and dialogues between them. I decided to choose this format mostly because the thoughts and ideas described in this book were born while working on real software projects and it seemed to be the most effective way to capture them: as a story.

Second, the book has many footnotes and references to other sources, both academic and professional. I tried to take and print the relevant quotes from most of the sources in order to illustrate the story of the book. I recommend that you read all footnotes—they are part of the story, not supplementary material.

Third, some footnotes are marked with the ★ sign—those are the materials that I suggest you read entirely, they are my favorite. Some of them are marked with 👎 signs—those I completely disagree with and mention them only to demonstrate how wrong some opinions can be.

Fourth, each section consists of a few semantic blocks with a few paragraphs in each of them. Each block has one side note, which relates exactly what I wanted to say by telling you the story. | You can read just the side notes similar to this one and the gist of the book will be clear.

Finally, pay attention: This book is *not* for managers, executives, testers, or just people who love to read. This is a technical book, with many very specific terms and concepts, which you can only understand if you are a software developer. This book is for programmers, who, like myself, write code for a living.

Chapter 1

Adrian

Being a programmer is fun. Being a software developer is pain. Computers are logical while people are not. Unfortunately, in the modern software industry, they don't pay for programming. They pay for software development, which means getting things done in teams, together with others. Teams consist of irrational people, not Java classes and methods. I'm going to get a job in one of those teams and survive there. I can write Java, but this won't be enough to be successful. There will be other skills required. Some of them I still have to develop.

Carriers and non-carriers

Deceitful formalities (16) – How soon can you start? (17) – Wrap everything up in one week (17) – Coding for them or for myself? (18) – I am not really lazy (18) – Interview the interviewer (18) – Three things I pay attention to (19) – The more they pay, the better (19) – Too small and too big are no good (20) – Politics (20) – Division of labor (21) – Desor's rats experiment (21) – Theft is not a sin (22) – Equity theory (22) – Look like a carrier, be paid like a non-carrier (23)

I say to the receptionist, "I have a meeting with Chris, he is expecting me." One day, I will have my own receptionist, and my own office, and my own programmers, and my own startup with investors and a big mission to accomplish. I will be famous and successful. Until that day comes, I need to pay my rent. These guys seem rich enough to treat me for the next few months or so, and they seemed to like my resume. Now I have to convince them that I'm dreaming about staying with them for the rest of my life.

> Since any software architecture is the product of people, to improve it, one, first of all, has to improve the architect.

"She, actually," says the receptionist, coldly. Chris shows up in a minute. We go to the meeting room, she offers coffee, I ask for a glass of water, she leaves, I automatically pull out my phone and check Facebook. She comes back with a glass and a dude in a dark t-shirt with the GitHub logo. I feel better. She says how excited she is and leaves. The dude's name is Adrian and he is a developer here. We start talking. He seems to be senior enough, according to his questions. I seem to be doing good. He is definitely behind me, technology-wise, so there is almost nothing to worry about.

"We need someone to fix our architecture," he summarizes in half an hour.

"You guys need someone to fix yourselves before you can do something with the architecture," I say to myself. "I'd be glad to help," I say out loud. "Your project seems very interesting, both technology- and business-wise. I don't really like to work in boring projects, no matter how much they pay. I usually fall in love with the product I work on and I want to fall in love with something interesting and cutting edge." Adrian seems to be very calm and melancholic; he just smiles back. Or maybe he is used to hearing this from every second person sitting in this room?

He asks a tricky question: "When are you available? How long will it take for you to finish your current projects? We are looking for a full-time person." He seems to be very proud of saying that; they think that being with them full time is going to be a privilege for me. I have already realized that I will have to sit in this office from nine 'til five if I want those paychecks in my mailbox. Until I have my own startup, that seems to be the way it is. This is already the third company this week that is telling me that. The previous two haven't given me their answers yet, even though they also seemed to like me. This dude looks much more desperate. I suspect that his servers are going down every second night and it's going to become my problem right after I sign the contract. I have to be careful.

"Probably a week will be enough to wrap everything up." I say what I have to say, even though I have no project, no employment, and no income at the moment. I can't tell him the truth. That's how this game has to be played. I must

> When loyalty is promised in one place it is betrayed in another, by the same person.

look very busy and demanded. On the other hand, how does a week to wrap everything up sound logical? What kind of project am I working on right now that I can leave in just a week? Obviously we both understand that it's a lie, but there is nothing we can really do about it.

"How long have you been with this company?" I ask him just to change the subject. "Two years,"Adrian says. My next question is; "Are you the creator of all this?"

"Yes, I was the first developer here. I met Tony two years ago, our co-founder and CTO. You will meet him for another interview." I see how much he respects that guy. Of course, the man with the check book. "Would love to meet him!" I say the usual and we wrap it up.

CHRIS emails me three hours later. Tony wants to see me tomorrow morning and says that Adrian told him good things about me. They seem interested. The other two companies are not saying anything, so I might end up working for Tony. I don't even know the salary yet, but that Craigslist ad said that it's "competitive."

What I really don't like to imagine is me working for someone. I'm fine with being in their office, with pretending that I'm interested, with laughing at Tony's jokes, and asking Adrian how his two kids are doing. But I don't want to code for them or, even worse, become responsible for their technical failures. And this is what they will try to do: to place as much as possible onto my shoulders.

> "How much can an employer provide?" is the right question a professional employee asks oneself.

I'm not really lazy. I love to code, but doing it for someone who is going to become a millionaire because of that—no, thanks. I value my life much more than the rent they will pay for. To be honest, I think that this exact attitude of mine was the real cause of the troubles I had in the previous office and a few offices before. They all wanted me to be a good employee and I just wanted to do what I love to do: making my own ideas real by writing Java code. I've been fired four times already and I'm just twenty nine. Not really an impressive career so far. Am I doing something wrong?

I've heard many times people saying that when an employer interviews you, you have to interview the employer too.[1] It seems right to me, but not because we have to be picky with the companies we join—they are all the same in the beginning, just different names, markets, and budgets. We have to "interview them back" in order to demonstrate that we are very interested in them specifically. It's very similar to dating:[2] you have to ask

---

[1] Paul Powers, *Winning job interviews*, Career Press, 2005: "Obviously, they are interviewing you, but, in reality, you are also interviewing them."; "Even if the interviewer doesn't ask you if you have questions, I want you to have some good ones prepared so that you can try to ask them."

[2] Steve Harvey, *Act Like a Lady, Think Like a Man*, Amistad, 2014: "When a man approaches you, he has a plan. And the main plan is to sleep with you, or to find out what it takes to sleep with you."

questions and pretend that you're interested in her soul, not only in her body.

Initially each new company, team, or project is a mystery. No matter how many questions you ask about their DevOps processes, management principles, and static analysis—all of that could either be a lie, their fantasies, or simply something that doesn't work the way they present it. I never really listen to what they say at the initial interviews. What I pay attention to is 1) the money they are ready to pay, 2) their size, and 3) the position they will place me into.

THE money question is obvious: the more they pay, the better. It's not only because I'm greedy and prefer a Mercedes-Benz over a Chevrolet, but mostly because more money means projects that are more valuable and interesting. Look at it from the marketing perspective: if they can afford to pay more than others, they found that money somewhere. Maybe they managed to invite big investors—this means that venture capital believes in their ideas; maybe they are generating a decent revenue already—this means that their clients are already appreciating them more than their competitors; or maybe their founder just inherited a few millions and invested them into this new crazy startup—this means that instead of generating pure fun in Vegas their dollars are heating up the market through the business I'm invited to.

In any of these cases, the money is the indicator of the importance the market is putting into this particular business. More money, in most cases, means that the project at this very moment is more important for the market than others. When the project you're working with starts running out of money, it's time to quit and move to another one that is more important to the market. This may sound disloyal, but it's only fair if you really care about people you're working for—your customers—not the bosses that cut paychecks for you every few weeks.

> The salary is the primary explicit indicator of the importance of your contribution to the market.

Picking a project that pays less and "looks more interesting" would be unfair and not logical. It's not up to the programmers to decide how interesting and valuable it is. The market, represented by paying clients or venture capitalists, has to make that decision. And they are making it every minute, delivering it to us via our salaries. When the salary goes up, the market is happy with what we're doing for it. When the salary goes down it's time to question ourselves: why are we still doing that for the market if the market doesn't appreciate it anymore?

THE second thing that is important for me is the size of the company: too small and too big are no good. When the team is too small, technical people wear too many hats, like writing code, configuring servers, preparing presentations for investors, moving furniture, and fixing the coffee machine. This may sound like fun, but career-wise it's degrading and a huge risk of wasting time. I will have to do too many things that are not really relevant to my professional profile, helping the team to survive. And the chances of survival are very low among small teams,[1] statistically speaking.[2] I prefer to stay away from projects with less than twenty technical people inside.

> Big companies are too political, small ones are too chaotic.

On the other hand, all huge companies have a problem of a different sort: politics. People don't work there, they fight against each other.[3] I will either survive there at the lowest level of the corporate hierarchy, wearing a "senior developer" title and getting a new mug once a year as a birthday present, or will become a

---

[1] Carmine Giardino et al., *Why early-stage software startups fail: a behavioral framework*, International Conference of Software Business, 2014: "More than 90% of startups fail, due primarily to self-destruction rather than competition."

[2] Erin Griffith, *On Message, Off Target*, Fortune, July 2017: "Cambridge Associates, a global investment firm based in Boston, tracked the performance of venture investments in 27,259 startups between 1990 and 2010. Its research reveals that the real percentage of venture-backed startups that fail has not risen above 60% since 2001. Even amid the dotcom bust of 2000, the failure rate topped out at 79%."

[3] ★Jo Owen, *Management Stripped Bare: What They Don't Teach You at Business School*, 3rd edition, Kogan Page, 2012.

master of covert fights in one particular group of morons. Neither option is attractive enough for me. Thus, if a company is bigger than a thousand people, I tend not to join.

THE third factor I pay attention to is the position they are offering me. And I don't mean the title, but the actual position in the hierarchy. All companies are built as hierarchies, no matter what that holacracy adepts are saying now.[1] It's always a boss on the top and then people who report to him down to the lowest level. Staying on the lowest level is what I always try to avoid. Not only because I have some dignity, but mostly because I am lazy. The lower you are in the hierarchy, the more work you have to do and the less money you get for it. This is how the division of labor works, not only in the software industry.[2]

Ergo, the lower the position and the more technical it is, the bigger the trouble will be: I will have to work for somebody instead of for myself. This is what I'm loathe to do. I have no problems in working hard, when I know that the result is mine. In software teams with a fat management layer, lower levels generate value that is consumed by the higher levels. What's the point of staying at the lower level?

Have you ever heard about the experiment Didier Desor with colleagues recently performed at the University of Nancy?[3] They put a few rats into a cage with no food inside. To get food, those poor rats had to get out of their cages through a small hole, swim

---

[1] Jaclyne Badal, *Can a Company Be Run as a Democracy?*, Wall Street Journal, April 2007: "Ternary runs itself as a democracy, and every decision must be unanimous."; "Ternary leaders, who adopted the system in reaction to experiences of corporate infighting at another small company where they met, insist that it works."

[2] Thomas Piketty, *Capital in the Twenty-First Century* Harvard University Press, 2014: "The higher one climbs in the income hierarchy, the more spectacular the raises. Even if the number of individuals benefiting from such salary increases is fairly limited, they are nevertheless quite visible, and this visibility naturally raises the question of what justifies such high levels of compensation."

[3] Didier Desor et al., *Potential Stock Differences in the Social Behavior of Rats in a Situation of Restricted Access to Food*, Behavior Genetics, Volume 25, Number 5, 1995.

to the food distributor through the aquarium, take some food and swim back in order to eat it, since it was not possible to eat right from the distributor. There were ten similar cages with five or six male rats in each cage. By the end of experiment, in all cages rats divided half-and-half into two groups: carriers and non-carriers. Carriers were swimming for food and non-carriers were stealing from them.

What does this story tell us? It is that you either work or steal and this is what nature expects of you. Rats were not aware of the Ten Commandments. They had no idea that stealing was a sin,[1] they were just stealing. It seems that nature has nothing against thievery—it is just its natural distribution of roles. Likewise, for some of us, working is the preferred activity. For others, theft is more customary.

> The higher you are in the hierarchy, the less you need to deliver and the more results of others are attributed to you.

Of course, we are not rats and our behavior is way more complicated, but the principle is the same: we either work or we take work products from others. Management hierarchies were invented in order to discipline this process and avoid constant fights like those rats had in their cages. We don't fight with our managers anymore, we just give them the value we produce,[2] believing in equity.[3] They, of course, also produce something, but the amount of value they

---

[1] *Exodus*, 20:15: "You shall not steal." The Ten Commandments, according to the book of Exodus in the Torah and in the Bible, are laws for life given by God to Moses on Mount Sinai to give to the People of Israel.

[2] Emile Durkheim, *The Division of Labor in Society*, 1893: "The division of labor is, then, a result of the struggle for existence, but it is a mellowed denouement. Thanks to it, opponents are not obliged to fight to a finish, but can exist one beside the other."

[3] J. Stacy Adams, *Toward an Understanding of Inequity*, The Journal of Abnormal and Social Psychology, Volume 67, 1963.

generate is obviously smaller while the wages are higher.[1]

Having this in mind, the most comfortable position for me in this modern system of "carriers and non-carriers" is to look like a carrier but be paid like a non-carrier. In other words, I like to look like a hard-working software engineer, while in reality doing almost nothing.[2]

The vast majority of software teams I've seen aren't really capable of forcing programmers to contribute at full speed. The management, especially at its highest levels, doesn't really understand the difference between Java and JavaScript. On the other hand, at the lower the level, it is more difficult to fool a manager by pretending to be writing code while actually writing a new Facebook post. That's why the higher my position, the better. Nobody will understand what I am actually doing and I can do what I want. I do contribute to the projects I am being paid for, but I prefer to do that when I feel like it and when it is really necessary. Not when it is 9am.

---

[1] Dennis L. Gilbert, *The American Class Structure in an Age of Growing Inequality*, 8th Edition, Pine Forge Press, 2011: "From 1980 to 2000, the real earnings of CEOs rose by over 600%—a remarkable increase in an era of stagnant wages. The gulf separating the typical CEO from the typical American worker has grown to colossal proportions The average CEO of a major corporation earned a stupendous 475 times the wage of an average blue-collar worker in 1999, up from roughly 42 times in 1980."

[2] Corinne Maier, *Bonjour Laziness: Why Hard Work Doesn't Pay*, Vintage, 2006: "In the biggest companies, seek out the most useless positions: those in consultancy, appraisal, research, and study. The more useless your position, the less possible it will be to assess your 'contribution to the firm's assets.' Avoid operational ('on-site') positions like the plague. The goal is to aim for something 'on the sideline': the kind of 'interdepartmental' positions that are of no consequence whatsoever and are subject to no corporate pressure. In short, keep out of sight."

The second interview

Impress and think vs. steal and dominate (24) – Why Chris is here? (24) – When are you going to hire me? (25) – Quality is critical, but it's not Tony's fault (26) – I'm selling myself high (27) – Am I going to abandon my open source projects? (28) – Responsibility (28) – Loyalty (30) – Agile (31) – Dictators vs Managers (32) – The more love they expect, the weaker they are (33) – My biggest career mistakes (33) – How I was fired for publishing my CV (33) – True professionals are never loyal (34) – The fake story about me being arrogant (35) – Pocket mistakes for job interviews (35) – Respect vs. management (36) – My questions (36) – My poker with Tony for the place in the hierarchy (36)

THE office looks nice, in a minimalist style. The pop art painting on the wall has the words "impress" and "think" on it. The rest is just abstract rectangles. Maybe I should be an artist instead? I'm sure can draw something similar. I can even put more words there, like "steal" and "dominate," but not as many people would want to buy it for their offices, I guess. Tony shows up. He is tall, in a black shirt and jeans, over forty, with a beard. No surprise, he smiles. I doubt he even knows who I am. Where is that Adrian, I wonder?

"Adrian has called in sick today, sorry about that," Tony says, and we walk through the corridor to one of their meeting rooms. The usual "coffee or tea" and I ask for a glass of water. He leaves and returns back in a minute with a glass.

Chris shows up—the woman I met before. Most probably, she is their HR director, which means they are not too small. I still can't see the size of the office. And I don't even know what they are working with. I probably should've done some research to prepare. I never do that and most likely offend my potential employers—they all want to see how interested we are in them. The truth is that I'm not, but it's not polite to act like that. I feel sorry, but it's too late: Tony and Chris are in front of me and I put my phone screen down on the table and smile.

> Very often, decision makers and influencers are not the ones with the official badges or the best skills.

And why the hell Chris is here? She wasn't with us when I was speaking with Adrian. I guess, it's for two reasons. First, Tony is her boss and she wants to show him how hard she is working to find new talent. Second, she will have some say in the final hiring decision. Thus, I have to impress her too?

Actually, this second interview will be much more important than the first one. Even though Adrian was the person who was capable of understanding my professional strengths and weaknesses, these people, knowing almost nothing about software development, are going to decide. And I'm sure that their decision will be based purely on emotions. That's what I have to be prepared for—to impress them and to help them fall in love with me.

"How was the interview with Adrian?" Chris starts.

This may look like an innocent question, but it's tricky. If I just say "It was great," they won't fall in love, because it will look like I'm not willing to share my feelings, either because I don't have any or because I feel something negative. Just "great" is not the right answer in this situation. Actually, in all situations being formally polite is not what attracts people.

On the other hand, telling them too much about how I really feel about that interview is risky, because I don't feel anything except, "when are you going to hire me?" And I don't find Adrian technically savvier than me, which is also something that they don't need to know.

I have to give them something in the middle. Something like, "It was interesting, especially this and that, but this and that puzzled me." That will demonstrate that I really remember what the interview was about, that I thought | Flattery is the most powerful instrument when dealing with the weak and stupid.

about it and their company for a few days, that there are some questions in my head that I want to find answers for, that I'm someone who is going to be committed and dedicated. I hate those words, but they work in this situation.

I go forward with this: "I actually enjoyed it, which almost never happens to me. Most interviews are boring and all about the candidate. However, with Adrian we talked like two fellow programmers, both about me and your project. What I didn't understand, though, is what your long-term plan is, software-wise?" I simply put the ball back into their corner. Everybody likes to talk about themselves and C-level people like Tony are all about plans and strategies. That's all they do—talk about long-term visions and missions. I'm sure he will be happy to tell me more about himself and the team.

"Well, that's a good point, let me explain how we see it," Tony swallows the bait and starts talking. Chris, I'm sure, has heard that story many times, but she looks extremely interested. Well, that's her boss and she has to work hard to prove that she is loyal, right?

WHILE Tony is explaining their global vision, I'm trying to prepare myself for the next question. The best defense is offense, so the best way for me to avoid questions is to start asking them. "So, you believe that quality is important for you now?" I interrupt him right after he mentioned how many innovations they made recently in the area of continuous delivery.

"It always was, but now it's absolutely critical. The user base is growing and we can't afford to jeopardize our reputation when servers are not responding."

> Quality and responsibility mean nothing unless they are attributed personally.

"Does that happen too often?" I pretend to be worried for their servers and their poor clients. Tony seems not to understand that the servers that are not responding are his personal fault, as a CTO. He should have been fired already. Interesting, how much those CTOs enjoy talking about quality and its importance, not understanding that the quality first of all means personal responsibility for its absence. For them this "quality comes first" is just a marketing slogan.

"Well, not really, but still we need higher quality." Obviously, he is lying. That's how most technically clueless CTOs behave. They are afraid to lose their warm seats and have to do two things at the same time: demand higher quality and be careful not to blame themselves for not having it. They can't say, "Our server farm is very unstable, it's my fault," because the next question the CEO or the board will ask is, "Why are we paying you half a million dollars a year, then?" And there will be no reasonable answer. On the other hand, they have to say something about us being responsible for the quality. Who "we" are, they prefer not to specify.

"It's great you understand the importance! It's very unusual to see a C-level executive so tech savvy!" I can't believe I'm saying that. However, it works. Tony is flattered and is ready to speak about quality for another half an hour. However, it seems that Chris understands what I'm doing.

"Can you tell us about your experience?" she interrupts him. That's an easy question, because they don't understand a thing in what I'm working with. I start telling them about the products I've been using, the frameworks, the tools, and the languages. They look very interested, keep nodding, but I know that it doesn't make any sense to them. It's time to impress them a bit. C-level guys, like Tony, love numbers and big splashy things they can remember. They want to feel proud because of hiring "good" people.[1] They must feel that they caught a big fish. That's what their job is all about: finding people on the market and then making them work, what else?

I give them a few open source products of mine. They are rather popular on GitHub. I tell them that I created that stuff in my free time and that the amount of my followers is growing. They look impressed. I'm sure they don't hear that very often in this room. Most programmers sitting in this chair are telling them stories about some dead startups they have spent their years at, calling out some names of some long-ago-fired CTOs they were reporting to. It's all boring and not impressive at all. I've got

---

[1] See footnote 3 on page 131: "So great job performance by itself is insufficient and may not even be necessary for getting and holding positions of power. You need to be noticed, influence the dimensions used to measure your accomplishments, and mostly make sure you are effective at managing those in power—which requires the ability to enhance the ego of those above you."

open source stuff, which is on the market right now. I'm known in the programming community and Tony understands that.

Chris again: "Are you planning to keep working on that open source library?" This is a tricky question. They obviously don't want me to spend time on anything aside from their business. They don't understand that I'm valuable to them mostly because I work in open source. They want to find somebody who is professional and put him on a chain. It's simply impossible. Just like girls prefer guys who other girls are interested in, but then they want to marry that playboy and be sure he stops seeing any other women. They don't understand that it's either impossible or will turn that attractive dude into a pet they can't love anymore. A paradox, right?

> Independence turns us into professionals, but is not appreciated when we join teams.

I'm a professional because I'm free, because I develop something on my own, because I'm on the market, trying new things every day. They understand that a programmer like that will definitely bring fresh air into their team. But they don't like the freedom to continue. They expect me to stop doing everything I was doing before and marry them forever. I can't do that. But I can't say that either. A very similar paradox, right?

I have to lie. "Well, it's just maintenance now, a few hours during my weekends. I simply can't abandon my products, but I obviously want to dedicate all of my time now to a more serious project." I called their project more serious and they feel proud. That's the answer they wanted to hear, I'm sure. Of course, it's not just maintenance. Of course, my own projects are way more important for me than their business. Of course, I won't spend just a few hours during weekends. But I haven't met a single business owner yet or an executive on a payroll who would feel comfortable with my honest answer: "My projects are way more important, so get used to it." Do they exist?

THE root of the problem here is that they can't manage us

engineers properly.[1] They can't control what we're doing and how many results we are producing simply because they are way behind in technology and absolute amateurs in management.[2] The only thing they can do is check whether we're in the office with guilt, also referred to as accountability,[3] on our shoulders. They don't really know[4] how to properly plan a project, how to assign tasks, how to validate that we actually deliver something valuable, how to make sure the quality of deliverables is acceptable, and many other things professional management has to do.[5]

---

[1] Tsuneo Furuyama, *Fault generation model and mental stress effect analysis*, Journal of Systems and Software, Volume 26, Issue 1, 1994: "71% of all faults are the responsibility of the project manager, the quality assurance manager, and senior management."

[2] Richard Barker, *The Big Idea: No, Management Is Not a Profession*, Harvard Business Review, Volume 88, Number 7, 2010: "Management is not a profession at all and can never be one."

[3] Jonathan Rasmusson, *The Agile Samurai: How Agile Masters Deliver Great Software (Pragmatic Programmers)*, Pragmatic Bookshelf, 2010: "A good agile team will always want to be held accountable for the results they produce. They know customers are counting on them to come through, and they won't shirk from the responsibility that comes with having to deliver value from day one."

[4] Robert N. Charette, *Why software fails*, IEEE Spectrum, Volume 42, Number 9, 2005: "Bad decisions by project managers are probably the single greatest cause of software failures today. Poor technical management, by contrast, can lead to technical errors, but those can generally be isolated and fixed."

[5] Capers Jones, *Software Project Management Practices: Failure Versus Success*, CrossTalk: The Journal of Defense Software Engineering, Volume 17, Number 10, 2004: "When comparing large projects that successfully achieved their cost and schedule estimates against those that ran late, were over budget, or were cancelled without completion, six common problems were observed: poor project planning, poor cost estimating, poor measurements, poor milestone tracking, poor change control, and poor quality control. By contrast, successful software projects tended to be better than average in all six of these areas. Perhaps the most interesting aspect of these six problem areas is that all are associated with project management rather than with technical personnel."

Instead, they popularize the myth[1] that software development is a very creative process[2] and cowardly rely on our desire to be "good"[3] and "do the right thing."[4]

They promote the philosophy that management processes are less important than the "greatness"[5] of people. They expect those mythical "great" programmers to be loyal, fully committed

---

[1] Gary H. Anthes et al., *Lessons From India Inc.*, ComputerWorld, April 2001: "There is this myth that software development is a creative effort that relies heavily on individual effort. It is not. It is just very labor-intensive, mechanical work once the initial project definition and specification stage is past."

[2] Craig Larman, *Agile and Iterative Development: A Manager's Guide*, Addison Wesley, 2003: "Most software is not a predictable or mass manufacturing problem. Software development is new product development. Since predictable manufacturing is the wrong paradigm for software, practices and values rooted in it are not helpful."

[3] 👎Alistair Cockburn et al., *Agile Software Development: The People Factor*, IEEE Computer, Volume 34, Number 11, 2001: "If the people on the project are good enough, they can use almost any process and accomplish their assignment. If they are not good enough, no process will repair their inadequacy—'people trump process' is one way to say this."

[4] 👎Jim Highsmith, *Agile Software Development Ecosystems*, Addison Wesley, 2002: "We accept that talented people, who are internally motivated, who must work in a volatile environment, who understand the product vision, will do the best they can do."

[5] 👎Mike Cohn, *Agile Estimating and Planning*, Prentice Hall, 2005: "Agile teams value individuals and interactions over processes and tools because they know that a well-functioning team of great individuals with mediocre tools will always outperform a dysfunctional team of mediocre individuals with great tools and processes."

to corporate values,[1] responsible, heroic,[2] solid thinking,[3] and simply ready to work under incompetent management[4] or without any at all.[5]

Instead, it is not loyalty or internal motivation that drives us programmers forward. We must write our code when the road to our personal success is absolutely clear for us and writing high quality code obviously helps us move forward on this road. To make this happen, the management has

> A weak management incapable of organizing the project right can only rely on people's heroism.

---

[1] See footnote 1 on page 128: "In effect, corporate culture programmes are designed to deny or frustrate the development of conditions in which critical reflection is fostered. They commend the homogenization of norms and values within organizations. Employees are selected and promoted on the basis of their (perceived) acceptance of, or receptivity to, the core values. More generally, employees are repeatedly urged and rewarded for suspending attachments to ideas and mores that do not confirm and reinforce the authority of the core values."

[2] Bach, James, *Enough about process: what we need are heroes*, IEEE Software, Volume 12, Number 2, 1995: "... the approach might be called the 'cowboy' or 'big magic' model. In this view, gifted people create software through apparently magical means, with no particular guidance or support. This approach also centers on heroes, but pathologically so. It doesn't do much to grow or nurture them. Rather, it tends to wear them out."

[3] Langdon Morris, *Agile innovation: the revolutionary approach to accelerate success, inspire engagement, and ignite creativity*, Wiley, 2014: "Although processes and tools can provide guidance and support for competent people to work effectively, nothing is more important than solid thinking and meaningful collaboration when it comes to creating something new."

[4] Alistair Cockburn, *Agile Software Development: The Cooperative Game*, 2nd Edition, Addison-Wesley Professional, 2006: "A well-functioning team of adequate people will complete a project almost regardless of the process or technology they are asked to use."

[5] Lyssa Adkins, *Coaching Agile Teams: A companion for ScrumMasters, agile coaches, and project managers in transition*, Addison-Wesley, 2010: "Here's how it works: You don't trust the team, so you tell them what to do. They do what you said, not really what they thought they should do. The results are not what you wanted, so you tell them what to do again, this time more explicitly. And the cycle continues. In this cycle, everyone loses trust."

to define the rules of the game, also known as "process,"[1] and make sure they are strictly enforced, which is much more difficult than "being agile."

I would compare a project with a country, which is either properly regulated by the laws or enslaved by a dictator whom everybody is supposed to love. What modern management is doing in most companies is the latter scenario. They expect us to love the customer and work just because of that. There are no laws, no discipline, no regulations, and no principles, because, like every dictator, they simply are not competent enough in creating them. Dictators just capture the power and rule by the force:[2] it's much easier than building a system of laws, which will work by itself.[3] The management in software projects also can't create a proper management system, since they simply don't have enough knowledge for that. Instead, they expect our love. Isn't it obvious

---

[1] See footnote 2 on page 121: "The word 'process' is viewed as a four-letter word by some people in the software development community. These people see 'software processes' as rigid, restrictive, and inefficient. They think that the best way to run a project is to hire the best people you can, give them all the resources they ask for, and turn them loose to let them do what they're best at. According to this view, projects that run without any attention to process can run extremely efficiently."; "Projects that don't pay attention to establishing effective processes early on are forced to slap them together later, when slapping them together takes more time and does less good."; "When a project has paid too little early attention to the processes it will use, by the end of a project developers feel that they are spending all of their time sitting in meetings and correcting defects and little or no time extending the software. They know the project is thrashing."

[2] David C. McClelland, *Power Is the Great Motivator*, Harvard Business Review, January 2013: "Power without discipline is often directed toward the manager's personal aggrandizement, not toward the benefit of the institution."

[3] Barrington Moore, Jr., *Social Origins of Dictatorship and Democracy: Lord and Peasant in the Making of the Modern World*, Penguin, 1966: "The author sees the development of a democracy as a long and certainly incomplete struggle to do three closely related things: 1) to check arbitrary rulers, 2) to replace arbitrary rules with just and rational ones, and 3) to obtain a share for the underlying population in the making of rules. The beheading of kings has been the most dramatic and by no means the least important aspect of the first feature. Efforts to establish the rule of law, the power of the legislature, and later to use the state as an engine for social welfare are familiar and famous aspects of the other two."

that rather soon that love turns into hate and we quit or the project collapses?

LET me see how much love these guys expect from me. Usually, according to my experience, the more they expect the weaker their management is. Which would be a good thing: they won't manage me, I will fake love, and they will pay me.

"Great, that's what we wanted to hear," Chris looks happy. If I am a match for them, it's her success first of all. She posted that Craigslist ad and I emailed her first. She doesn't want me to be a failure, especially after the first interview with Adrian. So, she is definitely on my side.

"We do understand the importance of the open source," Tony sounds very affirmative, even though, I'm sure, he never wrote a single line of open source code. Most likely he wrote some Pascal in the college and then just turned his career to management and money making. Now he "understands the open source." What can I say?

"Cool, this is also very unusual to meet a CTO who believes in open source!" I will keep flattering this guy. He seems to like what I'm saying. And Chris is on my side. I'm doing fine.

"Can you tell us about the biggest mistake you made in your career?" she asks and smiles. She most probably got this question from one of those "Top 100 questions to ask at job interviews" books. Well, I have to play ball and give them something. Of course, I won't tell them about last year's deployment scripts mis-configuration which exposed our test database credentials to production and a few thousand users lost their accounts for a few hours, while we were fixing the issue and re-deploying. We were lucky to find out the bug just forty minutes after the deployment. And it was totally my fault, since I created the scripts.

| Honesty in business is nothing else but a lack of qualification.

I also won't tell them the story when I was fired because my direct manager found my resume on a job site. It was hilarious, I still remember that day. I showed up in the office and he said, "We need to talk." You know that moment, right? You always feel the

33

smell of that last "talk." So did I. He said, "Dude, we found your resume on a job site and feel like you are not being loyal to us. We decided to let you go." What could I say? I was embarrassed. Not because I posted it there—every professional engineer must do that—but because I didn't make the C.V. anonymous enough.

SERIOUSLY, truly professional programmers absolutely must be on the market permanently, even when they are employed. Especially when employed. We must always be open to new opportunities, in order to stay in shape, to be able to compare options, to understand the market, and be better than others. We must see those others, we must go to job interviews, see what others have to offer and understand how good we are for them. If they stop calling us or stop offering jobs—it's a signal that something is wrong and we must improve.

Without that information we quickly become very limited to one office environment, one project, one technology stack, one team, and one boss. Of course, we will be effective in that closed territory, but eventually and very soon our effectiveness will start to decrease and we begin to degrade.

| A demonstrated ability to learn from mistakes is the most attractive trait of a team candidate. | Most employers don't understand that, just like they don't understand the importance of open source for us.[1] They act like those girls who get attracted to playboys and then lock them |

in the house, prohibiting any contact with other women. What do those playboys turn into? Boring husbands with a beer, on the sofa, in front of the TV. Without open source and without the market we can't be professionals.

---

[1] Alexander Hars et al., *Working for free? Motivations of participating in open source projects*, Proceedings of the 34th Annual Hawaii International Conference on System Sciences, IEEE, 2001: "Motivations for participating in open-source projects proved to be more complex than expected. While internal factors, such as intrinsic motivation, altruism, and identification with a community, played an important role, so did external factors, such as direct compensation and anticipated return. Factors that promised future monetary rewards, such as building human capital and self-marketing, were also more significant than expected."

We must be visible and constantly challenged.

I won't tell them those stories. Instead, I will tell them something else they will definitely like to hear. "Well, it happened two years ago, when I just joined my previous project. There was one guy who I didn't really like. It was just something personal, you know how it happens. He was really stubborn with everything I was suggesting, and we just didn't get along, even though he was in my team. I wasn't his boss, but I was the architect and had to direct him technically. It was almost impossible and I even asked the CTO to fire the guy. I wasted so much energy and emotions on regular fights with him. What happened later was a big surprise. A few of us stayed in the office later, we had a new release coming out. And that guy started to tell us about his own open source framework he was working with. I became interested and started to ask more and more. In a few weeks we became friends. He started to respect me after I respected him. That's the lesson I learned: don't tell people what to do until you know them enough and you earned their respect. Not treating that dude with enough respect was one of my biggest mistake in my professional career. Still feel bad about that. And we are still friends."

I see that Chris is ready to start crying. Tony is smiling. They are both idiots. Actually, the story is very close to being real, something like that really happened. And I do believe that the power you earn out of respect is way stronger than the power you get through your title. No, they are not idiots. It was a good story.

I always have something like that prepared for the job interviews. They all seem to be interested in our "mistakes" and every mistake always has to have a happy ending where the main guy, which is myself, learns something. The employer wants to see how we learn our lessons—this means that we are teachable and manageable. Nobody likes to work with stubborn people. Almost nobody knows how to work with them, to be precise. But those people are the best.

This story demonstrated my readiness to understand my mistakes, learn from them, and bring my knowledge to their company. Now Tony is sure that I won't have problems with his programmers: I will respect them. Will I really do that? Well, let's first see who they are.

> Management by respect is an attractive illusion most teams and bosses love to hear.

"You are right, we also prefer to respect our team instead of directing them," Chris summarizes with a quick smile. She looks very serious, like I'm a kid just learned something new and she is a teacher, happy to see that. "Do you have any questions for us?" Tony asks, expecting the answer, "Yes, of course!"

Now it's my turn. I want to know what I want to know: the money, the size, the position. "May I ask how many tech people are on the team?" I start with the most innocent one, to warm it up.

"Over fifty and we're growing. By the end of the year, we are planning to have eighty," Tony looks proud of those numbers. Indeed, fifty programmers in California means an annual payroll budget close to ten million. That's the number he will put in his resume when it will be his turn to find a new job. Or maybe he is the owner of this shop? I will find out later. He definitely looks like a loaded guy.

"How important will my position be on the team, in terms of possible contribution?" I ask this and I'm proud of myself. This is the right way to put the question without exposing my strong desire to be the main guy and do nothing. The question sounds like I'm very interested to contribute as much as possible and that's why I need a higher position.

"Well, we need your help in the back-end part of our product. We thought about a Senior Developer position. What do you think?" He looks at me. He wants to hire me. Now is the right moment to use it. I don't like the "Senior Developer" title at all. It means writing code eight hours per day. It sucks. I have to get a special status right from the beginning. It will be much more difficult to obtain it afterwards. And Tony is my guy. He's got a very powerful position and this is the moment he can promise me something I will use later.

"Adrian is the head of the back-end group?" I bet carefully.

"Yes, we planned to place you in his group," Tony calls my bet.

"I will report to him?" I bet again.

"Yes ..." Tony is prepared to raise, but calls in a second. "And to me, of course!"

> Aim for sound job titles, which usually mean vague responsibilities and more autonomy.

That's what I wanted. He is afraid of losing me. Through my question about Adrian he immediately understood that I don't like this idea. I don't want to report to Adrian, because this makes my position way lower and doesn't allow me to work directly with Tony. That's why he added that "to me", to put me at least on the same level as Adrian.

"Would be great to work with other groups too. I feel that I can contribute elsewhere, especially with DevOps. I can report to you and work next to Adrian, for example. What do you think?" I'm going "all-in."

Tony looks at Chris. Chris looks at Tony. "Let us think about all this and we'll get back to you," Tony folds. I'm sure he will accept that. And that will mean that I will be in a very privileged position, next to Adrian, without any personal responsibility for anyone. Something like an architect. Maybe even my title will be "Software Architect." They stand up and shake my hand. I go home. Did I do alright?

Open source

$140,000 a year (38) – Report and control (38) – Obey the boss (39) – Fear us, despise the enemy (41) – Discipline (41) – Fear of discipline (41) – Pollock for $140 million (42) – I'm too weak to steal, that's why I work (43) – Open source is a new territory (45) – How I started to open my code (47)

THE next day, as expected, I get an email from Chris. She says that I'm a great catch for them and they are a great opportunity for me. They are ready to pay $140,000 a year and also cover my medical insurance. It's a decent salary in Silicon Valley.[1] Let's do the math: $47,524 will be taken by the government as income tax, $42,000 I'm paying for my studio in Mountain View, $10,800 every year for my car loan. Hence, my pocket cash every month will be around $3,250. A hundred dollars a day. Not bad, but very far from being a millionaire.

> It's not the control that hurts, but the inability to apply it correctly.

Also the email says that my position will be "Software Architect" and I will report to Adrian and Tony. They seem to not understand that it's not possible to report to two people at the same time. It's only good—they are not expecting me to report at all. And I won't.

I've seen that situation many times, when people don't really understand the word "reporting" or simply don't want to understand it. They think that asking someone to report to them would look like an offense, like a demonstration of power, like control.[2]

---

[1] Tekla S. Perry, *Where Are the U.S. Firms That Pay the Best Salaries? Silicon Valley (Mostly)*, IEEE Spectrum, April 2017: "Google, based in Mountain View, at number 6 with a median total compensation of $155,250. Facebook, based in Menlo Park, at number 7 with a median total compensation of $155,000. Twitter, based in San Francisco, at number 22 with a median total compensation of $142,000."

[2] Mike Myatt, *The Most Misunderstood Aspect Of Great Leadership*, Forbes, December 2012: "Control restricts potential, limits initiative, and inhibits talent. Surrender fosters collaboration, encourages innovation and enables possibility. Controlling leaders create bottlenecks rather than increase throughput. They signal a lack of trust and confidence, and often come across as insensitive if not arrogant."

And they are right in many cases. Most of us employees are very sensitive to the word "control," believing that we are free and must not be controlled by anyone. We don't understand that the abusive component of management, which we are so much afraid of, comes not from those who want to control, but from those who don't know how to do it.

Any group of people needs a hierarchy of authority. It doesn't matter if the group is writing code or climbing a mountain.[1] The work of the group has to be coordinated in order to be effective and productive. No matter how smart the members of the group are, how much they love each other, and how many times they've done that work before, they need[2] instructions and accountability, distributed hierarchically. Someone on the top has to say what needs to be done and everybody else has to obey.[3] Of course, that someone on the top has to be smart and give clever instructions. Moreover, in order to be even more effective and productive, the leader has to collect enough information from the group members

---

[1]Laura Van Berkel, *Hierarchy, Dominance, and Deliberation: Egalitarian Values Require Mental Effort*, Personality and Social Psychology Bulletin, Volume 41(9), 2015: "We suggest there is an initial tendency to endorse hierarchy—it is easier, quicker, and more deeply ingrained. Egalitariansim is learned at an older age and is socially valued, but egalitarian values exist in the context of these older hierarchy values."; "People are well tuned to dominance and deference; they are central to social life."

[2]Emily Zitek, *The fluency of social hierarchy: the ease with which hierarchical relationships are seen, remembered, learned, and liked*, Journal of Personality and Social Psychology, Volume 102(1), 2012: "Social hierarchies are fluent social stimuli; that is, they are processed more easily and therefore liked better than less hierarchical stimuli."; "When social relationships are difficult to learn, people's preference for hierarchy increases."

[3]Christopher Boehm, *Hierarchy in the Forest: The Evolution of Egalitarian Behavior*, Harvard University Press, 2001: "If a stable egalitarian hierarchy is to be achieved, the basic flow of power in society must be reversed definitively ... it takes considerable effort to maintain that condition. Our political nature favors the formation of orthodox hierarchies—hierarchies like those of chimpanzees or gorillas, or humans living in chiefdoms or states."

before giving any instructions. But that's secondary.[1] The primary success factor of the group coordination is that everybody obeys and does what the boss says—also known as discipline. That's how all armies were organized[2] since the ancient times of Timur and Alexander. Isn't that how they won their battles?[3]

THE paradox of modern management is that we still want to win our battles, but don't want to hear words like "control," "obey," or "report." We believe that management will just happen somehow by itself, just because everybody is a good person doing "the right thing." This may be partially true, but, like in an army, even though loyalty and honesty of soldiers are appreciated, their accurate following of the orders given by their commanders is way more important. It's crucial.

| Clear rules of subordination lead to discipline, which leads to order, which leads to success. | When I hear my bosses saying that they are against control and want me to report to everybody and to no-one, I immediately realize that I will be managing my boss, not the other way around. Again, the army analogy will work here. |

If an officer is not smart and strong enough to structure his unit in such a way that every single soldier knows who to report to, the soldiers will manage the officer. They will create chaos, which will help them to do less, get more, and follow no orders. Eventually, the unit will lose the battle, the soldiers will be captured and the officer will be executed. Wouldn't

---

[1]Patrick Bolton et al., *Leadership, Coordination and Mission-Driven Management*, The Review of Economic Studies, Volume 80, Issue 2, 2013: "We argue that a key attribute of a good leader is a form of overconfidence, which we shall refer to as resoluteness. A resolute leader has a strong prior and is slow to change his mind in the face of new information about the environment in which the organization operates."

[2]★Sun Tzu, *The Art of War*, 5th century BC: "If a general shows confidence in his men but always insists on his orders being obeyed, the gain will be mutual."

[3]Flavius Vegetius Renatus, *De Re Militari*, 390 A.D.: "The ancients, taught by experience, preferred discipline to numbers. The excellence of their discipline made their small armies sufficient to encounter all their enemies with success."

he deserve that?

As Wei Liao Zi said in 200 B.C.:[1]

"If they fear us they will despise the enemy; if they fear the enemy they will despise us." This literally means that in a properly-organized military unit, soldiers are so afraid of violating the rules that the danger of the enemy is nothing comparing to that. And it's not because their officers are so violent and cruel, eager to punish and abuse. Not at all. It's because their commanders understand that the survival of the unit and the entire army depends on the discipline they can enforce. The more discipline and order, the higher the chances of survival.

Discipline means, first of all, clear and explicit subordination. I, as a soldier, must always know exactly who is my officer, who I report to and who can punish me if I'm doing something wrong. If I don't know that, I despise the officer, the team, the company, and the investors. Wouldn't it only be fair if I treat them like just yet another cash cow?

CHRIS is saying that I will report to Adrian and Tony at the same time. What do they expect me to think of them after that? I can only despise them like those ancient soldiers in the army of the Chinese emperor despised their commander.

They are afraid of telling Adrian that I will report to Tony, because Adrian will be offended, and I understand this. He was interviewing me and was expecting to be my boss. Now they are going to tell him that the situation has changed.

> Freedom and discipline must not contradict each other, but they usually do.

They don't even know how to explain that to him. Why, all of a sudden, is this new guy going to be next to him instead of beneath? They can't say that this is what the guy wants in order to join us. The next move Adrian can make is to blackmail them with some similar idea. For example, he may say that he wants to get a higher position just because he feels like it and they will be in a very tough spot—it will be very difficult to refuse if they

---

[1] ★Shawn Conner et al., *Military Strategy Classics of Ancient China*, Special Edition Books, 2013, p. 222.

just recently accepted my demand.

On the other hand, they are afraid of telling me that I will report to Adrian only, simply because they don't want to lose me. They don't have enough arguments to explain to me why it's not possible. For example, they don't have a clear written hierarchy of roles and responsibilities, where it would be obvious that my position is here and the area of influence for me will be exactly this one. They can't show me such a map. They don't know how to manage me, how to define my obligations and responsibilities, how to specify the limits of my authority.

That's why they say: "You will report to Adrian and Tony." They just told me that, "You are free to do whatever you want, there will be no boss above you." Am I happy? Yes, I am.

AFTER waiting a day, just to look serious, I accepted the offer, we signed the contract and agreed that I will start on Monday. Today is Monday. Adrian is not here. Well, it's just 9am and he is the boss of the group. Of course, he will show up later. One of the biggest perks you earn when you get promoted to a management position is the ability to be in the office closer to lunch.

> It is only natural that the majority works hard and makes less than the minority in charge.

I go around the office to see who is who. It's still almost empty, just a few people here and there. They look relaxed. The office is newly remodeled and some abstract paintings are on the walls. I recently found out that one of the most expensive paintings in the world was made by Jackson Pollock in his unique style of "drip painting." The name of the painting is *No. 5, 1948* and it was sold in 2006 for $140,000,000.[1] What is really interesting is that Pollock himself sold it in 1949 for just $1,500 and died in a car accident seven years later, when he was 44. You should see the painting to understand what I'm

---

[1] Carol Vogel, *A Pollock Is Sold, Possibly for a Record Price*, The New York Times, November 2006: "The Hollywood entertainment magnate David Geffen has sold a classic drip painting by Jackson Pollock for about $140 million."; "The art-world experts identified the buyer as David Martinez, the Mexican financier who bought a two-floor apartment in the south building of the Time Warner Center for $54.7 million recently."

talking about.

Doesn't this story prove my earlier point that there are carriers in this world and non-carriers? There are those who do the work (painting) and those who steal (reselling).[1] And the amount they steal is way bigger than the money working people are getting. Is it unfair? I don't know. It seems that nature itself invented that.

We, as animals, are designed to dominate and steal, if we can. If we are strong enough, we do it. On the other hand, to prevent us from being animals and constantly fighting for goods,[2] morality was invented.[3] We are taught that theft is something God Himself doesn't want us to do; it looks like the entire Universe is against thievery.[4] However, and maybe unfortunately, it's not

---

[1] Karl Marx and Friedrich Engels, *Manifesto of the Communist Party*, 1848: "Society as a whole is more and more splitting up into two great hostile camps, into two great classes directly facing each other—Bourgeoisie and Proletariat... In ancient Rome we have patricians, knights, plebeians, slaves; in the Middle Ages, feudal lords, vassals, guild-masters, journeymen, apprentices, serfs; in almost all of these classes, again, subordinate gradations."

[2] Travis Hirschi, *Causes of Delinquency*, University of California Press, 1969: "We are all animals, and thus all naturally capable of committing criminal act... the chicken stealing corn from his neighbor knows nothing of the moral law; he does not want to violate rules; he wants merely to eat corn... No motivation to deviance is required to explain his acts. So, too, no special motivation to crime within the human animal... is required to explain his criminal act."

[3] As attributed to Friedrich Nietzsche, but I couldn't find the actual source: "Morality is just a fiction used by the herd of inferior human beings to hold back the few superior men."

[4] Bernard Gert, *Morality: Its Nature and Justification*, Oxford University Press, 2005: "Since moral judgments can be made about all rational persons, it follows that morality is universal and that what seem to be different moral systems are simply specifications or variations of a universal morality or moral system."

true.[1,2] The Universe and God, if He exists, are totally in favor of it—that's how they designed this planet and us.

I'm not buying paintings for $1,500 and selling them for $140 million for one simple reason: I'm too weak for that. That's why my job is to write Java code, sitting in this office, making a hundred bucks a day. Well, to be honest, this position is many levels above those millions of people in the world who are barely making a hundred bucks a month.[3] Unlike rats, we are not divided half-and-half to carriers and thieves, but only a few percent of us are thieves, while the majority consists of carriers.[4] It seems that rats, which split fifty-fifty, are way more humane and ethical than us, aren't they?

ANYWAY, I find the most comfortable desk, which is empty and positioned the right way, meaning that I will be sitting with my back to the wall, so that nobody can see my screen. That's how it should be and it's very important—nobody should see my screen, ever. Let's call it privacy. It actually has nothing to do with privacy, it's solely about control. I don't want anyone to spy on me and then have a leverage against me in the organization; and

---

[1] George Edward Moore, *Principia Ethica*, Cambridge University Press, 1922: "When, Ethics presumes to assert that certain ways of acting are 'duties' it presumes to assert that to act in those ways will always produce the greatest possible sum of good. If we are told that to 'do no murder' is a duty, we are told that the action, whatever it may be, which is called murder, will under no circumstances cause so much good to exist in the Universe as its avoidance."

[2] Richard Joyce, *The Evolution of Morality*, The MIT Press, 2006: "We are interested in the hypothesis that human morality is the product of natural selection, not in the extravagantly implausible hypothesis that any morality must be the product of natural selection."

[3] The World Bank, *Poverty Overview*, October 2016: "According to the most recent estimates, in 2013, 10.7 percent of the world's population lived on less than US$1.90 a day... Half of the extreme poor live in Sub-Saharan Africa... A vast majority of the global poor live in rural areas and are poorly educated, mostly employed in the agricultural sector, and over half are under 18 years of age."

[4] Jill Treanor, *Half of world's wealth now in hands of 1% of population*, The Guardian, October 2015: "This is the latest evidence that extreme inequality is out of control. Are we really happy to live in a world where the top 1% own half the wealth and the poorest half own just 1%?"

I'm going to do a lot of things in this office, which have nothing to do with what they will pay me for. I will work with my open source projects and I will continue to work with my own startup. Am I allowed to? Is it ethical? What would those rats say?

Now I check my email and then look at a new pull request in my open source framework. Having a popular open source project is a lot of fun, but at the same time—a lot of stress. You can find many articles from open source maintainers, where they complain and explain.[1] No matter what they say[2] and what I feel now, being an open source maintainer, I truly believe that this is something every serious software developer must do—have their own open source project(s).

Twenty years ago, when I was a kid, the world didn't really know what open source was, since the majority of software was being created privately and for specific hardware.[3] Also, there was almost no Internet, and almost no tools with which to share the code.[4] Currently, the situation is totally different.[5] Take any commercial software product from the market, be it a mobile app, or a web site, and analyze its code. The majority of it would be coming from its dependencies—libraries and frameworks—while

---

[1] Nolan Lawson, *What it feels like to be an open-source maintainer*, https://goo.gl/6D7BAs: "You're reluctant to create new projects, because you know it will just increase your maintenance burden. In fact, there's a perverse effect where, the more successful you are, the more you get 'punished' with GitHub notifications."

[2] Karl Fogel, *Producing Open Source Software: How to Run a Successful Free Software Project*, O'Reilly Media, 2006: "Most free software projects fail."

[3] Joel West, *How open is open enough?: Melding proprietary and open source platform strategies*, Research Policy, Volume 32, Issue 7, 2003: "Computer platforms provide an integrated architecture of hardware and software standards as a basis for developing complementary assets. The most successful platforms were owned by proprietary sponsors that controlled platform evolution and appropriated associated rewards."

[4] Christopher Tozzi, *For Fun and Profit: A History of the Free and Open Source Software Revolution (History of Computing)*, The MIT Press, 2017.

[5] Jan Sandred, *Managing Open Source Projects: A Wiley Tech Brief*, Wiley Computer Publishing, 2001: "When you scrape the surface, open source software is everywhere. To me it is clear: All future networked information applications will be based on open source technology."

only a small portion would be written by its authors.[1]

We live in the world of software reuse. The amount of code companies are creating to achieve their business goals is increasing, while the percentage of proprietary code in it is decreasing.[2] What does it mean for us, programmers? One thing—we need to know what open source is and how to work with it.[3] We can't say anymore that, "My company is paying me to write code for their business, that's why I'm not touching open source." This statement sounds less and less logical, since it's impossible now to create any piece of software without taking something from the Internet for free.

Open source is not something you learn and understand in a few days. It's a wild territory with its own rules, principles, habits, and best practices. It's a landscape[4] full of risks, enemies,[5]

---

[1] William B. Frakes et al., *Software Reuse Research: Status and Future*, IEEE Transactions on Software Engineering, Volume 31, Number 7, 2005: "Most software systems are not new. Rather they are variants of systems that have already been built."

[2] Bernard Golden, *Why enterprises embrace open source*, CIO, June 2015: "Enterprise IT has a large and growing commitment to open source products in preference to proprietary alternatives."

[3] Stephanos Androutsellis-Theotokis et al., *Open Source Software: A Survey from 10,000 Feet*, Foundations and Trends in Technology, Information and Operations Management, Volume 4, Numbers 3–4, 2010: "The entire software market has been influenced at a global level as a result of open source software, affecting issues of monopoly, competition, and market placement."

[4] Barthélémy Dagenais, *Moving into a New Software Project Landscape*, Proceedings of the 32nd International Conference on Software Engineering (ICSE), IEEE/ACM, 2010: "Newcomers are explorers who must orient themselves within an unfamiliar landscape. As they gain experience, they eventually settle in and create their own places within the landscape. Like explorers of the natural landscape, they encounter many obstacles, such as a culture shock or getting lost without help."

[5] Jailton Coelho et al., *Why Modern Open Source Projects Fail*, Proceedings of ESEC/FSE'17, 2017: "The most common reason for project failures is the appearance of a stronger open source competitor."

fights,[1] failures, and frustration.[2] You can't just enter it tomorrow and declare yourself an expert. Nobody will listen to you, you won't get any help, you won't know where to ask for information, you will simply be lost.[3]

The open source market is a tool every professional programmer must know how to use. In order to know how to do it, you just need to do one thing: use it every day. And the best motive to be there regularly and frequently is to be the author of your own open source

> It's impossible to be a successful software developer without being an active user of open source products.

product, which is needed and appreciated by the community.[4] Being a user is one thing—being an author is a completely different ball game. If you've never tried that, you don't know open source.

I still remember when I made one of my Java libraries public a few years ago and soon found out that some programmers were still using Windows as their development platform. They started to submit bugs, complaining that the library didn't compile, didn't pass unit tests, and didn't work on their laptops. Initially I was

---

[1]Minghui Zhou, *Who Will Stay in the FLOSS Community? Modeling Participant's Initial Behavior*, IEEE Transactions on Software Engineering, Volume 41, Number 1, 2015: "The start of participation in a FLOSS project is fraught with difficulties, as the new contributors may not be familiar with project's practices and norms."

[2]Amanda Lee, *Understanding the Impressions, Motivations, and Barriers of One Time Code Contributors to FLOSS Projects: A Survey*, Proceedings of the 39th International Conference on Software Engineering (ICSE), IEEE/ACM, 2017: "The process of joining a FLOSS project can be daunting. Developers have to understand the submission process, interpret semi-automated rejection messages, and handle other difficulties."

[3]Igor Steinmacher, *The hard life of open source software project newcomers*, Proceedings of the 7th International Workshop on Cooperative and Human Aspects of Software Engineering, CHASE, ACM, 2014: "While onboarding an open source software project, contributors face many different barriers that hinder their contribution, leading in many cases to dropouts."

[4]Karim R. Lakhani, *Why Hackers Do What They Do: Understanding Motivation and Effort in Free/Open Source Software Projects*, MIT Sloan Working Paper No. 4425-03, 2003: "A clear majority (>61%) stated that their focal F/OSS project was at least as creative as anything they had done in their lives."

surprised since everything was fine on my machine, but then realized that they were using Windows. I had to make many changes both to the code and to the unit tests, just to make them compatible with this dying or already dead operating system. That's how I met open source. Who else would tell me the truth in such a brutal and honest way?

Morning stand-ups

The usual round in a standing circle (49) – Why do I waste my time? (50) – Guilt (51) – Empathy and exclusion anxiety (51) – Survival instinct (52) – Parents and teachers (53) – Mother figure (54) – Greed (54)

ADRIAN is already in the office and calls me to join their standup meeting. This is the ceremony many software teams learned from the modern Agile/Scrum[1] movement, without really understanding what it's for and how to do it. To be honest, I also don't know what it's for and how to do it either. I mean, how to do it right. If there is a way to do it right in the first place, of course.

There are twelve of us. We make a circle, standing and looking to the center of it. Needless to say that I feel a bit uncomfortable since everybody is looking at me.

"Morning, all. Please meet a new member of our team, he just joined us today," Adrian starts, everybody says, "Hi," and I reply with a more formal, "Hello."

"Let's do the usual round, I will start," Adrian takes the initiative. "I'm still working with the the database connection pool bug, hope to fix it today," Adrian finishes quickly with his hands in the pockets of his blue XXL jeans, staring at his shoes.

> Status checking meetings are a great tool to sync up the team when the management is weak.

"I am still implementing the XML retrieval interface, will need two more days because there are some issues with the unit testing, but I'll manage," says the tall guy in a white t-shirt.

"OK, please keep me updated, we need it as soon as possible," Adrian plays a big boss. It's obvious that these words won't help at all, the tall guy will finish when he can, not earlier.

"Sure," he answers very seriously. I'm sure he is smiling to himself now, after hearing these "orders" from Adrian for months. Adrian looks at the next guy in the line.

---

[1] Jeff Sutherland et al., *Scrum: The Art of Doing Twice the Work in Half the Time*, Currency, 2014.

"I am helping Tom to fix the bug with the database performance, we are close, but will require today and tomorrow, I think," the guy reports and Adrian looks satisfied.

"Tom, you are still not sure whether this is the query or Java?" Adrian asks and Tom, the guy standing next to me, says, "Most likely, it's Java, since all indexes are in place. We checked yesterday."

"Weird ... OK, we will discuss it later," Adrian says and the next victim is a fat dude in glasses.

"I'm still fixing yesterday's script problem." He is looking right at Adrian and is obviously nervous, "It works ... doesn't work, I'm sorry ... I will fix it today, I am close already."

"What script?" Adrian looks annoyed. The dude is not his favorite, I feel.

"XML convert ... I explained to you Friday ... it makes empty space bugs ..."

"But I told you that you should not work on that, it's not important for us now!" Adrian gets angry and starts to explain why it's not important.

OBSERVING all this patiently, I think: Why do I need to waste my time here? What do I need to listen to this "noise" for? This information is absolutely irrelevant to me. The only person who needs it is Adrian, since he is the manager of these programmers. If he needs to know what they are working with, he should ask them privately. Or even better, just ask them to update the status of the tickets they are working with.[1] Why does this tall guy needs to know what kind of bug Tom is fixing? Why do I need to know that the fat dude is fixing something that is not important? What difference does it make to me?

---

[1]Steve McConnell, *Rapid Development: Taming Wild Software Schedules*, Microsoft Press, 1996: "Tracking is a fundamental software management activity. If you don't track a project, you can't manage it. You have no way of knowing whether your plans are being carried out and no way of knowing what you should do next. You have no way of monitoring risks to your project. Effective tracking enables you to detect schedule problems early, while there's still time to do something about them. If you don't track a project, you can't do rapid development."

Let's pretend that I'm very loyal and really care about this business. Even in that case, why do I need to know what Tom is working on? Well, unless I work with Tom, of course. But, in that case, I will ask Tom. Not in the morning in front of everybody, but when it's needed, privately. Why do twelve people have to waste their time listening to my stories?

The only reasonable explanation I have is that the group needs this ritual in order to stay united. This standup meeting is not about sharing information—we don't understand and don't want to understand the majority of it anyway—it is for sharing emotions. We are all staying here, looking at each other, saying something about our yesterday's results and today's plans, explaining our mistakes, smiling, and laughing—but the key emotion is our guilt. This is what unites us.[1] This is the glue.[2]

| Status meetings exploit our emotions in order to keep the group together.

EMPATHY and fear are two primary sources of guilt.[3] First, we don't like to see others suffering;[4] second, we are afraid of being rejected from the group.[5] The combination of these two psycho-

---

[1] Roy F. Baumeister et al., *Guilt: An Interpersonal Approach*, Psychological Bulletin, Volume 115(2), 1994: "Guilt can be understood in relationship contexts as a factor that strengthens social bonds by eliciting symbolic affirmation of caring and commitment."

[2] Thomas J. Scheff, *The Emotional/Relational World: Shame and the Social Bond*, Handbooks of Sociology and Social Research, Springer, 2001: "If shame and the bond are the key components of social integration, then acknowledged shame would be the glue that holds relationships and societies together and unacknowledged shame the force that drives them apart."

[3] See footnote 1 on page 51: "We propose two sources: empathic arousal and anxiety over social exclusion. Both of these are important, powerful sources of affect and motivation in close, communal relationships."

[4] Martin L. Hoffman, *Development of Prosocial Motivation: Empathy and Guilt*, The Development of Prosocial Behavior, Academic Press, 1982: "It is intuitively obvious and there is considerable evidence that most people from an early age feel guilt after harming someone."

[5] Roy F. Baumeister et al., *Anxiety and social exclusion*, Journal of Social and Clinical Psychology, Volume 9, 1990: "Anxiety is seen as a pervasive and possibly innately prepare form of distress that arises in response to actual or threatened exclusion from important social groups."

logical stimuli keeps us motivated to stay loyal and contribute.[1]
If we would be working in isolation, just having tasks in front of us, what would motivate us not to be lazy? Our plans, agendas, schedules, tickets, requirements? I doubt that they would work as strong as the responsibility (read: "guilt") we feel in front of the team.[2] First, we don't want to let our colleagues down by, for example, not paying enough attention to some tasks, or ignoring certain problems, or just cutting corners. Second, we don't want them to think poorly of us and potentially reject us. It seems that these two reasons have the same root, though.[3]

It starts to develop the moment we are born, or even earlier. When we are small and vulnerable, our mothers, parents, teachers, and other authority figures are the providers of resources and protection for us. Since our primary objective, as living organisms, is to stay alive, we can't afford a rejection—it will immediately mean suspension of resources and then death. We have to be with them, love them, and keep them happy—in order to stay

---

[1] June P. Tangney, *Moral Affect: The Good, the Bad, and the Ugly*, Journal of Personality and Social Psychology, Volume 61, Number 4, 1991: "Other-oriented empathy—broadly or narrowly defined—is generally viewed as the 'good' moral affective capacity or experience because it is presumed to foster warm, close interpersonal relationships, to facilitate altruistic and prosocial behavior, and to inhibit interpersonal aggression."

[2] Vanessa K. Bohns, *Guilt by design: Structuring organizations to elicit guilt as an affective reaction to failure*, Organization Science, Volume 24(4), 2012: "We posit that several workplace features should be enhanced not to avoid negative affect, but rather to promote a specific form of negative affect that tends to be constructive (guilt)."

[3] Giovanni Novembre, *Empathy for social exclusion involves the sensory-discriminative component of pain: a within-subject fMRI study*, Social Cognitive and Affective Neuroscience, Volume 10(2), 2015: "Experiences of social rejection can activate regions of the brain so far observed during experiences of physical pain... this pattern of brain activation extends to the witnessing of the same type of social pain in others."

alive. Later, when we grow up,[1] psychologists call it empathy and claim that it is innate.[2] However, it seems to be just an artificial derivative[3,4] from the survival instinct—disappointing others is not in our favor.[5]

Parents need to train us to behave the way the entire society behaves. If they don't do that, the society punishes them, not us kids. To simplify the process of training, abstract categories—like guilt and shame—were invented.[6] When an infant spits his food on the floor, his mother raises her voice and the kid realizes that death is not so far away—the next step she could abandon him. However, the voice, as a primitive signal, works only with infants. Growing up, he easily figures out that some food on the floor doesn't lead to exclusion or death. Guilt, as a higher-level emotion, helps him connect his infantile fears with later adult mistakes: Every time he spits on the floor his mother

---

[1] Ronit Roth-Hanania, *Empathy development from 8 to 16 months: Early signs of concern for others*, Infant Behavior and Development, Volume 34, Issue 3, 2011: "Modest levels of affective and cognitive empathy for another in distress were already evident before the second year, and increased gradually (and not always significantly) across the transition to the second year. Prosocial behavior was rare in the first year and increased substantially during the second year."

[2] David Howe, *Empathy: What it is and why it Matters*, Palgrave Macmillan, 2013: "Empathic responses and pro-social behaviours therefore do seem to have a strong genetic component. These innate differences can be spotted even in young children, some of whom consistently exhibit pro-social behaviours that continue to be present throughout their lives."

[3] Tatiana Karyagina, *Empathy Development: Natural or Cultural?* Promises, Pedagogy and Pitfalls: Empathy's Potential for Healing and Harm, Inter-Disciplinary Press, 2016: "So, is empathy natural or cultural? My answer is that it is cultural. Its brain foundation is natural."

[4] Ariel Knafo, et al., *The Developmental Origins of a Disposition Toward Empathy: Genetic and Environmental Contributions*, Emotion, Volume 8, Issue 6, 2008: "Empathy was associated with prosocial behavior, and this relationship was mainly due to environmental effects."

[5] Robin Allott, *Evolutionary Aspects of Love and Empathy*, Journal of Social and Evolutionary Systems, Volume 15(4), 1992: "Empathy clearly increases fitness, has a value for survival, insofar as it serves as a mode of communication between members of a family, between members of a group or even between hostile individuals or groups."

[6] Jean Delumeau, *Sin and Fear: The Emergence of the Western Guilt Culture, 13th-18th Centuries*, Palgrave Macmillan, 1990.

raises her voice and says, "You can't do that, it's bad," or, in a more aggressive form, "You are a bad boy!"

> Our learned desire to do the right thing is way stronger than any other extrinsic motivation a business can offer.

Thus, the kid is trained that being bad or doing bad things, which disappoint his mother, means being guilty. Later, when he stands up in front of the team at the morning meeting, he subconsciously remembers that being guilty and disappointing these people may lead to exclusion, the raised voice of his mother, and potential death. His internal control, based on guilt, develops.[1]

For this poor fat dude, Adrian is the "mother figure." He doesn't even need to raise his voice, doesn't need to punish, doesn't need to threaten. All he needs to do is to say that he is disappointed. Guilt, which the fat dude was trained to feel, will do the rest. It will connect a small mistake in the Java code with the innate fear of death.

Thus, seeing the entire group standing up every morning triggers our guilt and helps us remember that we can't hurt the project, can't disappoint the manager, can't be selfish, can't be free to do what we want. We feel ourselves as part of the group and that the group may reject us if we go against it.

That's why I don't like these standups at all. Well, the good news is that I fully realize what's going on and prevent that guilt from kicking in. I'm just saying to myself, "You're not a kid, there is no mother or a teacher around. You're working here not because you're afraid of being guilty; you're here because they pay you. Make sure you do what's required to be paid more, that's it." In other words, I'm always trying to work because of greed, instead of because of guilt. I believe that selfish financial needs are much better motivators.

The bad news is that tomorrow I will have to say something at this standup show. And eleven people will look at me and listen to me very carefully. They won't understand a thing though, but they will try to look absolutely serious and detail-oriented. I will

---

[1] Francis Ivan Nye, *Family Relationships and Delinquent Behavior*, Greenwood Press, 1973.

be embarrassed, just like they are now; they will pay me back. This is what this show is about: to make all of us feel embarrassed and guilty for not being able to say "I've done everything you said, and I'm ready for your new assignments, Sir!"

Task tracking chaos

Silicon Valley (56) – Political correctness (56) – Inverse bullying (57) – The more loyal they look, the easier they betray (58) – Positive thinking (58) – My first coding task (59) – Does being hired by Facebook make one a good developer? (60) – Bao is bullying me (61) – Where are the requirements? (62) – Experts don't need transparency (63) – Experts vs. order (64) – The flow of information must be obvious (65) – I just need another scapegoat (65) – I suggest task tracking formalities (66) – Does Agile mean chaos? (67)

SILICON Valley is a small territory at the West of the United States. It's really tiny, about fifty by ten miles, with a total population of less than four million people. There is San Francisco (SF) to the North of it and San Jose (SJ) to the East; a big Highway, 101, connects these two cities. It will take you about fifty minutes to drive from SF to SJ if there is no traffic, which is usually at night. Otherwise, it may take two hours.

It really is a territory of villages. Even SF, one of the biggest cities in the US, mostly consists of town houses, with two or three stories. The rest of the Valley looks like it is still somewhere in the 1950s. Luxury cars parked in front of some of those retarded houses are the only thing that reminds you which century you are in. Have you watched "Silicon Valley," the TV series? Forget everything you've seen there—it's all lie, the Valley is absolutely not like that.

It's boring, primitive, ugly, depressive, shallow, discriminating, racist, and ... rich. All you can effectively do here is money. If you're looking for joy, fun, emotions, sincerity, empathy, friendship, or love—you have to look somewhere else.

The biggest problem, of course, is the political correctness insanity, which is escalating every year.[1] The very idea of P.C. seems to be noble—protecting those who can't protect themselves

---

[1] Gregg Henriques, *Political Correctness is All about Slave Morality*, Psychology Today, https://goo.gl/vUVafR, April 2016: "Over the past decade, I have found myself increasingly concerned with political correctness evolving into an oppressive righteousness that are in many ways deeply misguided and incomplete and there is definitely a need to push back against it when it spills over into absurdity."

against offense.[1] However, it has recently turned into a witch-hunt: anything you say or create[2] may be treated as an offense and you will be accused of being politically incorrect.[3] You can't think, joke, or do scientific research about men and women,[4] blacks and whites, smart and stupid, Americans and Mexicans, cute and ugly. You'd better not think or joke at all, to be safe.

The situation is very similar to the "good old" Soviet-Nazi time,[5] where both empires claimed freedom, but it existed only for those who agreed with the main discourse. In Silicon Valley, they don't imprison or execute you for your different thoughts, like Stalin and Hitler did; they ostracize you by firing[6] and public shaming. P.C. has become a very effective instrument for inverse bullying: former victims turn into offenders.[7] I'm often asking myself, is it what the tech sector really needs in order to be innovative?

| Political correctness is a disease quickly infecting the tech industry.

ADRIAN is here and interrupts my thinking. Damn, this is just

---

[1] Geoffrey Hughes *Political correctness: a history of semantics and culture*, Wiley, 2010.

[2] Roger Kimball, *The rape of the masters: how political correctness sabotages art*, Encounter Books, 2005.

[3] Sam Altman, *E Pur Si Muove*, https://goo.gl/sJAXYs: "It seems easier to accidentally speak heresies in San Francisco every year. Debating a controversial idea, even if you 95% agree with the consensus side, seems ill-advised."

[4] Bruce Rind, Archives of Sexual Behavior, Volume 37, 2008: "Research that steps outside the boundaries imposed by hegemonic cultural values and ideologies to question privileged constructions of sexuality may be accused of championing bigotry or abuse, while practicing pseudo-science."

[5] Doris Lessing, Sunday Times, May 10, 1992: "Political Correctness is the natural continuum of the party line. What we are seeing once again is a self-appointed group of vigilantes imposing their views on others. It is a heritage of communism, but they don't seem to see this."

[6] Nitasha Tiku, *James Damore's Lawsuit is Designed to Embarrass Google*, Wired, January 2018.

[7] David G. Green, *We're (Nearly) All Victims Now! How political correctness is undermining our liberal culture*: "Groups who have been politically recognised as victims are starting to use their power to silence people who have had the cheek to criticise them."

the second day and he already wants something from me. He is definitely doing this because he feels responsible to give me some work to do. I'm ready and I'm scared. I have to fight back, or I will be turned into a regular programmer and my life for the next year or so in this office will be miserable.

"You got a moment?" he starts in a traditionally polite way.

"Sure, what's up!?" I reply loudly, pretending to be fully ready to do whatever is necessary for him, for this business, for the company, for the country, and for human kind. I have to show that readiness, this is what makes people happy. I would actually say that the more loyal and ready to help a person looks and behaves, the higher the chances of selfishness and betrayal. Don't trust those who say that they are interested in helping you, in working with you, in dedicating their time to your project, in being loyal and committed. They are lying and you can't really rely on them. Trust those who are saying that they hate working with this stupid project, that they are here merely because of money, that they are fed up with this source code base, this team, this project, and this programming language. Those people are telling you the truth and you can really rely on them when things go South.

> Strong management, first of all, means readiness to admit that coercion is inevitable.

The "positive thinking," which is popular now,[1] is what people

---

[1]Barbara Ehrenreich, *Bright-Sided: How the Relentless Promotion of Positive Thinking Has Undermined America*, Metropolitan Books, 2009: "A good 'team player' is by definition a 'positive person.' He or she smiles frequently, does not complain, is not overly critical, and gracefully submits to whatever the boss demands."

hide behind[1] when they can't or don't want to tell the truth.[2] If and when I assemble my own team, I will be looking only for skeptical people—even though they may look "negative" on the surface—they can't lie or don't want to.

Now I'm lying to Adrian, expressing my readiness to help. If I would be telling him the truth, I would say: "Dude, leave me alone for now. I have been in this office for just two days. Can't you give me at least two weeks of free time, pretending that I'm learning the product? Nobody will notice anyway." However, Adrian is not strong enough to handle that truth and forces me to do what he wants anyway.

HE explains, "There is an API for the payments that has some issues. Maybe you can fix them. I don't really know what's wrong. Bao can explain. It's all in Java so I figured you can help us right away." He is waiting for my question. What did I understand? Not so much. There is some Bao, there is some Java code with bugs, they expect these bugs to be fixed soon, they want to make me responsible for not fixing them, I must be ready to become a scapegoat.

"Who is Bao?" I start with the most neutral question.

"Ah, he is from the payment group, I can introduce you," Adrian doesn't move, doesn't stand up, doesn't rush to introduce

---

[1] Oliver Burkeman, *The Antidote: happiness for people who can't stand positive thinking*, Text Publishing, 2012: "The effort to try to feel happy is often precisely the thing that makes us miserable. And that it is our constant efforts to eliminate the negative—insecurity, uncertainty, failure, or sadness—that is what causes us to feel so insecure, anxious, uncertain, or unhappy."; "In order to be truly happy, we might actually need to be willing to experience more negative emotions—or, at the very least, to learn to stop running quite so hard from them."

[2] Gabriele Oettingen, *Rethinking Positive Thinking: Inside the New Science of Motivation*, "People who positively fantasize about the future—and that's probably all of us—thus put themselves in a double bind. On the one hand, they inadvertently relax and fool their minds into thinking they've attained their wishes. Meanwhile, their dreams lock them cognitively into these same wishes, sustaining their fantasies by avoiding information that might otherwise prompt them to step outside, get some perspective on their wishes, and perhaps resolve to take a different path. The result all too often is frustration, failure, and, at the extreme, a deep-seated feeling of being stuck."

me.

"Did he develop the code?"

"No, no, another guy. He quit in March. Hired by Facebook. He was a good developer." I wonder what exactly makes that guy a good developer? The fact that he was hired by Facebook or maybe the code that he left behind is just awesome.

"Really? Did he work here for long?"

"About a year. He was very to himself, always in his headset. I don't miss him," he laughs. Me too. But my question still remains: Why he was a "good developer?" I'm always interested what people say about me when I leave. Even programmers, like Adrian, who are supposed to be objective and judge fellow workers by their results, don't really pay attention to the deliverables produced. Instead, they value others by very vague social behavioral factors, like "was hired by Google," or "was cycling to the office," or "was dating a guy," or something similar. I've never heard people saying that there was a guy who "was always writing unit tests first" or "was really good in UML." I don't blame them, it's a good thing to remember—doesn't really matter what the quality of your code is, your political views or your sense of humor are much more important. Isn't it unfortunate?

> Your social achievements are much more important the the quality of code you produce.

I reply, "Sounds scary to me. Did you ever see that code?" I'm smiling, but I'm really scared. He said that they expect me to "help them right away" and now I will be fixing something a Facebook guy created last year sitting in his headset. No way.

"Yeah, I saw it, of course!" Adrian is obviously lying.

"OK, give me access and let me talk to Bao. Where is the guy?" I stand up and Adrian does the same, but way slower. "He shows up later," Adrian makes a sorry look, but this is good information for me—it's possible to "show up later" in this office.

"No problem, let me see the code and I'll do everything I can," I say, cheerfully, and return to my desk.

I<small>N</small> a few minutes an email arrives from Adrian with my login and password to their internal Git repository. I check out the repo and open it in IntelliJ IDEA. A few hundred Java files, the code looks ugly, and it's one of the frameworks I hate. I have no desire to even touch it. Let's see who Bao is and what he has to say. Adrian introduces us. Bao looks like he's forty. Bold, tall, and a bit Asian. Do I like him? I don't know yet, but he seems like a guy with a big ego. Rather friendly, though.

"There is a concurrency issue in the database connection pooling. You just fix it. It should be easy," Bao says looking me right in the eye. Now I know where the trouble will be coming from in this office. There is so much wrong with his words that I don't even know where to start.

"How do you know?" I try to stay calm.

"Listen, I've been a software engineer for over fifteen years. Trust me, I know what I'm talking about," he stops and smiles very friendly, without any intent to continue and explain me why he thinks there is an issue specifically in the connection pooling. And why the hell he is telling me where the problem is instead of explaining what it is? "Man, stay calm, don't lose your temper," I say to myself.

"I'm going to learn a lot from you, then!" I reply with a smile and he doesn't smell the sarcasm.

"Listen, you should ask me for advice if you don't understand something. I'm the most skillful programmer in this company," he doesn't smile anymore. Is he joking? Doesn't seem so. He really means it. Looks like this dude is way more concerned about his position in the hierarchy than about the technical problem he expects me to solve. It's much more important for him to see himself above me than in delegating the task in a way that it can be completed better. It doesn't mean he doesn't want the task to be completed, but he sees power as the key instrument in making this happening. First, he has to climb on top of me, then he will direct me. What should I do? Fight back, what else? But not in an open fight, where I will most certainly lose.

> Knowledge sharing, which is not structured and formalized, is inevitably full of frustrations and bottlenecks.

"That's what I've heard," I stop smiling and flatter him in the dirtiest way I can.

"Right," he swallows and I reckon that his mind is totally clouded by self-obsession.

"What are the symptoms of the issues? Do you have them reported somewhere?" I always expect some formalities between the task specifier and the task performer. In this particular situation they are the only way to protect me against this crazy dude. I must not allow him to tell me what to do, on the technical level. He must specify the requirements and my code will satisfy them. Otherwise, if I allow him to deal with my "concurrency issue" as he sees fit, he will become the bug fixer and I will be the slave and the scapegoat. I must prohibit any discussions about the internals of our API and allow him to only talk about the exposed issue. There must be some bug tracker, I believe, where the bug is reported and there must be a reporter. Maybe Bao is the reporter, but probably not. There are over twenty programmers in his department under his management. I'm sure he is not writing any code, ever, and can't personally experience any issues with the API. So, the question is, where are the requirements?

"Listen, just check the synchronization in the pool and fix it. If you know Java and databases, it shouldn't be a problem for you," he says and turns his head away from me, looking into his laptop. "Excuse me, there is something urgent going on now, let me know when the concurrency issue is fixed and we will check on our side," he reads some emails and I look at his face from the side.

"All right, give me some time ... " I stand up and slowly walk away.

How do I feel? Like I've been raped. I get back to my desk and try to analyze what just happened. Bao has enough power in this company, because he is a head of department, he has worked here for much longer than I have and he has the information I need to solve the problem my boss, Adrian, expects me to. If I don't solve it, for any reason, the blame will be on me. Bao understands this. If I don't manage to extract the information from Bao, I won't even be able to explain that he sabotaged me, because he will say that he told me what to do and what to fix. If I don't know how to fix it, I'm not a professional Java programmer, just like he just said. That will be enough for Tony to make his organizational decisions. Will he fire me? Not right away, but my position of power in the team will be seriously damaged.

Can I go to Adrian and complain? Complain about what? Well, I can say that Bao doesn't explain what the problem really is and just tells me what to do. Will that surprise Adrian? I don't think so. They've worked together for a long time, so they know how things are organized here. They both are perfectly aware of the chaos that allows Bao to do what he just did. Yes, right, the root cause of this situation is the lack of management structure.

Indeed, if the bug would have been already reported somewhere in a bug tracker, it would have an author, symptoms, history of changes, severity and priority, and all the other attributes a proper bug should have, as Dr. Myers

> A strictly formal bug tracking system prevents speculation with information.

taught me in his book,[1] the role of Bao would be minimal. He would simply have no say, since he would not own any information. Everything would be freely-available in the ticket history. I would just open it up, read through it, fix the concurrency issue—if that is really what's going on and Bao is not lying—and close the ticket. Of course, such transparency would seriously affect Bao's position, since way fewer people will come to him for "advice," as he calls this, but in reality they are coming to demonstrate their respect and submissive position to the great expert, who "knows things!"[2]

---

[1]★Glenford J. Myers et al., *The Art of Software Testing*, 3rd Edition, Wiley, 2011.

[2]★Scott Adams, *The Dilbert principle: a cubicles eye view of bosses, meetings, management fads & other workplace afflictions*, Harper Business, 1996: "A good way for ineffective people to cling to power in an organization is by creating a monopoly on information. This information should seem important, but not critically important. In other words, your co-workers should want the information you're withholding, but not so badly that they'll choke you to death when you prevent them from getting it."

WAIT, maybe there is a ticketing system somewhere and Bao just didn't tell me about it. "Do we track issues somewhere?" I ask Adrian and use "we" instead of "you idiots" to look loyal and polite.

"Yes, sure, customer support records all bugs coming from users and posts them to JIRA, but they are not really good at explaining them correctly," he smiles.

"What about technical bugs inside the departments and between them?"

"Nah, we don't track them, since it's always easier to explain face-to-face. We are in the same office!" He seems to be proud of that. Well, I can understand him. He is part of this chaos and he is in a very similar position to Bao. He is not that crazy about power, but he definitely enjoys being an expert too.

I noticed that in the previous companies I've been before, the chaos always favors the people that stay longer. They usually are not the best people, but the most stable and adaptive, just like Adrian and Bao. They accumulate knowledge about the product and don't want to share it with anyone for free. Any documenting or bug tracking rules and systems scare them because they are an obvious threat to their jobs. The more these guys share, the less important they are.

> The higher the price of information in a software team, the less effective the team is.

Let's take this example again. If the problem had already been described in a ticket, I would not go to Bao, would not be introduced to him, would not need to listen to his schizophrenic stories about how skillful he is. He would just become a regular nobody, instead of a big boss and a very smart expert, who can explain what the problem is like nobody else can.

We, newbies and young programmers, don't like chaos because it makes us dependent on experts. We have to beg for information and feel bad if Bao or Adrian don't love us.

Needless to say, this situation hurts the company for so many reasons. First of all, those experts usually are over-paid and the top management can't really do anything with them. Tony can't fire Bao easily, because only Bao knows what the "concurrency issue" is about. The very presence of experts turns management upside down. It's not Tony anymore who manages the organization, but Bao. Second, the presence of these information owners or experts seriously demotivates others who are not interested in becoming experts or begging for help and data. I'm one of them. I don't want to talk to Bao anymore. I would rather see him suffer or dead. I'm very angry, but if we think deeper, he may not be a bad person. He is just protecting his job, his paycheck, his family. He might be a bigger victim of this chaos than myself.

The guilty person is Tony. He is the CTO and he is responsible for establishing the rules of work in his organization. He must ensure that the flow of information is very well-explained, formalized, documented, and easy to understand. He didn't manage to do that and that's why the team created its own rules, which look like, "Bao knows how to do it." These rules are ugly, counter productive and work against Tony and the organization. I blame him, first and foremost. Isn't that fair?

THE good thing, though, is that I know what to do. I have to complain about the chaos, not about Bao. I won't fight with Bao because I will definitely lose since his position is absolutely stronger than mine. However, I will try to put him on my side, together with Adrian, and introduce the rules of bug tracking in this team. Then, these rules will kill them both, in a good way: they won't be experts anymore, since the information will become more available and transparent. The ticketing system will contain the knowledge about the software, the bugs, the issues, the problems, risks and solutions. Personal face-to-face meetings won't even be required if everything is in writing, formally documented. The power of these guys will be diminished.

I have to do it nicely, though, to neutralize their fear of losing their jobs. Will it be possible? I'm not sure, but I will try.

What to do with this task in the meantime? I think I have to find another scapegoat, who will be ready to replace me in this tough spot.

"Do you know who knows the most about concurrency issues in our back end?" I ask Adrian. The question is pretty risky, since it may sound like I don't know anything about concurrency and I can't afford doubts at the beginning of my trial period in this team. That's why I emphasize the "in our back end" part. The question should sound like I know a lot about concurrency, but need some help to understand the problem with this specific case.

"Try Tom, he solved some issues a month ago." Adrian is my guy, unlike Bao.

I find Tom, he is a young dude with Gucci glasses and a few layers of stickers on his MacBook. Let's try to make him help me and do my job.

> The only way to get rid of knowledgeable experts is to formalize information flow.

"Hey," I smile, "can you please help me? I can't really figure out where to start." I have to be honest with the guy and explain everything to him so that he feels responsible for helping a friend. "Bao said that there are some concurrency issues in our payment API, but didn't really say what's wrong. Do you know what he is talking about?"

"Yes, sure, let me see," he immediately opens up a new IDEA window and scrolls through the code. He says something about some classes, trying to explain to me what is where. I don't listen but keep nodding and saying, "yeah." All I need now is for him to take responsibility for this issue. Then, he will go to Bao and they will figure something out. I'm sure Bao already treats Tom as his subordinate and won't play that rank-pulling game he did on me.

"So, do you think it's fixable?" I ask after ten minutes.

"Yes, I'll take care of that, don't worry," he feels great because he can help a friend.

"Thanks, dude, appreciate it," I go back to my desk.

I get back to Adrian: "Look how difficult it is for us to figure out what Bao is talking about! I had to talk to him today again about this problem, even though he already explained everything to Tom a few months ago. How about we ask Bao and his programmers to report bugs to us only through the ticketing system?" I say and realize that this move is right, since Bao is a competitor for Adrian. They simply can't like each other. I will help Adrian in this fight and he will be on my side.

"Look," I continue, "he tells programmers from our department, who are supposed to report to you only, what to do. He tried to do the same with me. Instead of properly formulating the problem, he told me to go figure it out by myself, and only thanks to Tom did we manage." Adrian listens. "This is not how it should be. Instead, everything they don't like in our code and products should go through the ticketing system. Let's make sure every single problem and task that comes to us has a ticket. By the way, I'm sure Tony will like this initiative, it will give us more discipline." Tony is his boss and Adrian is definitely interested in bringing new ideas to him.

"We tried that last year, but it didn't really work out," Adrian replies with a lack of interest. Most likely, I'm not the first one who is suggesting this. "Because nobody creates those tickets, they just go and talk to each other. Maybe we are just not as disciplined as you expect us to be." Adrian smiles and I realize that the most undisciplined person is right in front of me.

| Agility is not an excuse for a lack of task tracking rules and systems.

"How do you know what the team is working on at the moment? How do you dispatch tasks and track their results?"

"That's why I'm in the office all day long without holidays," he laughs, feeling very proud of that. "That's why we have standup meetings every morning, to keep things under control."

"So, there is no official tracking of tasks, right?"

"No, we are Agile," Adrian smiles and I don't understand whether it's sarcasm or he really thinks that Agile means no task tracking.

What else can I say? That's how it works in most companies. This poor Adrian is not alone. He is not really a manager. He was a programmer for a few years and then was promoted to this management position. He hardly knows anything about project management, but has got a big heart. He can't let Tony down just because he can't do it. He is a good guy and that's why he is a manager. Can we blame him for managing the team without tasks, tracking, rules, requirements, and any discipline? I don't think so. Again, the person to blame here is Tony, who didn't structure the company right.

Is this situation fixable? Can I do something with this, being an architect or just a programmer? I seriously doubt it. This situation is not unique for this particular company. Most or almost all software teams work like that and call it Agile. They just don't have any discipline at all, don't have any rules, any regulations, any plans, schedules or formalities. Every morning, they just make a standing circle around their manager, who used to be a programmer, and call it a day.

[Handwritten margin notes: FIX B / CORE TEAM / HARD FORMALIZATION OR RFQ's AND TASKS / AGILE ≠ CHAOS]

Chapter 2

Dennis

I'VE been here for almost two months already. Just like I predicted earlier, not only is the management messy, but so is the code base and all of the technical processes. The right word would be *ad hoc*—not messy or chaotic, like I initially thought. It's not a total mess. There are some rules, some agreements, some habits, but they were created by the team, not the management on top of it. This may not sound like such a bad idea, but it actually is. The process we have now is motivated solely by the qualities of people participating in it. For example: Bao was the author of the deployment script, so that's why he is responsible for deploying the product to production; Tom was using Hibernate at his previous job, so that's why we also use Hibernate; Dennis doesn't like Bao, so that's why Dennis doesn't work with the tasks coming from Bao's department; Bao doesn't like me, so that's why he doesn't invite me to his meetings, and so on. Who is managing who?

Automated testing

What are unit tests for? (70) – TDD (71) – Merging the garbage (72) – Branching (72) – Code reviews (73) – Merging script (74) – Test coverage (74) – Safety net (76)

W<small>E</small> are doing things the way we do them because that's the most comfortable way for us to do them or it's the only possible way. Business reasons come second, if ever. Tony, our CTO, can't say that we must do something in a certain way, because this is how our customers need it. Instead, he can only ask us what can we do and then bring it back to the customers. In most cases, he doesn't bring back anything. There is no process enforced. The process just happens. And it always happens in our favor. We, the programmers, are happy, but the business suffers.

Dennis is a Greek programmer sitting next to me. He came to California with a work visa about six years ago and, since then, got married, had two kids, and changed companies a few times. He is a good programmer and a very passionate guy. Somewhere around thirty. He doesn't seem happy about his job here and told me a few times already that he was going to quit soon. He didn't explain why and I didn't ask. It's usually better to stay away from those who are ready to leave, strategically speaking. But these people usually are the most honest about their problems and you can learn a lot from them. They have almost nothing to lose.

> Automated testing is a safety net that protects the program from its programmers.

"I fixed that two weeks ago! What's going on?" Dennis screams and hits the desk.

"What's up?" I smile. I'm always interested to hear a story from a frustrated programmer.

"Look, I spent my whole day to fix this stupid bug and now it's back!" He looks at me, frustrated. What can I say?

"Did you cover it with a unit test?" I ask.

"What do you mean, dude?"

"Do you know what unit tests are for?[1] Well, any automated tests, actually," I pretend to be surprised, but I'm not. I've seen the code base and realized already that unit testing here is a very rare exception, not a rule. They write them sometimes and mostly for fun.[2] Nobody really understands the real reason behind automated testing.[3]

"You mean test-driven development? Yes, I know what it's for, dude!"

"No, not that, forget the TDD, just tests." Again, I'm not surprised. Most people confuse them for each other.[4] Automated tests and TDD are two different things,[5] but they usually stay very close to each other, maybe thanks to the book.[6]

"How is that related to this silly situation, dude?"

"The automated tests are protecting you and everybody else

---

[1] Terry Shepard et al., *More testing should be taught*, Communications of the ACM, Volume 44, Issue 6, 2001: "Testing typically takes 50% or more of the resources for software development projects. Curiously, far less effort and resources of the software development portion of a typical undergraduate curriculum in computing is allocated to testing."

[2] Andy Hunt et al., *Pragmatic Unit Testing in Java with JUnit*, The Pragmatic Bookshelf, 2003: "Many programmers feel that testing is just a nuisance: an unwanted bother that merely distracts from the real business at hand—cutting code."

[3] ★Michael C. Feathers, *Working Effectively with Legacy Code*, Prentice Hall, 2004: "Code without tests is bad code. It doesn't matter how well written it is; it doesn't matter how pretty or object-oriented or well-encapsulated it is. With tests, we can change the behavior of our code quickly and verifiably. Without them, we really don't know if our code is getting better or worse."

[4] David Janzen et al., *Does test-driven development really improve software design quality?* IEEE Software, Volume 25, Number 2, 2008: "Misconception #1: TDD equals automated testing."; "Because TDD has helped propel automated testing to the forefront, many seem to think that TDD is only about writing automated tests."

[5] David Janzen et al., *Test-Driven Development: Concepts, Taxonomy, and Future Direction*, Computer, Volume 38, Number 9, 2005: "Automated testing involves writing unit tests as code and placing this code in a test harness or framework such as JUnit. Automated unit testing frameworks minimize the effort of testing, reducing a large number of tests to a click of a button."; "With TDD, the programmer writes the unit tests prior to the code under test. As a result, the programmer can immediately execute the tests after they are written."

[6] Kent Beck, *Test-Driven Development by Example*, Addison Wesley, 2003.

from the very situation you're experiencing right now. Any bug you fix, or any functionality you add, you're supposed to cover with a test. Simply put, you have to create another piece of code that runs and fails if the functionality doesn't work or the bug is still there," he listens and looks into his laptop. "If you would've created such a test two weeks ago," I continue, "nobody would be able to break that code again."[1]

"How so?"

"Well, they would be able to do that, but the build would not pass, and, ideally, they wouldn't be able to merge their changes."

I feel like I'm saying something obvious,[2] but he doesn't look like he's understanding.

"What do you mean wouldn't be able to merge? How is the build related to the merge?"

"In our case they are not related, but, in an ideal world, changes get merged into the the 'master' branch only if and when they don't break the build."

"Get merged by who?"

"There has to be script that does that. Say you create a new branch and make your fixes, together with the test. They don't break the build, since both the changes and the test present in your branch. You make sure the test passes. Then, we start a script, which merges your branch with the 'master' and runs the

---

[1] Kent Beck, *Embracing change with extreme programming*, Computer, Volume 32, Number 10, 1999: "Instead of activities that evaporate into the ether as soon as they are finished, you record the tests in a permanent form. These tests will run automatically today, and this afternoon after we all integrate, and tomorrow, and next week, and next year. The confidence they embody accumulates, so an XP team gains confidence in the behavior of its system over time."

[2] Laurie Williams et al., *Test-driven development as a defect-reduction practice*, 14th International Symposium on Software Reliability Engineering (ISSRE), 2003: "New functionality is not considered properly implemented unless these new (unit) test cases, and every other unit test case written for the code base, run properly."

so called 'pre-flight' build[1] again. If everything is clean, the script pushes the changes to the 'master.' Then, someone else ... Nah, not 'someone else.' Let's make the story more realistic. Let's say Tom creates a new branch and makes some changes that break the code you just fixed. Then we start a script for Tom's branch. The script merges Tom's changes to the 'master' and runs the build. Your test, which you added earlier, fails, because Tom broke the code. The script complains to Tom and the master stays untouched. Tom will have to make sure his code is compliant with your test if he wants his code to get into 'master.'"

"Yes, but Tom can remove my test."

"That's possible, yes, but that's what code reviews are for.[2] Before we give the code to the script we have to pass it through a more or less formal code review, preferably by two people. If the test gets deleted the reviewer will notice that and ask for a reason. Maybe you should be the reviewer, if his changes are touching the code you created."[3]

"What if Tom just commits to the master branch without

---

[1] Bob Aiello et al., *Agile Application Lifecycle Management: Using DevOps to Drive Process Improvement*, Pearson Education, 2016: "Preflight builds enable the developer to run the build privately on his or her machine before turning the code over to the build engineering team to verify that the code will compile on the build platform. Preflight builds save a lot of time by identifying anomalies without the volleyball game of tossing the build over the net to operations—only to have them toss the build back when it fails."

[2] Georgios Gousios, *Work Practices and Challenges in Pull-Based Development: The Integrator's Perspective*, Proceedings of the 37th International Conference on Software Engineering, IEEE Press, 2015: "A member of the project's core team is responsible to inspect the changes and integrate them into the project's main development line. The role of the integrator is crucial. The integrator must act as a guardian for the project's quality."; "The quality phenomenon manifests itself by the explicit request of integrators that pull requests undergo code review, their concern for quality at the source code level and the presence of tests."

[3] Alberto Bacchelli et al., *Expectations, Outcomes, and Challenges Of Modern Code Review*, Proceedings of the 35th International Conference on Software Engineering (ICSE), IEEE Press, 2013: "When the context is clear and understanding is very high, as in the case when the reviewer is the owner of changed files, code review authors receive comments that explore deeper details, are more directed and more actionable and pertinent, and find more subtle issues."

running the script?" he smiles.

"We must make it technically impossible, via Git configuration.[1] Nobody should be able to push to master, only the script."

"So, in order to merge anything every one of us must run the script? Where will this script be installed? I don't get the technical details."

> The master branch must be read only for everybody except the machine that merges everyone's changes in.

"Ideally, it shouldn't be just a simple bash script, but a server or a bot, installed somewhere and available to everybody through a web interface or something similar. You should not literally run the script, but, instead, push a button somewhere."

D<small>ENNIS</small> shrugs: "But we don't write those automated tests, anyway, dude."[2]

"That's a different story. Of course we don't, because there is no motivation. If you had written that test two weeks ago, it wouldn't help, anyway. Tom, if it was him, would easily break your test and push to the master. Not because Tom is evil, but because there is no script in front of him."

"Your system looks like an extra hassle for programmers. Nobody will like that," Dennis smiles.

"Well, yes, it is an extra hassle, and a big one. When the system is big and the test coverage is pretty high, it becomes rather difficult to make any serious changes without breaking someone else's tests."

> High test coverage, while increasing the quality of software, inevitably slows down development.

"And you think that's good? What is test coverage, by the way?"

"It's the percentage of code touched by unit tests when we

---

[1]Scott Chacon, Pro Git, 2nd Edition, Apress, 2014: Chapter 8: Customizing Git, An Example Git-Enforced Policy, Server-Side Hook.

[2]Kent Beck et al., *Test infected: Programmers love writing tests*, Java Report, Volume 3, Number 7, 1998: "Every programmer knows they should write tests for their code. Few do. The universal response to 'Why not?' is 'I'm in too much of a hurry.'"

run them.[1,2] Let's say you have ten Java classes and no unit tests. Your coverage is 0%. Then, you create your first test which calls some methods in one of those classes. It doesn't touch other classes. Your coverage is 10%. Then you create another test, which also touches the same class and nobody else. Your coverage still is 10%. Eventually you will have many tests, which will touch all ten classes and your coverage will be 100%.[3] Usually, the number of tests is bigger than the number of classes they test. Of course, the metric isn't that simple, it doesn't work only by classes. It also takes into account lines of code, by paths, by methods, and so on.[4] Doesn't really matter. You get the idea."

"Yeah, yeah, I got it," he leans back and puts his hands behind his head. "So, what is our coverage now?" he smiles and looks into the monitor.

---

[1] *SWEBOK*, Chapter 4: "Control flow-based coverage criteria are aimed at covering all the statements, blocks of statements, or specified combinations of statements in a program. The strongest of the control flow-based criteria is path testing, which aims to execute all entry-to-exit control flow paths in a program's control flow graph. Since exhaustive path testing is generally not feasible because of loops, other less stringent criteria focus on coverage of paths that limit loop iterations such as statement coverage, branch coverage, and condition/decision testing. The adequacy of such tests is measured in percentages; for example, when all branches have been executed at least once by the tests, 100% branch coverage has been achieved."

[2] ISTQB, *International Software Testing Qualification Board*, version 2.0, 2007: "Coverage is the extent that a structure has been exercised as a percentage of the items being covered. If coverage is not 100%, then more tests may be designed to test those items that were missed and therefore, increase coverage."

[3] Christian R. Prause et al., *Is 100% Test Coverage a Reasonable Requirement? Lessons Learned from a Space Software Project*, Proceedings of the 18th International Conference on Product-Focused Software Process Improvement (PROFES), 2017: "100% coverage is unusual but achievable."; "100% coverage is sometimes necessary.", "100% coverage brings in new risks."; "Don't optimize for the 100%-metric."; "100% coverage is not a sufficient condition for good quality."

[4] Muhammad Shahid et al., *A study on test coverage in software testing*, Proceedings of the International Conference on Telecommunication Technology and Applications (CSIT), Volume 5, 2011: "There are about 12 coverage item types like statement, branch, block, decision, condition, method, class, package, requirement, and data flow coverage."

"It's close to zero and this is the main[1] problem. That's where your frustration is coming from. Without decent test coverage, this situation will keep repeating and you can't really do anything about it."

H<small>E</small> exclaims, "I can find who broke my code, just look at the Git history!"

"Yes, you can, but what good will it do? They will tell you that they were fixing some important bug and accidentally broke something you did. So what? They feel sorry. This feeling won't stop them from breaking your code again tomorrow. They didn't do it intentionally. It was an accident. Automated tests were invented exactly to prevent such accidents. They are sometimes compared with the safety net electricians put above the road when they are fixing high-voltage cables. If they accidentally drop the cable it won't fall down on the ground and won't hurt anyone. Instead, the net will catch it. Unit tests play exactly the same role—they catch you when you drop something accidentally. What you are suggesting is catching them after they already broke the code. It's too late. The automated test will catch them one step earlier."

"Yeah, sounds like a good philosophy, but we are far away from there."

"It's never too late to start," I want to make it simple for him, even through it's not simple at all. I can't really imagine how a team with zero testing mentality and a lot of "legacy code"[2] can start writing unit tests and achieve some decent coverage. He didn't ask me what decent coverage is, but I believe that it is somewhere over 80% code, lines-wise,

| In most projects, high test coverage is not achievable because of management weaknesses.

---

[1]Laura Inozemtseva, *Coverage Is Not Strongly Correlated with Test Suite Effectiveness*, Proceedings of the 36th International Conference on Software Engineering (ICSE), 2014: "Coverage alone is not a good predictor of test suite effectiveness; in many cases, the apparent relationship is largely due to the fact that high coverage suites contain more test cases."

[2]The term allegedly was first used by computer scientist George Olivetti to describe code maintained by an administrator that did not develop the code. However, I wasn't able to find proof.

and over 60%, method-wise.[1] So, I'm way more pessimistic than I want to look.

---

[1] StackOverflow question: *What is a reasonable code coverage % for unit tests (and why)?* https://goo.gl/yZtFxp

Rewards and punishments

Nobody writes unit tests (78) – Quality must be enforced in order to happen (79) – The business doesn't need quality (79) – We must do what the business says (80) – How can they punish us? (81) – $100 for each ticket closed (81) – Don't judge people, judge their results (83) – Punishment without a logic (83) – How to punish a kid right (84)

D<small>ENNIS</small> thinks for a few seconds and says, "Nobody will write tests, man. Nobody really cares about the code being broken. We are paid to fix it. The more frequently it's broken, the more the company needs us. If the code becomes more stable, the company will need less programmers and we will lose our jobs. So, man, we don't need any tests." He laughs.

He is joking, but he is very close to the truth. Indeed, that's exactly how it works and we both perfectly understand it. It's job security.[1] Programmers on payroll don't need the code to be maintainable, because it's against their primary motivation:[2] to stay with the company for as long as possible, be needed, and paid as high as possible.[3] The motivation of the company is exactly the opposite, though: to have as few programmers as possible and pay them as little as possible.

If the company doesn't explicitly require their programmers to follow certain rules and principles, which will guarantee the

---

[1] Diomidis Spinellis, *Job Security*, IEEE Software, Volume 26, Issue 5, 2009: "It seems that writing code that nobody else can comprehend can be a significant job security booster."

[2] Pankaj Bhatt, *Dynamics of Software Maintenance*, ACM SIGSOFT Software Engineering Notes, Volume 29, Number 5, 2004: "In some situations, lack of maintainability is linked to job security of the existing maintenance programmer(s)."

[3] Arthur L. Carpenter, *Programming for Job Security: Tips and Techniques to Maximize Your Indispensability*, Proceedings of the Twenty-First Annual SAS Users Group International Conference, Volume 19, 1996: "In general, easily maintained programs require fewer programmers and one of the fewer programmers could be you. It is possible to write programs that no one else could possibly maintain. Programs can be written that produce results that cannot be predicted from either a quick or even fairly careful inspection of the code. Once you know these techniques and have learned to properly apply them, your job will be secure for as long as your programs are in use."

desired quality of code and its maintainability, the programmers will make their code as dirty as they can.[1] This may sound counter intuitive, but Dennis got it perfectly right: the quality won't show up by itself—it has to be enforced.

"You're right, man, quality must be enforced, otherwise it won't happen. We programmers must be required to write tests, otherwise we won't do it," I suggest.

"OK, how can you motivate me to write those tests, huh?"[2]

"I think that the only way is to reject your code if it doesn't contain enough tests."

> Quality won't happen voluntarily. It must be enforced.

"How can you check that?"

"There must be a rule that every change goes through a code review.[3,4,5] You write something and then someone reviews it. The reviewer rejects it if there are no tests."

"OK, let's say, you review my code and reject it. I will immediately go and complain to Masha. She will tell you to accept it right away."

"Who is Masha?"

---

[1] Harold Davis, *Visual Basic 6 Secrets*, Wiley, 1998: "There are armies of maintenance programmers still keeping legacy mainframe programs going ... If maintenance is not considered as a very important aspect of any substantial project, it is going to mean very big trouble in the years to come. Just as the 'Year 2000 Problem' has stirred legions of COBOL programmers out of their comfortable retirements, VB programs written today without taking maintenance into account should be considered your ultimate job security."

[2] Joy Shafer, Proceedings of Pacific NW Software Quality Conference (PNSQC), 2011: "How do you start unit testing if your team has never done it before? The first thing you'll need, as is the case with many of these recommendations, is management support. Your managers need to communicate to the development team that unit testing is required- not optional. To facilitate the on-boarding process, you'll want to implement an appropriate measurement and reward system."

[3] Tom Gilb et al., *Software Inspection*, Addison-Wesley, 1993: "A software review is as a nonexecution-based approach for scrutinizing software products for defects, deviations from development standards, and other problems."

[4] ★Karl E. Wiegers, *Peer Reviews in Software: A Practical Guide*, Addison-Wesley Professional, 2001.

[5] Jason Cohen, *Best Kept Secrets of Peer Code Review: Modern Approach. Practical Advice*, Smart Bear, 2006.

"The lady that gives me a headache every few days," he grimaces. "She is the product owner or the product designer, I don't really know. But she tells me what to do feature-wise. She will just tell me that some feature must be online on Friday and your review results will just be ignored, man, I'm telling you," he giggles.[1]

He is damn right, I can understand that. The business is always right, no matter what we technical people think about it. We work for the business, we get paid by the business, and we must do what they say. In the short term, though. In the long term, the priorities must be different.

"Yes, and she will be perfectly right. She is our customer and she doesn't care about our code reviews. We must care about them, and ..."

"But she will force us to break our process," he interrupts.

"Yes, man, if it's not strong enough!"

"What do you mean?"

> The business has to share its goals with employees through a system of rewards and punishments.

"Look, we have to make sure that when she comes with a new idea, one of us picks it up and starts working on it. In most cases, that's you, as I understand. Right?" He nods. "OK, right, then you implement it somehow and submit your changes for a review. I review your code and reject it. Then, she shows up and asks, where is the feature, why isn't it implemented yet? You will tell her that it's my fault, right?"

"Of course," he smiles.

"No doubt, and she will come to me and try to force me to ignore the review and accept your changes, right?"

"You bet, she will."

"What will I do?" I'm asking rhetorically, "I will tell her to

---

[1] Elfriede Dustin, *Implementing automated software testing: How to save time and lower costs while raising quality*, Pearson Education, 2009: "The primary challenge today of testing software is that customers want more software functionality to be delivered faster and cheaper, while at the same time they expect the quality of the software to at least meet if not exceed their expectations."

get lost."

"Seriously?" he smiles.

"A hundred percent, dude," I'm exaggerating a bit, but on purpose, "and she will go to Adrian or Tony, to complain about us. If they are strong enough, they will put the blame on you and punish you."[1]

"Punish me? With a whip or what? Seriously, how will they punish me?"

"Dude, I don't know, there has to be some mechanism of punishment. Maybe they will fire you?"

"For one failed code review?" he stares at me.

"No, not for just one, but there has to be some mechanism."

"Like what?"

"I don't know, maybe some negative points, maybe some penalties. Something.[2] The point is that the company has to track your performance. And, of course, it has to not only punish you, but also reward you somehow."[3]

"That sounds better, man."

EVEN though it's difficult to imagine how a traditional company can implement an explicit reward policy, I try to improvise. "I bet. Imagine, you get a hundred bucks for each ticket closed in time and you don't get them if it's not closed in time. So, your reward is those hundred bucks and your punishment is the absence of

---

[1] Saul Axelrod, *Effects of Punishment on Human Behavior*, Academic Press, 1983.

[2] James Andreoni, *The Carrot or the Stick: Rewards, Punishments and Cooperation*, American Economic Review, Volume 93, Number 3, 2003: "While rewards alone have little influence on cooperation, punishments have some. When the two are combined the effect on cooperation is dramatic, suggesting that rewards and punishments are complements in producing cooperation."; "Thus designing an institution around rewards only and omitting an option for punishments may be a mistake."

[3] Thomas S. Bateman et al., *Job Satisfaction and the Good Soldier: The Relationship Between Affect and Employee "Citizenship,"* Academy of Management Journal, Volume 26, Number 4, 1983: "Any covariance between job satisfaction and job performance emerges only when satisfaction results from performance-contingent rewards. Any notion that satisfaction 'causes' performance is regarded as naive folk wisdom, not supportable by the empirical record."

them. Well, the punishment may be even stronger, if, say, for every failed task, you lose a chance to get the reward next time. Something like that. Nobody will take money out of your pocket if you fail to finish in time, but will pay you only if you actually stay within the timeline."

"I'm not sure I like it, though," he slowly replies. "It sounds rather harsh.[1] I will be stressed all day thinking about how to complete my task in time.[2] Moreover, money is not the only thing that motivates me.[3] Also, what about other activities that may distract me?"

"That's your problem. You should deal with them somehow on your own."

"Dude, stop it. That's not how software teams work."

"OK, tell me how software teams work. They consist of people responsible for nothing, awarded with nothing, and never punished? This literally means no management and it leads to the problems you experience everywhere."

"What problems?"

"No tests, dude! What did we start from? Did you forget?"

"Sorry, I lost my train of thought. We don't have tests because

---

[1]C. W. Von Bergen et al., *Contemporary Workplace Punishment and Discipline Recommendations*, International Journal of Interdisciplinary Research, Volume 1, Number 1, 2012: "Although it is generally accepted that supervisors and managers should avoid punishment for its supposed negative side effects, this paper illustrates that once again conventional wisdom with respect to correcting worker misbehavior is wrong and that truth is not always politically correct or as reassuring as one would like."

[2]See footnote 1 on page 29: "42% of all design faults were directly attributable to programmer stress."

[3]Sarah E. Bonnera, *The effects of monetary incentives on effort and task performance: theories, evidence, and a framework for research*, Accounting, Organizations and Society, Volume 27, 2002: "The fundamental hypothesis that predicts a positive overall relation between the presence of monetary incentives and task performance is that incentives increase effort and increased effort leads to improvements in performance (either in the short run or the long run). Furthermore, a number of mechanisms have been proposed for explicating the incentives-effort link, including expectancies, self-interest, goal setting, and self-efficacy. In contrast to this fundamental hypothesis, empirical evidence indicates that monetary incentives frequently are not associated with increased effort and improved performance."

nobody punishes us?"

I think for a second: "Well, yeah, exactly that. Look, you have no motivation[1] to complete the task in time, because there are no rewards and no punishment. Simply put, nothing really happens if you do it right and on time, or just do it a bit later, or even never. The only thing that can really happen is they fire you. But this won't happen, we know that, provided the company has money. There is a deficit of programmers on the market and you're a good developer. So, you will stay here until you quit voluntarily. In such a situation, there is absolutely no way to motivate you to write those tests, unless you are a truly responsible person by nature.[2]

But, even in that case, you will lose your motivation quickly because you will see that others are not writing the tests and commit broken code right into your beautiful classes. Simply put, in order to make all of us write tests we need to devise a degree of separation between

> Punishment demotivates when it comes from people rather than a system of well-defined rules.

those who write them and those who don't. We need to find a way to objectively value people by their results, which means that we will reward those whose results are better and punish those whose results are worse. If we find a way to detect that and respond with some motivational instrument, like money, the problem will be solved. The moment you don't write the tests, fail to commit your changes in time, and make Masha unhappy—you personally will be punished."

"And this punishment will stress me so much that I will stop working at all," Dennis replies after a short pause.

"Yes, maybe, but I doubt it. You're not the type of person who would be demotivated by a punishment. I'm talking about a punishment that has a logic."

"A logic?"

---

[1] Victor Harold Vroom, *Work and motivation*, 1964.

[2] Edward L. Deci, *Intrinsic Motivation*, Plenum Press, 1975: "Intrinsically motivated activities are ones for which there is no apparent reward except the activity itself. People seem to engage in the activities for their own sake and not because they lead to an extrinsic reward. The activities are ends in themselves rather than means to an end."

"Yes, a punishment without a logic behind it is what demotivates people.[1] A punishment that is triggered by emotions is what turns people away from the person who punishes them. On the other hand, if the punishment has some logic behind it and is not motivated by anger or any other emotions, we tend to take it as a lesson, not as an abuse."

"Interesting," he leans back and sips from his cup.

I feel thirsty too and open a bottle of mineral water. "Let me give you an example. You have kids, right?"

"Yep, two boys," he smiles.

"Imagine you tell one of your kids that he has to clean up his room every Sunday. You also tell him that, if he doesn't do it, you will withhold half of his weekly allowance. Then, later, you find out that his room is messy on Sunday evening. You tell him that he is punished and gets only half of his weekly allowance, just like you agreed before. This is the first scenario. Now the second one. You don't discuss anything with the kid. You just show up in his room on Sunday, being very angry and start screaming that his room is messy and he is punished now and you will decrease his allowance by 25%. This is the second scenario. In the first one, the punishment is twice as big, but the kid will take it much easier. Moreover, he will learn something from it. In the second scenario, he will just hate you for punishing him and won't learn a thing. Well, he will learn that his dad is very emotional and it's better to stay as far away as possible from him on Sundays. He won't connect the fact that his room is messy with the punishment. Instead, he will connect your rage and anger with it. Exactly the same happens with us programmers. We have no problem with being punished based on rules and hate being punished situationally, when the management just feels like it."

"Maybe I will take it rationally, but most people will complain about the very idea of punishment, I guarantee you that," he sips

---

[1]Vikram Sethi et al., *What causes stress in information system professionals?*, Communications of the ACM, Volume 47, Issue 3, 2004: "Clear communications about performance and reward expectations were noted by many of our respondents as useful in reducing stress levels."

again and looks at me.

"Yes, they will, but do we really need those people?" I ask, smiling. "They are lazy, anyway, let's just get rid of them," I'm joking, but he doesn't smile. "Listen, dude, you must remember that punishment always goes together with rewards. They must be balanced, just like Machiavelli taught us.[1] Just punishments alone will ruin the team as fast as just rewards. There must be a balance. You, as an owner of a task, must know what you get when you do it right and what you lose if you fail. And the balance must be as accurate as possible. If someone complains about punishment, remind them about the reward. If they keep complaining, fire them.[2] They are obviously not oriented towards achieving results, but only interested in having a good time in the office."[3]

> Rewards and punishments must be balanced and regularly reviewed for consistency.

---

[1] See footnote 4 on page 101.

[2] ★Steve McConnell, *Problem Programmers*, IEEE Software, Volume 15, Number 2, 1998: "Tolerating even one problem programmer hurts the morale and productivity of good developers. Problem programmers are often viewed as having 'low productivity,' but both software research and software experience suggest that such an assessment is too optimistic. Next time you need to improve productivity, don't look for what you can add, look for what you can take away."

[3] Frederick Herzberg et al., *The Motivation to Work*, 2nd Edition, John Wiley, 1959.

Vague requirements and laziness

Who is guilty? (86) – Lesson learned (86) – She doesn't know what she wants (86) – Punishment hurts when the scope is vague (87) – Definition of Done (87) – It's our responsibility (88) – Product owners are always vague (88) – A programmer is just a tool (89) – Time machine example (89) – Refining the requirements (89) – Prototyping (90) – We must kill weak ideas (90) – Profit (91)

D<small>ENNIS</small> thinks for a while and says: "All right, let's say I get the idea, but how will it help the business if I will be punished for the failed feature? Masha won't be happy and the feature won't be delivered."

"Yes, initially nobody will be happy, but we will know exactly who is guilty—it is you. We will punish you and then will see what we can do with the feature. Maybe we'll skip the code review or will agree that the feature can go to production without any tests; it will depend on many factors. We will do what we are doing now, anyway. But the lesson will be learned by you. The chance of failure with the next task will be lower, since you will be very motivated not to fail again."

Punishment only harms and demotivates when the scope of work is unstable or poorly defined.	"It looks like I will be the only one motivated if you're going to always punish me. It's not fair." He seems offended a bit. "Besides, what if Masha doesn't know what she wants?[1] She says 'Do it this way,' I do it, she comes back, re-

views, and makes modifications, or completely changes the idea. She is very moody: one day she likes it, tomorrow she doesn't. You are still going to blame me for failing a task? You think it's fair?"

"Well, don't be surprised, but yes."

"Nah, man, it's simply stupid, nobody will work like that. Our

---

[1] ★Karl E. Wiegers, *Software Requirements*, 3rd edition, Microsoft Press, 2013: "Don't expect your customers to present a succinct, complete, and well-organized list of their needs. Analysts must classify the myriad bits of requirements information they hear into various categories so that they can document and use it appropriately."

tasks are too vague to apply your punishment model. We don't know how much time the task will take, what exactly needs to be done, and exactly how to make our customers happy. Too many unknowns."

"You're right, give me a few minutes," I leave him, go make some tea, and think a bit. What was this discussion about? I think I managed to convince this guy that automated testing is a good thing and, in order to guarantee it everywhere in the code base, we need to motivate programmers to write tests. In order to motivate them we need to put a quality checking gate in front of them, with a code review and a script that merges their changes only if they look good. The problem is still with the understanding of the reward-punishment mechanism. Dennis is right, it's not easy at all, because the tasks have no explicit borders. We simply don't know what to reward or punish programmers for. If we do that without an explicit formula, they will get offended instead of being motivated.

WHEN I return with a cup of tea, he is standing in front of the window, looking outside. "I have an answer, which you may not like," I say to his back. "It's the responsibility of a programmer to make sure the tasks he is working with have explicit borders.[1] There is a well known term, which you most certainly have heard:

---

[1] Steve McConnell, *Code Complete: A Practical Handbook of Software Construction*, 2nd Edition, Microsoft Press, 2004· "It's fine to hope that once your customer has accepted a requirements document, no changes will be needed. On a typical project, however, the customer can't reliably describe what is needed before the code is written. The problem isn't that the customers are a lower life-form. Just as the more you work with the project, the better you understand it, the more they work with it, the better they understand it. The development process helps customers better understand their own needs, and this is a major source of requirements changes. A plan to follow the requirements rigidly is actually a plan not to respond to your customer."; "If your requirements aren't good enough, stop work, back up, and make them right before you proceed."

definition of done."[1]

It's your fault if the requirements you are working with are not clear enough.

"Yes, I've heard of it. What is it?"

"It is just another name for the borders of the task. Each task must have clear exit criteria—we must know when it's time to stop working with it. If you're a professional programmer, you must not start working on a task in which definition of done is not clear enough for you. It's our responsibility, as engineers, to make sure everything we're working with has explicit borders and well-defined exit criteria."[2]

He turns back to me: "But she can't specify a task clearly, that's the issue. Don't you understand? She very often needs my help to figure out how those features have to work. Sometimes she is just experimenting and we're throwing a lot of code away. How can we put any borders around that? It's just impossible."

"She is a product owner. That's how they usually think and behave. They are creative and must improvise and experiment. We can't change her and we shouldn't blame her. She has all the rights to do what she does: use you as a tool to achieve her results."[3]

---

[1] Kenneth S. Rubin, *Essential Scrum: A Practical Guide to the Most Popular Agile Process*, Addison-Wesley Professional, 2012: "Conceptually the definition of done is a checklist of the types of work that the team is expected to successfully complete before it can declare its work to be potentially shippable."

[2] Karl E. Wiegers, *More about Software Requirements: Thorny Issues and Practical Advice*, Microsoft Press, 2005: "An ill-defined scope boundary can have serious consequences."

[3] Hossein Saiedian, *Requirements engineering: making the connection between the software developer and customer*, Information and Software Technology, Volume 42, Number 6, 2000: "We need to understand the realities of requirements elicitation and analysis. User-specified requirements are often vague, ambiguous, and incomplete."; "Ultimately, it is the customer that decides our fate whether we like it or not and whether or not we think they are qualified to proceed without us. Without the customer's business and dollars, we cease to exist."

"What? A tool?"

"Yes, man, a tool. They use us to create the software they need in order to please their clients. We are their resources, tools, instruments—call it whatever you want—but don't get offended by that, it's business. It is your job to be useful to her. If she comes to you and asks to create a time travel machine, you must not promise her to do it tomorrow. However, you must not say that you won't do it, either. You must know how to deal with the client and any type of request. This is part of your job description: dealing with vague requirements."

> A good programmer knows how to be a useful tool for the business that pays.

THE time machine example may help me illustrate the point: "So, she needs a time machine. This requirements specification obviously has a number of serious problems, that's why it can't be implemented immediately. If I were the programmer, I would tell her that we can definitely try to help, but need to do some preliminary work beforehand."

"Like changing some fundamental laws of physics, right?"

"No. The work we have to do first is to refine the requirements. We need to know what exactly the time machine is, how far in time should it travel, forward or backward, how will it be tested in order to be accepted, how big our budget is, how much time we have to build it, what our available resources are, and so on. The requirements must be clear, just like the IEEE standard wants."[1]

"OK, let's say everything is clear, we know exactly what kind of the time machine we need. What's next?"

"Well, it will never happen. Right at this stage everything will simply fall apart. Masha will understand that the amount of resources she has won't be enough to complete this task. She will also realize that she doesn't know how exactly this time machine should work in order to be accepted as a result. There will be many other issues which will destroy the project right at the stage of requirements specification."

---

[1] *IEEE Recommended Practice for Software Requirements Specifications*, IEEE 830-1998, IEEE Computer Society, 1998.

"I'm destroying projects?" Dennis smiles.

"Well, yes, by creating something for her that doesn't really work in the end. Instead of spending time for requirements specification and documentation, you just create a prototype and demonstrate it.[1] Then, she says that this is not what she wants and you throw the code away. I believe it's called 'specification by example'[2] and this is how you help her."[3]

"Ruin the ideas?" he keeps joking.

> By being skeptical about requirements and new ideas, a programmer helps the business fail fast.

"Yes. Not every idea makes sense business-wise. If we don't kill most of them, the best one won't ever see the market, because we will spend our resources equally between all of them, the good and the bad.[4] Instead, we must do our best to kill the bad ones as soon as possible. The sooner, the better. Experimenting helps us do exactly that: kill the wrong ideas earlier. But our intention is not to kill ideas! Our main intention is to do as little as possible. Because we are lazy."[5]

---

[1] Stephen J. Andriole, *Fast, Cheap Requirements Prototype, Or Else!* IEEE Software, Volume 11, Number 2, 1994: "Throwaway prototyping (sometimes called exploratory prototyping) is always cost-effective and always improves specifications. The process has nine steps: elicit initial requirements; model requirements; identify constraints; prioritize initial requirements; design; evaluate designs; specification; interactive prototyping; and requirements validation."

[2] Gojko Adzic, *Specification by Example: How Successful Teams Deliver the Right Software*, Manning, 2011.

[3] See footnote 1 on page 87: "If the requirements are especially bad or volatile and none of the suggestions above are workable, cancel the project."

[4] James Johnson, *My Life Is Failure*, Lulu, 2016: "It should be noted that organizations should not shy away from risky projects. An organization that has no failures will never be a leader in the marketplace, since it is not pushing its technology fast or far enough. A kill switch lets you do risky projects while minimizing losses. In fact, it could step up the amount of projects. To paraphrase Thomas Edison, 'The secret to success is failing fast.'"

[5] Eric S. Raymond, *The Cathedral and the Bazaar*, Knowledge, Technology & Policy, Volume 12, Number 3, 1999: "While I don't claim to be a great programmer, I try to imitate one. An important trait of the great ones is constructive laziness. They know that you get an A not for effort but for results, and that it's almost always easier to start from a good partial solution than from nothing at all."

Hᴇ smiles and scratches his head, "What?"

"You heard me," I take a little pause. "Look, we agreed that we are tools, business-wise, right? In other words, you are the service provider and Masha is your client. If this is how things work, your primary objective, as in any business, is to spend less and make more. This literally means deliver as little as possible and get paid for as much time as you can. This is also known as making profit."

"Are you sure you can say that in the office, dude?"

"Don't worry, I'm not saying anything against the business. Listen up, let me finish, and you will understand that I'm right."

> A profitable programmer writes less code and closes more tickets and projects.

"You can't be right by saying that programmers must be lazy, dude, it's insane. I need to hit the bathroom, one minute," and he leaves.

Egoism and altruism

Be lazy, don't waste time (92) – Transactional and transformational leadership (93) – Equity theory (95) – Egoists (95) – Altruists (95) – Balance (96) – Why are altruists worse than egoists? (96) – Loving wife example (97) – Fail fast (97) – Fail Safe (97) – We must encourage egoism (98) – "One can only lean of what resists" (99) – Decomposition of complexity (99) – "You have to become an egoist" (99) – Rewards and punishment (100) – Carrots and sticks (100) – People are "fickle, hypocritical, and greedy of gain" (100) – $20 per closed ticket (101) – "It is not for us" (101) – To fix the system, we have to fix its people (102) – Surrender (102)

He comes back and I continue: "Here's the point. We are doing this with Masha not because we are good or bad. We just don't want to waste our time on something with questionable reasons. We want to work as little as possible at the same time closing as many requests and projects as we can.[1] The proofs of concept you're doing for Masha are also perfect indicators of your laziness— you don't want to write production code until you make sure the requirements are stable and signed off by your client. Being lazy is not just an emotion, but a perfectly reasonable business attitude.[2] If we would be eager to write more code and do that as soon as

---

[1] Fred C. Kelly, *The Man of the 'One Best Way': How Frank Gilbreth studies men and their ways*, Popular Science Monthly, Volume 97, Number 6, 1920: "Most of the chance improvements in human motions that eliminate unnecessary movement and reduce fatigue have been hit upon by men who were lazy—so lazy that every needless step counted."; "So-called expert factory workers are often the most wasteful of their motions and strength. Because of their energy and ability to work at high speed, such men may be able to produce a large quantity of good work, and thus qualify as experts, but they tire themselves out of all proportion to the amount of work done."

[2] Philipp Lenssen, *Why Good Programmers Are Lazy and Dumb*, https://goo.gl/KZcA2W, 2005: "I realized that, paradoxically enough, good programmers need to be both lazy and dumb."; "Lazy, because only a lazy programmer will avoid writing monotonous, repetitive code—thus avoiding redundancy, the enemy of software maintenance and flexible refactoring."; "A good programmer must be dumb, because if he's smart, and he knows he is smart, he will: a) stop learning b) stop being critical towards his own work."

possible, we would only harm the business."[1]

"I don't get it, dude," he looks concerned.

"Look, a group can achieve something only when its members contribute to the cumulative result and take some value back. It's obvious, right? You write code, they pay you. I write code, they pay me. Masha designs a product, they pay her. Of course, it's not only money. There are many other intangible values we give to the group and take back. It's a rather complicated set of transactions,[2] but they are transactions—this is what is important to understand, no matter what those laissez-

> The key success factor is the fairness of transactions between the project and its members.

---

[1] Jeff Atwood, *How to be Lazy, Dumb, and Successful*, https://goo.gl/NQGw2B, 2005: "Being lazy and dumb isn't just good career advice: it's the key to running a successful software business, too."

[2] James A. Odumeru, *Transformational vs. Transactional Leadership Theories: Evidence in Literature*, International Review of Management and Business Research, Volume 2, Issue 2, 2013: "Transactional Leadership, also known as managerial leadership, focuses on the role of supervision, organisation, and group performance; transactional leadership is a style of leadership in which the leader promotes compliance of his followers through both rewards and punishments."

faire,[1] charismatic,[2] and transformational[3] leadership adepts say.[4]

---

[1] Anders Skogstad et al., *The Destructiveness of Laissez-Faire Leadership Behavior*, Journal of Occupational Health Psychology, Volume 12, Number 1, 2007: "The results indicate that laissez-faire leadership may be more of a counterproductive leadership style than a zero type of leadership style, associated with a stressful environment characterized by high levels of role stress and interpersonal conflicts. When workplace stressors and interpersonal problems are not dealt with, they may even escalate into bullying, resulting in high levels of psychological distress among those involved and even among those observing the bullying. Organizations should not only prevent and manage abusive and aggressive leadership, but they should also be aware of the potentially negative effects of laissez-faire leaders, who create work environments with high levels of interpersonal stressors."

[2] Jay A. Conger et al., *Toward a Behavioral Theory of Charismatic Leadership in Organizational Settings*, The Academy of Management Review, Volume 12, Number 4, 1987: "Administrators act as caretakers responsible for the maintenance of the status quo. They influence others through their position power as legitimated by the organization. Leaders, as opposed to administrators, direct or nudge their followers in the direction of an established goal. Charismatic leaders, however, transform their followers (instead of nudging them) and seek radical reforms in them in order to achieve the idealized goal."

[3] Bernard M. Bass, *From Transactional to Transformational Leadership: Learning to Share the Vision* Organizational Dynamics, Volume 18, Number 3, 1990: "Transformational leaders have better relationships with their supervisors and make more of a contribution to the organization than do those who are only transactional. Moreover, employees say that they themselves exert a lot of extra effort on behalf of managers who are transformational leaders. Organizations whose leaders are transactional are less effective than those whose leaders are transformational—particularly if much of the transactional leadership is passive management-by-exception (intervening only when standards are not being met). Employees say they exert little effort for such leaders."

[4] ★Gary Yukl, *An Evaluation of the Conceptual Weaknesses in Transformational and Charismatic Leadership Theories*, Leadership Quarterly, Volume 10, Number 2, 1999: "It is evident that charismatic and transformational leadership theories provide important insights, but some serious conceptual weaknesses need to be corrected to make the theories more useful. They do not describe the underlying influence processes clearly, nor do they specify how the leader behaviors are related to these processes. It seems that instrumental compliance is most important for transactional leadership, internalization is most important for transformational leadership, and personal identification is most important for charismatic leadership. However, the relevance of these and other influence processes for each type of leadership is still largely a matter of speculation."

The group works and moves forward when everybody who is in it gives and takes something: rewards, pleasure, appreciation, positive emotions, fun, knowledge, safety, self-fulfillment or simply cash."[1]

"Yes, so?"

"The equity theory says that they will give as much as they can only when they take back an equal amount of benefits.[2] Well, they can't take back exactly the same amount, or there will be no business and no profit, but they must feel that the amount of results they produce is fairly similar to the amount of appreciation they take back home."

I take a small pause and continue: "As a member of a group you may have two extreme attitudes: either be an egoist or an altruist.[3] As an egoist you will demand everything and give nothing back, you will steal from the group. Of course, the group won't tolerate you for too long, provided its other members are strong enough to fight back and eject you. They may also force you to start contributing. I'm sure you have seen a lot of those situations in the software business, when some lazy programmer is not doing anything, but is getting a decent salary for quite a long time."

"Yes, a lot," he sighs.

"There you go. The alternative attitude is altruism, which means that you contribute everything you can and ask almost nothing back. The group will, of course, give you something, but way less than you deserve. I'm sure you have seen such situations

---

[1] Abdul Qayyum Chaudhry et al., *Impact of Transactional and Laissez Faire Leadership Style on Motivation*, International Journal of Business and Social Science, Volume 3, Number 7, 2012: "So the workers are more motivated in those banks where transaction leadership style is used."

[2] See footnote 3 on page 22.

[3] James H. Davis et al., *Toward a Stewardship Theory of Management*, Academy of Management Review, Volume 22, Number 1, 1997: "Both agents and principals in agency theory seek to receive as much possible utility with the least possible expenditure. Given the choice between two alternatives, the rational *agent* or principal will choose the option that increases his or her individual utility."; "Given a choice between self-serving behavior and pro-organizational behavior, a *steward*'s behavior will not depart from the interests of his or her organization."

too, when someone literally lives in the office, fixing all the critical issues, constantly fire-fighting, and earning way less money than others who barely touch the code."

"That's me," he says, sadly.

> Both altruism and egoism of team members are the symptoms of a defective management system.

"Well, yes, you're on the altruistic side of the scale, and it's not good.[1] But I also think that neither egoism nor altruism is good. There must be a balance. When someone behaves like an egoist and the team tolerates that, it's a weakness of the team. It basically means that the management in the team is too stupid, weak, or both. The management can't organize the process such that egoistic people would be punished earlier."

"Here comes the punishment again?" he smiles.

"Yes, exactly. If you act like an egoist and the team doesn't punish you, it's a defect in the process, and it must be fixed. On the other hand, if you act like an altruist, it is another type of a defect in the system, even more critical than the first one, but less visible and that's why it's more dangerous."

THE concept seems to surprise him, but I continue: "Are you aware of the fail fast[2] philosophy?"

"Yes, it's about throwing exceptions instead of trying to recover from an error."[3]

"It's not only about coding. The fail fast concept can be

---

[1] See footnote 3 on page 131: "Not only may outstanding job performance not guarantee you a promotion, it can even hurt."

[2] Eric Ries, *The Lean Startup: How Today's Entrepreneurs Use Continuous Innovation to Create Radically Successful Businesses*, Currency, 2011.

[3] Jim Shore, *Fail Fast*, IEEE Software, Volume 21, Number 5, 2004: "Failing fast seems like it could result in pretty fragile software."; "Over time, more and more errors will fail fast, and you'll see the cost of debugging decrease and the quality of your system improve."

applied to anything, from life situations to Java programming.[1] Say, you are married ..."

"I am married!" he interrupts.

"Right, let's say your wife says that she is not happy about you coming back from work so late. There are two tactics for your response. Fail safe: Even though there is obviously something wrong with your relationship, you try to save it; you promise her that you will try to return home earlier; the conflict is suppressed until later. Fail fast: You ask her whether she doesn't love you anymore and why; you try to ruin your marriage as soon as possible, since there is already the first sign of disagreement between you guys."

"That's an awesome idea, dude. I would have killed my marriage three years ago if I listened to you," he smiles.

"Yes, you would have killed this one and found a new wife, which would be more loving and understanding. No offense,

> Quality increases when defects immediately lead to failures, which then get fixed.

I'm just using this situation as an example. In fail fast, when there is even a smallest reason for a failure, we use it and fail. We don't try to recover what is already broken, we help it die. It will learn something from it and improve fast, or it will actually come to its end. To the contrary, the fail safe approach begets troubles. In the short term, it helps, but in the long run it only degrades quality, because problems accumulate."

He stands up and stretches his back: "Interesting. So, what about altruists?"

"Altruists are fail safe guys. Egoists are fail fast creatures. We already agreed that a properly functional team is balanced: members of the group contribute as much as they take back. Then, one day in such a great team a 'defect' shows up—someone stops

---

[1] Yegor Bugayenko, *Elegant Objects*, Volume 1, CreateSpace, 2016: "I think that stability and robustness can only be achieved if errors are revealed and immediately reported. The sooner we find the problem and the faster we crash, the better the overall quality will eventually be. To the contrary, the longer we conceal the problem, the bigger the trouble will become."

getting back as much as they deserve—the motivational system is broken. Egoists will reveal this defect quickly, because they will stop working while the money will continue to come to their pockets anyway. The team will die pretty soon since it will run out of money and there will be no progress. Or it won't die and will fix the defect quickly, by introducing some new more effective motivational scheme. On the other hand, let's consider what happens if altruists discover the same defect: They will continue to contribute more than they get back and the system won't feel it anyhow. The project won't die immediately, since there will be no short term damage, the budget won't be wasted, the amount of contribution from the altruists will remain high. However, in the long term this defect will kill the project and the team."

"How?"

Altruistic behavior of team members harms the project, while egoistic one makes it stronger and helps it survive.

"Well, these altruists will quit eventually.[1] Aren't you frustrated by your situation in this team?"[2]

"True," he sighs.

"The same will happen with all the best people, and the system won't learn anything. It will slowly degrade and lose the best talents. To survive, the management system must be designed with the fail fast philosophy in mind, which means that egoistic behavior must be encouraged."

---

[1] Michael Babula, *Motivation, Altruism, Personality, and Social Psychology*, Palgrave Macmillan, 2013: "We can delineate from the evidence presented that the biggest threat to our psychological development to exocentric altruistic motivation is structural violence in the form of needs frustration. It produces a vicious cycle whereby large numbers of people can be turned from their drive to exocentric altruism into xenophobia."

[2] Robert H. Moorman, *Relationship Between Organizational Justice and Organizational Citizenship Behaviors: Do Fairness Perceptions Influence Employee Citizenship?* Journal of Applied Psychology, Volume 76, Number 6, 1991: "Fairness perceptions, particularly those derived from interactional justice, are instrumental in predicting the occurrence of citizenship. Therefore, managers should be aware of the benefits of behaving toward subordinates in a manner perceived as fair. Managers should be concerned with how they treat their employees because employees' perceptions of that treatment could affect the occurrence of citizenship behaviors."

"And how is that exactly?"

"The business must encourage programmers to be lazy and fight for their own interests all the time. By laziness here I mean a permanent intent to do less and get more. If everybody behaves like that, the business will be constantly facing the problem: how to manage those lazy and greedy people. The business will either die or invent a very effective and strong mechanism, which will be very beneficial for both programmers and the business. It will be balanced. The moment it loses its balance, egoists will immediately take advantage and the business will have to fix the mistake in order to survive. So, what I'm saying is that a professional developer must be egoistic and lazy, to help the business be effective and stay alive longer. The business doesn't need us to be helpful altruists. To be able to rely on us it needs us to be selfish and always ready to push back. As Stendhal said long time ago: 'One can only lean on what resists.'"[1]

HE takes his coffee from the table, sips, and thinks for a while. "Well, sounds logical, what can I say. But how does it solve the original problem of Masha being too vague and unclear with her requirements?"

"Well, it's easy, you just have to push her back every time you don't find her ideas clear enough. And if they look clear, you need to break them down to smaller pieces, which your laziness is ready to accept. Simply put, when the task is too big or unclear, you must suggest to do something smaller instead and call it a day, just because you're an egoist and don't want to help anyone for free," I smile.

"So you're saying that it's my fault that the tasks Masha is giving me don't have borders?"

"Exactly, and you do that because you're an altruist."

"I have to become an egoist?"

"Yes."

"Well, it's an interesting philosophy, but I'm not sure Tony will like it," he smiles.

"You are right, I don't think he will, unfortunately."

---

[1]Stendhal, *Le Rouge et le Noir*, 1830.

"Can we try to convince him that we will be lazy, starting tomorrow," he laughs.

"No, this won't work, but we can convince him that we need a system of rewards and punishment. Now, as you know, nobody is motivated to complete any tasks. We work mostly out of our natural altruism. Just like you. The moment the company starts rewarding for results and punishing for their absence, the egoism will start to grow," I respond and his phone rings.

Dennis picks up the phone and I think about the system we can introduce in a company like this. Can they really handle this idea? Are they ready to be rewarded and punished? Honestly speaking, everybody and everywhere communicates according to this pretty old "carrot and stick" model, but very few can admit it.[1] Even if it's an artist who paints on a canvas and says that only his feelings drive him. Such an artist still has a carrot and a stick. The carrot is the appreciation and recognition delivered by the society. The stick is the lack of them, if the painting is not good enough. Any job, no matter what the industry is or the amount of creativity it requires, is done because there is a potential reward and an unwanted punishment. That's how we are designed to behave, no matter how much we may not like it.[2]

> Carrot-and-stick is the best motivational model to encourage egoism in a team.

The business, if it's smart enough, must deploy the right

---

[1] Bernard M. Bass, *Leadership, Psychology, and Organizational Behavior*, Harper, 1960: "There are two ways to change the level of motivation of others—by threats of punishment, or by the promises of reward."

[2] Daniel H. Pink, *Drive: The Surprising Truth About What Motivates Us*, Riverhead Books, 2011: "Indeed, the very premise of extrinsic incentives is that we'll always respond rationally to them. But even most economists don't believe that anymore. Sometimes these motivators work. Often they don't."

carrots and sticks.[1] For simple jobs, like changing oil in a car, it will be easier. For more complex jobs, like creating a new encryption algorithm, it will be much more difficult. But nevertheless, it's necessary to do. We can't, like Trotsky suggested,[2] just rely on people's innate desire to work, without any sticks and carrots. People are not like that, no matter how well we think of them.[3] Machiavelli said five hundred years ago that people were "fickle, hypocritical, and greedy of gain."[4] Nothing has changed since then.

I'M ready to suggest something and hope that it will work. "How about this," I say when he hangs up the phone. "We just do two things. First, all tasks must go through tickets. Anything anyone wants us to do must have a ticket number. Moreover, we don't do anything unless it has a ticket number. And the second rule: for each closed ticket the person who closes it gets a bonus. Let's say, $20," I smile.

"This won't work, but we can try."

"Why not?"

"I don't know, you will see, let's talk to the boss," and Adrian moves his chair closer to us.

"I heard your discussion, guys, it won't work," he says.

"There you go," Dennis smiles, happily.

"Why?"

---

[1] Steven Kerr, *On the Folly of Rewarding A, While Hoping for B*, Academy of Management Journal, Volume 18, Number 4, 1975: "This is not to say the all organizational behavior is determined by formal rewards and punishments. Certainly it is true that in the absence of formal reinforcement some soldiers will be patriotic, some presidents will be ecology minded, and some orphanage directors will care about children. The point, however, is that in such cases the reward is not *causing* the behaviors desired by is only a fortunate bystander. For an organization to *act* upon its members, the formal reward system should positively reinforce desired behaviors, not constitute an obstacle to be overcome."

[2] Leon Trotsky, *My Life: An Attempt at an Autobiography*, 1930.

[3] Ángel Medinilla, *Agile Management: Leadership in an Agile Environment*, Springer-Verlag, 2012: "Money is not the main motivator, but a hygiene factor, and workers want to be proud of their work and enjoy it through self-organization, learning, vision, and connecting to others."

[4] ★Niccolò Machiavelli, *Il Principe*, 1513.

"Because it's very difficult to define tasks, especially when we don't really know what is required. Moreover, we change priorities frequently. In the morning Dennis has to work with one task and a few hours later it's something else. We need to be more agile than you're suggesting," he smiles.

"Do you really think it's wrong by itself, or there are some specific issues in our particular case?"

"I don't know ... we have bigger problems now ... we can try it next year, I think," he answers and I understand that he is right. It's impossible to change the management system without changing the managers who built it.

> To effectively fight with a management chaos one has to be ready to fight with the people inside it.

The management is the product of people who created it. The chaos we have now in this company was created by these very people. Both Adrian and Dennis are parts of the system. Thanks to them it works like it works. If I really want to change something, I have to either make sure they go away, or their way of thinking is changed.

Fixing the system without fixing people that work in it would be a huge trauma for them; they will do everything they can to prevent it from happening. It's not the chaos that I have to fight with. It's the people in charge. Do I really want to start this fight? No, I don't. Maybe next year, just like Adrian said, I smile to myself and call it a day. The conversation is over.

"Right, let's postpone it for now," I say to Adrian and smile to Dennis.

He looks surprised: "You surrender so fast?"

"I don't surrender, we will get back to this discussion later, don't worry."

Conflicts

The situation manages us, not the other way around (103) – RESTful API conflict (103) – Conflicts are progress catalysts (104) – Conflict resolution techniques (105) – Win-lose (105) – Lose-lose (105) – Win-win (106) – Compromises are evil (106) – Are there any conflict resolution procedures? (106) – Technical leader (106) – Lack of the architect role (107) – Responsibility and authority (107) – Democratic voting (107) – Hierarchical team decision making (108) – Discipline is stressful (108) – Effective architect (109)

ANOTHER two weeks and I start to understand the problem this team is suffering from: the lack of management. Everything is *ad hoc* here, which means that things happen the way they would most likely happen in any particular point in time. The situation manages us, not the other way around. However, it would not be fair to say that there is no process at all. It definitely exists and is based on some principles, but they are pretty primitive and derived from good old force: whoever is stronger wins and we do what that person says.

Here is an example, last week we were delivering a new version of the order processing microservice. We added a few new RESTful entry points to it, which were going to be used by Bao and his guys to retrieve the history of an order. A few of his developers said that the way we package the payload in JSON is not data complete.

> Conflicts, as technical progress catalysts, must be encouraged; their resolution procedures must be explicit.

They wanted to see all possible data in one response, while we made it possible to access all data only through a number of micro-requests. They said it's too much and too verbose. They wanted us to give them every single data we had, in one JSON response. Their point was that this is our internal interface and we know exactly that the data will be required. What is the point of making five requests if just the first one would be sufficient? Long story short, we were right and they were wrong, as we saw it. Bao saw it in the opposite way.

Adrian was saying that the server must dictate the design and it must be universal. Bao was saying that the microservice must do what its clients are asking it to do. They are the clients and we are the service providers, we must satisfy the requirements. He had a point, right? Not surprisingly, they called a meeting. There were eight people in the meeting room and it took over three hours[1] to resolve this technical conflict.

It's obvious[2] that conflicts are what push progress forward.[3] Without conflicts nothing would ever be achieved in this world.[4,5]

---

[1] Nicholas C. Romano et al., *Meeting analysis: Findings from research and practice*, Proceedings of the 34th Annual Hawaii International Conference on System Sciences, 2001: "Many reviews and surveys reveal that meetings dominate workers' and managers' time and yet are considered to be costly, unproductive and dissatisfying."

[2] John M. Levine, *Social Foundations of Cognition*, Annual Review of Psychology, Volume 44, 1993: "Socio-cognitive conflict occurs when individuals have different responses to the same problem and are motivated to achieve a joint solution. The intellectual development produced by socio-cognitive conflict reflects extensive cognitive restructuring rather than mere imitation, as indicated by subjects' ability to generalize responses from one domain to another, to employ novel arguments that were not mentioned during interaction, and to profit from interaction with peers at the same or lower levels of cognitive development."

[3] Bernard Mayer, *The Dynamics of Conflict Resolution: A Practitioner's Guide*, Jossey-Bass, 1946: "Conflict is not in itself a bad thing. There are many reasons why it is a necessary part of the growth and development of individuals, families, communities, and societies. Conflict can help build community, define and balance people's needs as individuals with their needs as participants in larger systems, and help them face and address in a clear and conscious way the many difficult choices that life brings to them."; "By facing major conflicts, addressing them, reorganizing as necessary to deal with them, and moving on, social organizations adapt to changes in their environment."

[4] Kenneth Cloke et al., *Resolving Conflicts at Work: Eight Strategies for Everyone on the Job*, John Wiley & Son, 2005: "Every conflict you experience at work will present you with an opportunity to significantly improve your personal life, expand the effectiveness of your organization, increase the satisfaction of your friends, coworkers, and customers, and release you from impasse."

[5] Stefan Schulz-Hardt, *Productive conflict in group decision making: genuine and contrived dissent as strategies to counteract biased information seeking*, Organizational Behavior and Human Decision Processes, Volume 88, Issue 2, 2002.

Hegel said[1] two hundred years ago that "war is progress, peace is stagnation," which, as I understand it, means that without making and resolving a conflict neither side of it would be interested to grow, develop, become better, improve, and even survive. The war, as the most extreme form of a conflict, is what motivates us to do all that. The goal is not to eliminate the war and find peace—this will only lead to stagnation. The goal is to find the most civilized, constructive, and effective forms of it.[2]

THERE are a number of techniques and a few outcomes a conflict resolution may produce.[3] All of them belong to three categories:[4] win-lose, lose-lose, and win-win.[5]

When we started the discussion, Bao wanted to resolve the conflict in a "win-lose" way by using force. He insisted that we made a mistake and had to fix it. He didn't want to hear any reasons and was even using his voice. If we would agree with him we would lose and he would win. This would not be a perfect result, since our entire logic behind our design would be ignored. Also, such a win-lose outcome would hurt programmers' motivation on Adrian's side, since they would realize that Adrian is weak. How much they would trust him in the future?

Then, they tried to make a compromise, which is a very typical mistake most conflicts make, because it leads to losses on both sides and that's why it is called "lose-lose." It was suggested to

---

[1] Georg Wilhelm Friedrich Hegel, *Phenomenology of Spirit*, 1807.
[2] David M. Schweiger, *Group approaches for improving strategic decision making: A comparative analysis of dialectical inquiry, devil's advocacy, and consensus*, Academy of Management Journal, Volume 29, Number 1, 1986: "On the one hand, conflict improves decision quality; on the other, it may weaken the ability of the group to work together."
[3] Jacob Bercovitch, *Conflict Resolution in the Twenty-first Century: Principles, Methods, and Approaches*, University of Michigan Press, 2009.
[4] Heidi Burgess, *Encyclopedia of conflict resolution*, ABC-CLIO, 1949: "The game theory terms win-win, win-lose, and all-lose describe possible outcomes of a two-party game or dispute."; "People can be expected to voluntarily accept dispute settlements only if they emerge as winners. This is why the goal of dispute resolution is often a win-win settlement."
[5] ★Rita Mulcahy, *PMP Exam Prep, Eighth Edition: Rita's Course in a Book for Passing the PMP Exam*, 6th Edition, 2015.

decrease the amount of HTTP requests from five to three. Such a consensus would neither be in favor of our design philosophy nor in Bao's one. It would be in favor of no philosophy. It would be just a workaround to make everybody happy and relax. This is what all compromises are about: calm everybody down and throw everyone a small bone so that they would just shut up. How much value does it bring to the architecture?

A compromise sacrifices technical correctness for the sake of emotional peace making, which makes it the worst conflict resolution technique.	Finally, we made a "win-win" decision. We agreed that the first HTTP request would have an optional argument, which would instruct the server to deliver the entire result in one JSON payload, omitting the necessity to make any more consecutive HTTP requests. Thus, both sides won. Adrian won be-

cause the API remained designed the "right way," according to his understanding. Bao won because his team got an ability to retrieve the entire data set with one request.

Every conflict must produce a win-win outcome and must never be resolved through a compromise, which makes both sides suffer in some way. Even forcing one side to do what the other side wants is better than a compromise. If we would force Bao to accept our design it would not break the design approach Adrian suggested, which, in the eyes of at least one group of programmers, was correct.

However, the key issue was that our conflict didn't have any predictable resolution mechanism. We simply didn't know what to do. We didn't know who had enough power to say what's right and what's wrong. Bao was using his voice, Adrian was ready to cry, Dennis was laughing and most probably thinking about quitting as soon as possible, and I was trying to understand why this situation is so common for so many teams. It was a mess. We didn't know who the boss was. Not the boss who pays the salary, but the technical boss, also known as the architect.

Any software project must have a technical leader, who is

responsible for all technical decisions made by the team and have enough authority to make them.[1] Responsibility and authority are two mandatory components that must be present in order to make it possible to call such a person an architect. In our situation the role of the architect was not occupied, that's why we had such a long fight, which, lucky for us, ended with a long meeting and a more or less correct design decision. If there were an architect, he would just listen to both sides, collect their opinions and make an immediate decision, taking full responsibility for it. Everybody, including Adrian, Bao, myself, and both teams, would just had to agree and obey.

If that architect needed a meeting, he would call it. If he needed a written explanation of the design decisions we were suggesting to make, he would request it. If he needed a proof of concept, he would require us to develop it. This decision would be his business. He would know that he would pay the full price if the decision would appear to be incorrect.

> Just by making the architect role explicit, a team can effectively resolve many technical conflicts.

Responsibility means an inevitable punishment for mistakes; authority means full power to make them. Not only the architect, but any person in the team must have them both. However, the architect must be responsible for the entire technical solution under development.

M<small>OST</small> software teams don't have such a role. Instead, they prefer to make technical decisions in a "democratic" way, sometimes even

---

[1] Grady Booch, *Object Solutions*, Addison-Wesley, 1996: "Every project should have exactly one identifiable architect, although for larger projects, the principal architect should be backed up by an architecture team of modest size."

by collecting votes from every single programmer involved.[1] Needless to say, there is no place for responsibility in such a situation. Nobody will make responsible and thoughtful decisions when they know that there is no personal reward for success and punishment for failures.[2]

A massive waste of time is yet another negative outcome of this "democratic" team decision making process. We've spent over thirty staff-hours on something that a smart architect would resolve in just an hour. If I were that architect, and Adrian came to me with Bao asking to help them resolve the conflict, I would ask them both to explain their positions. And I would ask them to do that in writing, not verbally. They would spend half an hour each, top. Then, I would ask them to show me how the entire API of the microservice is designed. That would take another half an hour or so. Then, I would need more information about how much time the re-design would take. I would ask them for as much information as I would need and they would provide it. Everything they would write for me, of course, would stay in our project documentation for future generations. Then, I would just make my decision and inform them about it.[3] My decision, with the reasoning behind it, would also stay in the project files.

However, most teams and programmers don't want to have such a structured and disciplined decision making process simply

---

[1] Jie Lu et al., *Multi-objective Group Decision Making: Methods, Software and Applications With Fuzzy Set Techniques*, Imperial College Press, 2007: "Majority rule. Some group decisions are made based on a vote (maybe in an informal way) for alternatives or individual opinions following a period of discussions. The majority's opinion is as the solution of the group for the decision problem. This method can make a group decision fast, and follows a clear rule of using democratic participation in the process."

[2] Linda Klebe Trevino, *Ethical Decision Making in Organizations: A Person-Situation Interactionist Model*, Academy of Management Review, Volume 11, Number 3, 1986: "If organizations are interested in encouraging moral action, they should promote individual responsibility for action consequences at every level of the organization."

[3] Sharolyn Converse et al., *Shared Mental Models in Expert Team Decision Making*, Individual and Group Decision Making: Current Issues, 1993: "In hierarchically structured teams where final decision authority is retained by a single individual, the team functions to provide the decision maker with assessments and information that are crucial to the situation."

because it's no fun. It's boring. There are no meetings, no arguments, no fights, no scandals, and no time wasting. Just pure work. Who would like it when you are are on a payroll? We all know that discussing technical decisions is the most time consuming process and the least stressful at the same time. Meetings take hours and require very little attention from its participants, simply because the decision is not yet made, nobody owes anything to the boss, there is nobody yet to blame, and you can always pretend that you are thinking, while dreaming about your next vacation.[1]

> To make technical decisions, a result-oriented team needs a strong architect and a decision making process, not meetings.

Having a professional software architect in the team with full authority and responsibility is much more stressful for the entire team, since that person won't organize long meetings and won't promote democracy. Instead, the architect will collect information in writing and will always try to blame those who provided wrong data. The process will be formalized and not free for its participants—everybody will have to pay for their mistakes and won't be able to get away with just attending a meeting and pretending to be very interested. However, the obvious question is whether this is what programmers and their bosses truly want.

---

[1] Lawrence G. Votta Jr., *Does Every Inspection Need a Meeting?* Proceeding of the 1st ACM SIGSOFT symposium on Foundations of Software Engineering, 1993: "We have found that inspection meetings are not as beneficial as managers and developers think they are. Even worse, they cost much more in terms of product development interval and developer's time than anyone realizes."; "Although synergy is firmly believed to be the major justification for holding inspection meetings, experimental evidence shows that little or no synergy actually occurs."

Manual testing

Testing, testing, and testing (110) – How many bugs do you find per week? (111) – What is the goal of testing? (111) – No bugs philosophy (111) – Test scripts (111) – Testers must prove that the software is broken (112) – Testing is a sadistic process (113) – Failed vs passed (113) – A test is successful when the product is broken (114) – xUnit frameworks (114) – Quality Assurance doesn't mean testing (114) – ISO 9001 (115) – Fake job titles (116) – Testers and coders are equally important (116) – The gate keeper misconception (117) – Unlimited amount of bugs (118) – Testing is not discrete (118) – Inverted motivation (119) – Testing and coding as parallel processes (119) – Testing deliverables (121) – Does testing have deliverables? (122) – We need bugs! (122) – We may pay for the bugs (123) – Focus on bugs only (124) – Testing metrics (124) – Priorities (125)

JYOTI is the lead of a small manual testing group in the company. I met her a few days ago. I come to her desk to chat about testing. This subject interests me a lot, even though I never worked as a tester.

"What's up?" I start.

"Not much, how are you doing?"

"Listen," I jump straight to the point, "I want to know what you think about the testing process and its quality here. Can you tell me what's going on and what the problems are?" I take an empty chair next to her.

"No problems, we are just very busy testing, and testing, and testing," she smiles.

"That's no good, you need some rest. Don't you think that the quality of our software is low and that's why you are testing so much?"

"I don't know," she carefully responds, "But you can always improve it."

"That's what we need testers for, I believe, to tell us what is wrong so that we can improve it. How many tickets do you usually file, say, per week?"

"Me personally?"

"No, the entire group. You have three testers and yourself,

right?"

"Yes, there are four of us," she says, "and we don't really count the tickets. I can count them for you now, if you want."

"No, I'll do it myself later. Aren't you interested in this metric? Aren't bugs your primary result?"

"What do you mean?" she smiles.

"I'm absolutely serious," I am a bit surprised that she laughs. "As far as I understand, the goal of testing is to find bugs and report them, the more the better."

"No," she exclaims, "the goal is to make sure the software doesn't have bugs, that's what testing is for. Who needs a software with bugs?"[1]

> The biggest mistake a tester can make is to think that the goal of software testing is to confirm that the software works as intended.

"How can you, in a testing group, make sure the software doesn't have bugs?"

"When they are ready to release a new version, they ask us to test it. We go through all features and test how they work. If we find that something is broken, we tell them and they fix it. Then, when everything is clear, we give them a green light and they release. This is how we guarantee that a broken product won't be released. That's why they call us Quality Assurance, because we assure quality. See?"

"So, basically, if you say that there are no bugs, the quality is high and they can release, right?"

"Correct."

"How do you know that everything works as expected and you don't miss something critical?"

---

[1] Watts S. Humphrey, *Reflections on Management: How to Manage Your Software Projects, Your Teams, Your Boss, and Yourself*, Pearson Education, 2010: "Some people mistakenly refer to software defects as bugs. When called bugs, they seem like pesky things that should be swatted or even ignored. This trivializes a critical problem and fosters a wrong attitude. Thus, when an engineer says there are only a few bugs left in a program, the reaction is one of relief. Suppose, however, that we called them time bombs instead of bugs. Would you feel the same sense of relief if a programmer told you that he had thoroughly tested a program and there were only a few time bombs left in it? Just using a different term changes your attitude entirely."

"We have a list of test procedures we always complete. Let me show you," she shows me a few pieces of paper with a long list of items, most of which have some marks and comments. "We go through this entire list and make sure each test passes."

I scratch my head thinking about my next question. She is so wrong and on so many levels that I don't even know where to start. I see three obvious issues in what I've heard so far.

FIRST of all, it is her understanding of the philosophy of testing. Dr. Myers said, "despite the plethora of software testing tomes available on the market today, many developers seem to have an attitude that is counter to extensive testing," and then added that, "testing is the process of executing a program with the intent of finding errors."[1] It seems that Jyoti, like many others,[2,3,4,5] doesn't understand this very principle. She believes that the job of a tester is to prove that the software is bug free, while it has to be the other way around: The job of a tester is to prove that the

---

[1] See footnote 1 on page 63.

[2] Nick Sewell, *How to Test a System That Is Never Finished, Agile Testing: How to Succeed in an Extreme Testing Environment* by John Watkins, Cambridge University Press, 2009: "If something is to be delivered, then it is the testers who make the final decision as to whether or not that something is delivered into the live environment."

[3] Antonia Bertolino, *Software testing research: Achievements, challenges, dreams*, Proceeding of Future of Software Engineering (FOSE), 2007: "Testing is an essential activity in software engineering. In the simplest terms, it amounts to observing the execution of a software system to validate whether it behaves as intended ..."

[4] James A. Whittaker, *What Is Software Testing? And Why Is It So Hard?*, IEEE Software, Volume 17, Number 1, 2000: "Software testing is the process of executing a software system to determine whether it matches its specification and executes in its intended environment."

[5] David Gelperin, *The growth of software testing*, Communications of the ACM, Volume 31, Number 6, 1988: "We distinguish the four major testing models."; "One model says we test to demonstrate that some version of the software satisfies its specification, two models say we test to detect faults, and the fourth says we test to prevent faults. These three goals need not conflict and, in fact, are all present in the prevention model."

software is broken.[1] The better testers are doing their jobs, the more bugs they manage to find and report.[2]

Moreover, the more critical and severe the bugs are, the better. A tester must be motivated to break the software. Myers even called testing "a destructive, even sadistic, process," because it always requires to think negatively towards the product under testing, expecting it to fall apart and looking forward to bugs and failures. Jyoti and her guys are doing exactly the opposite, going through the list of procedures, which they call test scripts or scenarios, expecting the software to do the expected. Moreover, since the output everybody expects from them is the "green light" for deployment, they obviously want to produce it as soon as possible. It's only logical that in order to do it faster they will tend to find as few bugs as possible.[3] How will that guarantee higher quality?

When you test your blood for syphilis, the sheet of results your doctor hands you out, says "failed," provided you're healthy. If the results sheet, God forbid, says "passed," this means that you're infected. The presence of syphilis makes the test positive, not its absence. Exactly the same should happen in software engineering: the presence of a bug should make the test positive and "passed."

However, Jyoti just told me that they "make sure each test passes." See how wrong this statement sounds? She puts it all

---

[1] ★Rex Black, *Pragmatic Software Testing: Becoming Effective and Efficient Test Professional*, Wiley, 2007: "Software testing is not about proving conclusively that the software is free from any defects, or even about discovering all the defects. Such a mission for a test team is truly impossible to achieve."

[2] Naresh Chauhan, *Software Testing: Principles and Practices*, Oxford University Press, 2010: "The immediate goal of testing is to find errors at any stage of software development. More the bugs discovered at an early stage, better will be the success rate of software testing."

[3] Boris Beizer, *Black-Box Testing: Techniques for Functional Testing of Software and Systems*, Wiley, 1995: "Anything written by people has bugs. Not testing something is equivalent to asserting that it's bug-free. Programmers can't think of everything especially of all the possible interactions between features and between different pieces of software. We try to break software because that's the only practical way we know of to be confident about the product's fitness for use."

upside down. But if she would say it right, she would immediately realize how wrong her attitude toward testing is. She would have to say that, "We make sure each test fails," but a test fails when there are no bugs. Thus, to make them fail you just need to not touch anything and discover no bugs, that will immediately guarantee you the results you're looking for: they all will fail![1]

| The goal of testing is to confirm that the software is broken and explain where exactly. | The product under testing and the test itself must always have reversed statuses. When the product is broken, the test is successful. When the product works fine, the test is broken. It is broken because it can't do what it is designed for: break the product. The same is true for all tests, either automated or manual, working with software or blood samples.

However, all xUnit frameworks, as it was suggested in the famous book,[2] use the reverted terminology and say those tests "pass," when they find no bugs. They also use green color for those tests and the red one for the ones that managed to crash, which they label as "failed." The problem is with the wording here. They are speaking about the product under test, but relate the verbs to the test. More logical names would be "works" and "crashes," because they would describe the behavior of the product, not the test. The product under tests doesn't "pass," it "works;" it doesn't "fail," it "crashes." The test "passes" when the product "crashes," and "fails" when the product "works." This would be the correct logic.

THE second problem is that she labels testing as quality assur-

---

[1]★Boris Beizer, *Software Testing Techniques*, 2nd Edition, International Thomson Computer Press, 1990: "The probability of showing that the software works decreases as testing increases; that is, the more you test, the likelier you are to find a bug. Therefore, if your objective is to demonstrate a high probability of working, that objective is best achieved by not testing at all!"

[2]See footnote 6 on page 71.

ance, while these are two different things.[1] Testing is a process of 1) making experiments, 2) comparing actual results with expected ones, and 3) documenting observed inconsistencies. Quality assurance (QA), on the other hand, is a much more broad concept,[2] which, according to ISO 9000,[3] is "focused on providing confidence that quality requirements will be fulfilled." Testing is not the only thing we have to do in order to assure the quality requirements are fulfilled.[4] There are many other activities in software development that must be accomplished in order to assure quality, for example: code reviews, static analysis, requirements validation and verification, even planning and technical decision documenting. Everything we do must be focused on quality and this is what real QA people are responsible for taking care of: making sure everything we do in the company has the required level of quality, including testing itself.

We don't call laboratory technicians who are taking our blood samples "quality assurance" engineers, right? They don't assure anything, they just take tests. They do help the society stay healthier, but they are just a small part of that "health assurance" process. They only diagnose syphilis, that's it. They don't cure it, they don't know what patients are going to do with those test results, they don't even attempt to re-test infected patients.

If this company would ever decide to obtain ISO 9001 certifi-

---

[1] Bernard Homès, *Fundamentals of Software Testing*, Wiley, 2012: "Tests are sometimes mistaken with quality assurance. These two notions are not identical: 1) quality assurance ensures that the organization's processes are implemented and applied correctly; 2) testing identifies defects and failures, and provides information on the software and the risks associated with their release to the market."

[2] Alan Gillies, *Software Quality: Theory and Management*, 3rd Edition, Lulu.com, 2011.

[3] The International Organization for Standardization, *Quality management systems—Fundamentals and vocabulary*, ISO 9000:2005.

[4] ★Cem Kaner, *Lessons Learned in Software Testing: A Context-Driven Approach*, Wiley, 2001: "Your team may be called 'quality assurance.' Don't let that go to your head. Your test results and bug reports provide information that facilitates the assurance of quality on the project, but that assurance results from the effort of the entire team."

cation,[1] just saying that we're testing our software would be very far from enough to get it. Just having a group of manual testers, who are doing regular experiments and reporting bugs, is just a small part of the QA system we must have in place in order to be certified.

> Quality assurance guarantees that all processes adhere to the required quality standards, including programming, designing, and testing.

Thus, by hearing Jyoti saying that they are called "quality assurance engineers," I realize that neither her, nor the management above her, really understand what quality assurance is and how to do it right. Maybe this QA title makes them proud of their work?[2] Maybe the management thinks that testing is something secondary in the entire landscape of software development activities? Look at the number of programmers we have in this company, which is definitely over fifty and the number of testers, which is just four. This is definitely an imbalance. I'm not saying that there should be fifty testers, but four comparing to fifty is an absolute mistake. Tony obviously thinks that programmers are creating the product and testers are helping them,[3] while the right way of thinking is that programmers and testers are creating the product together. Their roles are equally important.

Moreover, the job of a tester requires more skills and experience than the job of a coder, if we are talking about professional testers

---

[1] Craig Cochran, *ISO 9001 in Plain English*, Paton Professional, 2008.

[2] Cynthia F. Cohen, *Managing Conflict in Software Testing*, Communications of the ACM, Volume 47, Issue 1, 2004: "The lack of status and support makes the tester's job more difficult and time consuming, as the struggle for recognition becomes part of the job itself."

[3] Marnie L. Hutcheson, *Software Testing Fundamentals: Methods and Metrics*, Wiley, 2003: "In recent years, software development has been driven by entrepreneurial pressures, schedule, and constantly evolving production definition. For these and other reasons, management is not always convinced that testing is necessary or worthwhile. In many types of development effort, testing by an independent test group is not believed to be worthwhile or to add value."

and coders.[1] Unfortunately, however, the management doesn't understand it and doesn't know what kind of obligations the testers must have, what to expect from them, how to measure the quality of their work,[2] how to motivate them, how to pay them so that they stay interested, and what they are for.[3] That's why the management just throws them a bone in the form of a shiny "quality assurance" title.

THE third issue is that she believes that the software must be released when testers approve it, which is a common misconception.[4] Most software teams think that the role of a tester is to be a "gate keeper" and prevent the buggy software from being

---

[1] John D. McGregor, *A Practical Guide to Testing Object-Oriented Software*, Addison Wesley, 2001: "In many ways, being a good tester is harder than being a good developer because testing requires not only a very good understanding of the development process and its products, but it also demands an ability to anticipate likely faults and errors."

[2] Barbara Kitchenham, *Software Quality: the Elusive Target*, IEEE Software, Volume 13, Number 1, 1996: "Quality is a complex concept. Because it means different thing to different people, it is highly context-dependent. Just as there is no one automobile to satisfy everyone's needs, so too there is no universal definition of quality Thus, there can be no single, simple measure of software quality acceptable to everyone. To assess or improve software quality in your organization, you must define the aspects of quality in which you are interested, then decide how you are going to measure them. By defining quality in a measurable way, you make it easier for other people to understand your viewpoint and relate your notions to their own. Ultimately, your notion of quality must be related to your business goals. Only you can determine if good software is good business."

[3] ★Peter Farrell-Vinay, *Manage Software Testing*, Auerbach Publications, 2008: "Testing is very expensive and its results are often embarrassing. So there are many politically-adept people ready with plausible arguments explaining why testing can be reduced, curtailed, or its implications glossed-over If you think such politically-adept people are really too dim to bother with, then either you've just left university, have led a very cloistered life, or have only worked for really great companies."

[4] Kshirasagar Naik et al., *Software system testing and quality assurance*, Wiley, 2008: "On the one hand, we improve the quality of the products as we repeat a test–find defects–fix cycle during development. On the other hand, we assess how good our system is when we perform system-level tests before releasing a product."

released to production,[1] which is a mistake. Dr. West said that "software is released for use, not when it is known to be correct, but when the rate of discovering errors slows down to one that management considers acceptable."[2] This principle is derived from the postulate that any software, no matter how simple it is, has a very big amount of problems not yet discovered and fixed.[3] Philosophically speaking, I would even say that there is an unlimited number of defects yet to be discovered.

| The decision to release the product must not be made by testers or programmers, but the manager who observes the dynamics of bug finding and fixing. | Some may argue with this statement, but if we look at the IEEE definition of software quality, it will not sound as crazy: it is "the degree to which a system meets specified requirements or user expectations."[4] In other words, anything that doesn't work as written in the documentation is a bug. Moreover, anything |

that doesn't work as we would expect it to work is also a bug. See how broad the definition is? If there are just a few users, their expectations are more or less predictable and can be satisfied to some degree. If there are thousands of users, or even millions, you can imagine how diverse their expectations might be.

It's impossible to discover and document all defects, no matter

---

[1] ☞Elfriede Dustin, *Effective Software Testing: 50 Specific Ways to Improve Your Testing*, Pearson Education, 2003: "In most software development organizations, the testing program functions as the final 'quality gate' for an application, allowing or preventing the move from the comfort of the software-engineering environment into the real world."

[2] ★David West, *Object Thinking*, Microsoft Press, 2004.

[3] Bill Hetzel, *The Complete Guide to Software Testing*, Wiley, 1993: "There will *never* be a way to be sure we have a perfect understanding of what a program is supposed to do (the expected or required results) and that *any* testing system we might construct will always have some possibility of failing. In short, we cannot achieve 100 percent confidence no matter how much time and energy we put into it!"

[4] IEEE Std 610.12-1990, *IEEE Standard Glossary of Software Engineering Terminology*, IEEE Computer Society, 1990.

how much time and how many resources we have.[1] We can discover the most critical, the most visible, and the most obvious, but we can never find them all. That's why the output of testing can't be discrete. It's not either "yes, it works," or "no, it doesn't work," if we are talking about a piece of software with any decent complexity.

That's why the positioning of the testing phase after the implementation one is a terrible mistake most software teams are doing. They expect testers to be discrete gate keepers,[2] in just a few hours or days saying that the product is either good or bad. Of course, the effectiveness of such a testing is very low, because the time is limited and the motivation is inverted.[3]

---

[1] Paul Ammann et al., *Introduction to Software Testing*, Cambridge University Press, 2017: "Software testing is inherently complicated and our ultimate goal, completely correct software, is unreachable."; "One of the most important facts that all software testers need to know is that testing can show only the presence of failures, not their absence. This is a fundamental, theoretical limitation; to be precise, the problem of finding all failures in a program is undecidable."

[2] See footnote 4 on page 115: "Some testers dream of having veto control over the release of the product. They deserve to be punished by having their wish granted. The problem is that when testers control the release, they also must bear the full responsibility for the quality of the product. The rest of the team will relax a little bit, or maybe a lot. If any bug sneaks by the testers and out the gate, the rest of the team can (and will) shrug and blame the testers. After all, why did the testers ship such a buggy product? On the other hand, if the testers delay the release, they bear intense scrutiny and pressure for being such quality fanatics."

[3] William E. Lewis, *Software Testing and Continuous Quality Improvement*, 3rd Edition, Auerbach Publications, 2009: "A 'testing paradox' has two underlying and contradictory objectives: 1) To give confidence that the product is working well 2) To uncover errors in the software product before its delivery to the customer (or the next state of development). If the first objective is to prove that a program works, it was determined that 'we shall subconsciously be steered toward this goal; that is, we shall tend to select test data that have a low probability of causing the program to fail.' If the second objective is to uncover errors in the software product, how can there be confidence that the product is working well, inasmuch as it was just proved that it is, in fact, not working! Today it has been widely accepted by good testers that the second objective is more productive than the first objective, for if one accepts the first one, the tester will subconsciously ignore defects trying to prove that a program works."

The right positioning would be parallel, when the programming phase is running simultaneously with the testing one. Programmers create new code and fix the existing one while testers break the product and report bugs. When the product is still young, it is easier to break it and the volume of bugs is high, testers easily discover them and report. Then, when the code becomes more stable and most critical bugs are fixed, breaking it becomes more difficult and the speed of bug reporting decreases. At that point the management makes the decision to release,[1] looking at the metrics.[2] Adrian will always say that everything is great and the release is ready. Jyoti will always say that there are many bugs

---

[1] Johanna Rothman, *Release Criteria: Is This Software Done?* STQE Magazine, March/April 2002: "It's possible to create a software product your customers will want to use, and to know when you're done creating it. You don't have to play the 'when-can-we-release-the-product' game. When you use release criteria to know when a project is done, you have taken potentially hidden decisions and made them public and clear. Make your release criteria objective and measurable, so everyone on the project knows what they're working toward. Use the criteria as you progress through the project and up to the final release. Then you can say, 'Release it!' with pride."

[2] Stephen H. Kan, *Metrics and Models in Software Quality Engineering*, Addison-Wesley, 2002: "After going through all metrics and models, measurements and data, and qualitative indicators, the team needs to step back and take a big-picture view, and subject all information to its experience base in order to come to a final analysis. The final assessment and decision making should be analysis driven, not data driven. Metric aids decision making, but do not replace it."

and they just need more time to find more of them.[1] Tony will say, "enough," and push the button.[2]

Now I want to convince her that she is wrong. "What do you think is your primary objective, as a lead of the testing group?" I ask.

"To make sure our software is of high quality. We validate that all features work as expected," she answers and smiles. "I just showed you the list of our test scripts, remember?"

---

[1] Zhang, Xihui et al., *Sources of Conflict between Developers and Testers in Software Development*, Proceedings of Americas Conference on Information Systems (AMCIS), 2008: "The software testing process is inherently adversarial, setting the stage for inevitable developer-tester conflict. Tensions may arise between developers and testers because they often have different and even divergent goals that are difficult to synthesize. Software developers and testers are very different from each other in terms of mindsets, goals, experiences, and perceptions of their relative importance. First, developers and testers often have different mindsets, as developers always think in terms of 'building' something, whereas testers devise means of 'breaking' what developers build. Second, developers and testers typically have distinct goals due to the difference in their job functionality. Developers usually seek to maximize 'efficiency,' that is, to get the work done with the least amount of effort; for example, building the same functionality with the least number of lines of code or in the shortest amount of time. In contrast, testers usually seek to maximize 'effectiveness,' that is, to deliver the end product with the best quality. Third, developers and testers may differ in work experience; for instance, it is not uncommon that more seasoned developers work side-by-side with less experienced testers. And finally, developers and testers may have different perceptions of their relative importance in the organization; for example, testers often feel that they have to constantly work to gain the same level of respect as that of developers."

[2] ★Steve McConnell, *Software Project Survival Guide*, Microsoft Press, 1998: "The question of whether to release software is a treacherous one. The answer must teeter on the line between releasing poor quality software early and releasing high quality software late. The questions of 'Is the software good enough to release now?' and 'When will the software be good enough to release?' can become critical to a company's survival. Several techniques can help you base the answers to these questions on a firmer footing than can the instinctive guesses that are sometimes used."; "By comparing the number of new defects to the number of defects resolved each week, you can determine how close the project is to completion. If the number of new defects in a particular week exceeds the number of defects resolved that week, the project still has miles to go."

"Right, but how do you measure your contribution to the quality of the product we create? Let me put it simply," I decide to be more explicit. "What is your indicator of success? For us programmers it's easy: if we release new features or fix bugs in time, we're good. If we delay, we're not good and Tony is not happy. When and why Tony is happy or angry about your results and deliverables?"

"We don't have deliverables, we test your deliverables. What are you getting at?"

"I think that the deliverables of testers are the bugs they find. We programmers are writing code, this is our output, our deliverables. But the code can't be called complete and ready for production if there were no bugs found in it. That's why ..."

"What?" she interrupts, "You need bugs in order to release the product?" she seems very surprised.

> The primary deliverables of a testing group are the bugs they find and document.

"Yes, of course. If I create a product and find no bugs in it, this will only tell me that the bugs will be found by my users and they will be upset," I pause and think how to explain all that to her. "Listen, you will definitely agree that there are many bugs in any software, no matter how good the programmers are, right? They make mistakes because they are people. Not everything can be tested with automated tests and they don't always write them. That's why, when the code is written, it is expected that there are some amount of critical bugs, some amount of minor bugs and a very big number of cosmetic or non-important bugs. The question is just who will find them first—our testers or our users—even though the density of bugs is not the only quality metric, of course.[1] Hence, if I would be the CEO of my own company and would have two departments, one with programmers and one with testers, I would pay the first one for the features

---

[1] Sunita Chulani et al., *Deriving a Software Quality View from Customer Satisfaction and Service Data*, European Conference on Metrics and Measurement, 2001: "Customer's quality expectations are not typically based on size and complexity of the product they buy and their satisfaction can be influenced substantially by other product attributes that are not typically mapped to defects (e.g. ease of installation and use, timely support, etc.)"

they deliver and the second one for the bugs they find."

"You would pay for the bugs?" she smiles.

I smile too, even though it's not a joke at all. "Well, why not? If the deliverables of the testers would be bugs, why shouldn't I pay for them? That would help them understand what their contribution is to the overall result. They would know exactly how high the quality of their work is. If the company would count the bugs you find, classify them, and somehow make a correlation between your paychecks and the numbers you produce, you would be very interested in finding more of them, and making sure they are more critical and important, wouldn't you?"

"Well, I don't know, the amount of bugs we find depends on so many factors," she returns me the most popular excuse I usually hear.[1] "We just can't predict it. Just numbers don't say enough about the work we do here. We also do the regression testing before each release and it consumes a lot of time and we don't find too many bugs in most cases. Bugs are not the only deliverable we produce. We do many other things," she says and I feel how proud she is.

---

[1] Rex Black, *Managing the Testing Process: Practical Tools and Techniques for Managing Hardware and Software Testing*, Wiley, 2009: "When you consider another objective of testing—to find bugs—the real question is, 'Have we found enough bugs?'."; "Unfortunately, we can't know what we don't know. If it were possible to know all the bugs in advance, the entire test effort would be unnecessary. Suppose, though, that you could estimate the total number of bugs in the system under test. Or, perhaps you could measure the bug-finding effectiveness of your test system. There are three techniques for solving these problems ..."

"But bugs are the most important thing I would expect my testers to deliver, if I were the CEO. And not only testers, actually.[1] I would want them to focus on just bugs, since everything else would not be as valuable for me. You know, I would even ask them to stop doing any regression testing and focus only on finding bugs in the functionality programmers create. I think testers must not do anything aside from discovering bugs and breaking the product. Moreover, I think testers and programmers must not interact," I say this to shock her a bit, "and should stay completely independent. Now, Adrian and Bao and other programmers literally tell you what to do, asking you to test their changes when they need it, correct?"

"Well, yes," she nods.

> The best way to motivate testers to find more and better bugs is to pay them for each one.

"I would not allow them to do that. I would make your department responsible only to me, the CEO, and would ask you to report me about your key metric: the amount of bugs you find. Programmers would not have any say in what you do. They would know that you exist, and you test what they write, and they have to fix the bugs you report, but they can't tell you when to test and what to test."

"And my only metrics would be bugs found?"

"Well, it's not a simple metric. It's not just a number, because bugs are different. They have different severity and priority, some of them may be rejected because they are wrongly reported or duplicate previously reported ones. The metric should take all of

---

[1] Henry Lieberman et al., *Will Software Ever Work?*, Communications of the ACM, Volume 44, Issue 3, 2001: "Future software development should increasingly be oriented toward making software more selfaware, transparent, and adaptive. Software will still contain some bugs (though perhaps fewer), but users will be able to fix them themselves by interacting with the software. Software developers will have better tools for systematically finding out where bugs are, and the software itself will help them in correcting the bugs. Interacting with buggy software will be a cooperative problem-solving activity of the end user, the system, and the developer."

that into account.[1,2] Moreover, I would also somehow take into account the percentage of bugs that were fixed."[3]

"You don't think the job we're doing now has value," she asks sadly.

"Unfortunately."

"Hm... really?" she is not upset, just very concerned, if I read her right.

"Look, I'm not saying you're not good testers or quality assurance engineers, as you call it. Not at all. I'm just saying that your priorities are not set correctly, unfortunately. I think they keep you busy with things that are less important than the bugs you and your guys can find."

"Did you talk to Tony about that?"

"Not yet, I wanted to talk to you first. Think about all this and let's try to talk to Tony next week, OK?"

"OK," she nods.

---

[1] See footnote 1 on page 123, page 109: "A common metric of test team effectiveness measures whether the test team manages to find a sizeable majority of the bugs prior to release. The production or customer bugs are sometimes called *test escapes*. The implication is that your test team missed these problems but could reasonably have detected them during test execution. You can quantify this metric as follows:"

$$DefectDetectionEffectiveness = \frac{bugs(test)}{bugs(test) + bugs(production)}.$$

[2] Capers Jones, *Software Defect Removal Efficiency*, Computer, Volume 29, Issue 4, 1996: "Serious software quality control involves measurement of defect removal efficiency (DRE). Defect removal efficiency is the percentage of defects found and repaired prior to release. In principle the measurement of DRE is simple. Keep records of all defects found during development. After a fixed period of 90 days, add customer-reported defects to internal defects and calculate the efficiency of internal removal. If the development team found 90 defects and customers reported 10 defects, then DRE is of course 90%."

[3] ★Cem Kaner et al., *Testing Computer Software*, 2nd Edition, Wiley, 1999: "The best tester isn't the one who finds the most bugs or who embarrasses the most programmers. The best tester is the one who gets the most bugs fixed."

Equality and slavery

Two bosses (126) – "Just lie, it's not so difficult" (126) – The finger (126) – The slavery paradigm (126) – Modern instruments of enslavement (127) – Doing the right thing (128) – Do the right thing (128) – "Always be helpful" lie (129) – Stop working for the boss, work for yourself (129) – Different roles vs. emotional equality (129) – Guilt is the modern stick (129) – Don't let them fire you, keep it under control (130) – Greed (130) – Inner motivation (130) – Overtime (130) – The project is your boss (131) – Who do you work for? (131) – Coercion is all they know (131) – Methods of punishment (132) – Innate desire to have a master (132) – Forget the managers (132)

D<small>ENNIS</small> sits next to me: "Can you explain this thing to me, dude? This morning, Bao told me to add new fields to that JSON. Then, later, Adrian said that I have to help Tom prepare Friday's release. I told him that I'm busy but he said that it's important. Now, Bao will say that I'm not doing what's necessary. I can't work like that. They are giving me tasks at the same time and I can't understand who I'm working for. In the end, I work 'til late, but still look like an unreliable person," he starts doodling in by note book. "Damn it, I will quit soon anyway,"

"Can't you just tell them to get lost?"

"How?"

"Just tell one of them that you're busy and don't have time. Just lie, it's not so difficult."

"Come on, this is not what my mom taught me to do," he seems surprised. "Don't joke, dude, I really want your advice."

"I'm absolutely serious. You're not supposed to be a good boy in order to be helpful for the project."

> Management by force, also known as slavery, doesn't disappear just because we claim to be civilized and free.

"How else would I be helpful if I don't work and code just like those guys want me to? They will fire me if I don't work—you know this better than me," Dennis shows me the paper with the doodling, there is a fist with a middle finger pointing right in the air.

"Yes, that's exactly what you have to show them when you feel they are not acting in favor of the project. Listen, here is the ugly truth: You, like almost everybody else, get used to the paradigm of management through coercion, also known as slavery. People manage people for ages, and the only way to make one work and make profit for somebody else that they have developed so far is the good, old, force-coercion strategy.[1] A long time ago, its primary form was a physical act of violence and a literal threat of death. Even though those instruments aren't applicable anymore, most probably due to social justice and better education,[2] the fundamental principle is still in place,[3] just in a different form."

"Are you saying that I'm a slave?"

I smile. "Well, with the help of Christianity,[4] humanism, and then socialism we advanced our instruments of enslavement. They are not based on physical violence or corporal punishment anymore. Their new names are responsibility, accountability, empathy, team spirit, compassion, and even love. The boss doesn't need to beat you up with a stick if you don't meet the deadline. It's enough to tell you that you're disappointing the team and betraying our

---

[1] John R. Schermerhorn Jr. et al., *Exploring Management*, 5th Edition, Wiley, 2015: "A force-coercion strategy uses the power bases of legitimacy, rewards, and punishments as the primary inducements to change."

[2] Eric Williams, *Capitalism and Slavery*, The University of North Carolina Press, 1944: "The rise and fall of mercantilism is the rise and fall of slavery."

[3] John P. Kotter, *Choosing Strategies for Change*, Harvard Business Review, July 2008: "When speed is essential and the change is unpopular, using coercion—though risky—may be the only option."

[4] See footnote 2 on page 151: "The Christian faith is from the beginning a sacrifice: sacrifice of all freedom, all pride, all self-confidence of the spirit, at the same time enslavement and self-mockery, self-mutilation."

values.[1] Thanks to your christian upbringing, you will feel as bad as those tortured slaves in ancient Rome."[2]

"Dude, are you sure you got it right? First, I'm an atheist. Second, I'm doing the right thing because I like it way better than being lazy."[3]

> The innate desire to always "do the right thing" is the primary merit of a good slave.

"Of course you do. This is what centuries of education and training did to you, your parents, your grandparents, and so forth, down to those ancient soldiers and slaves who lived here thousands years ago. You're trained to feel good when you are doing the right thing and are being useful.[4] A long time ago, people didn't feel good about it; they needed regular punishments and rewards. Now, we enjoy being slaves—also known as good employees."[5]

---

[1] ★Hugh Willmott, *Strength is Ignorance; Slavery is Freedom: Managing Culture in Modern Organizations*, Journal of Management Studies, Volume 30, Number 4, 1993: "When corporate cultures are 'strengthened', employees are encouraged to *devote* themselves to its values and products, and to assess their own worth in these terms. By promoting this form of devotion, employees are simultaneously required to recognize and *take responsibility* for the relationship between the security of their employment and their contribution to the competitiveness of the goods and services that they produce."; "Insofar as they are drawn to the allure of technocratic informalism, employees come to *discipline themselves* with feelings of anxiety, shame and guilt that are aroused when they sense or judge themselves to impugn or fall short of the hallowed values of the corporation."

[2] ★Jerry Toner, *How to Manage Your Slaves by Marcus Sidonius Falx*, Profile Books, 2015.

[3] Dennis W. Organ, *Organizational Citizenship Behavior: The Good Soldier Syndrome*, Lexington Books, 1988: "OCB is an individual behavior that is discretionary, not directly or explicitly recognized by the formal reward system, and that in the aggregate promotes the effective functioning of the organization."

[4] ★Friedrich Nietzsche, *Zur Genealogie der Moral: Eine Streitschrift*, 1887: "Slave morality is essentially a morality of usefulness."

[5] See footnote 1 on page 101: "Whether dealing with monkeys, rats, or human beings, it is hardly controversial to state that most organisms seek information concerning what activities are rewarded, and then seek to do (or at least pretend to do) those things, often to the virtual exclusion of activities not rewarded."

"You, too?"

"Me, too. We all are in the same trap, including Adrian, Bao, Tony, and everybody else. The good old carrot-and-stick management concept hasn't been changed for ages, but now it is in its ugliest form. We hide its real face behind those always-be-helpful and do-the-right-thing masks. We are slaves, buddy, just like our forefathers, or even worse."

"OK, what is your point? Is there any light at the end of this tunnel?"

"Sure, that's what I'm heading to. To be productive, effective, and happy you should stop working for the boss and start working for yourself. That means ..."

"Four hour workweek,"[1] he interrupts.

"No, it's not about that. I'm talking about your attitude towards the project, its owner, and yourself. You must not feel like you owe them something or that they are superior than yourself anyhow. We are in this project all together, they contribute with the management, you and me contribute with Java programming. We have different roles, but we are equal in our rights and contribution. However, this is not how the world works.[2] So, everything I'm saying now, I'm addressing to you only. Take it as my personal advice: You must not work because of guilt."

He thinks for a second. "What has guilt got to do with all this?"

"Guilt is the modern stick. We don't beat employees up, we use guilt. What else is the do-the-right-thing philosophy based on, man? Guilt is what pushes you forward and makes you feel bad when Adrian or Bao are disappointed. Without guilt you would just show them the finger and go home. The consequences would be minimal, because you're a good programmer and they can't really find a replacement easily. You know that better than me."

"I guess you're right," he thinks and says after a pause. "But

---

[1] Timothy Ferriss, *The 4-Hour Workweek*, Harmony, 2009.

[2] See footnote 1 on page 128: "In the installation of corporate culture/HRM/TQM programmes, every conceivable opportunity is taken for imprinting the core values of the organization upon its (carefully selected) employees. To the extent that succeeds in this mission, corporate culturism becomes a medium of nascent totalitarianism."

eventually they would fire me."

> Free people work when they see profit for themselves, not when they feel obliged or guilty.

"Eventually, yes. But you're not that stupid. You would not let the situation go that far. You would keep it under control and would give them what they want, from time to time. Some people are doing exactly that, and you hate them for that. You are sitting in the office till late, while they go home earlier. You're working hard, while they are being lazy. However, the salaries are the same or they are even getting more. They work out of greed, not guilt."

"Greed? Hm ..." he stands up and stretches his back. "What is that supposed to mean?"

"This means that free people, not slaves, work when they find it profitable for themselves. I think it's only fair to call them 'greedy,' while you are 'guilty.' Well, you are for sure, if you feel depressed because Bao or Adrian are not happy about your results."

"No, no, dude, I'm not happy because I see that I'm not as good engineer as I want to be. They just give me a feedback of my work, either positive or negative. It's not guilt, dude, it's just normal boss-employee relationship that must have an established flow of results and responses. If they never tell me where I'm wrong, I will stop working or will produce very bad results. I think you misunderstand what's going on here," he sits down right on my desk.

He has a point, but I continue, "Look, do you think that you are writing bad code or not enough of it?"

"No, I work for two bosses and stay late every day!" he exclaims.

"See! If we ask the project, what do you think it would tell us about Dennis's job?"

"Dennis is the best programmer ever, no doubts about that!" he exclaims sarcastically, not being far away from the truth. He indeed is a good programmer and he works overtime almost every day.[1] Overtime by itself don't mean anything, but I saw his code: He definitely is one of the best in this company.

"See? The project likes you, the project is paying you, the project is giving you tasks, the project is your boss. However, you feel bad when two guys are ruining your day with their demands and orders. Where is the logic?[2] Why is your real boss, the project, satisfied with your results, but you're depressed?"[3]

"These two guys," he looks over his shoulder. "I hope they don't hear us, are the representatives of the project, aren't they?"

"Apparently not, if they don't deliver the right message to you. As we both know, the project gives you a five-star review, while they constantly give you negative remarks. It seems they have no idea what the project really needs from you, or they are hiding that information. My point is that you should work for the project, not for the boss. It is difficult, because bosses always try to make you work for them, triggering your guilt instincts. I guess it's obvious why they are doing that."

"Not really, why?"

"Because they have no idea how to manage people otherwise. All they know how to do is to make you feel scared of them. Then you will just 'do the right thing' and they will harvest the results.

> Very often managers are just a noise, while the real boss is the project, which we work for and which pays us.

---

[1] Edward Yourdon, *Death March*, Pearson Education, 2003: "If bonuses and extended vacations are a motivator, then overtime during the project would normally be considered a 'de-motivator.' But, it's almost inevitable on death march projects; indeed, it's usually the *only* way that the project manager has any hope of achieving the tight deadline for the project."

[2] Dennis W. Organ, *A Reappraisal and Reinterpretation of the Satisfaction-causes-performance Hypothesis*, Academy of Management Review, Volume 2, Number 1, 1977: "Satisfaction more generally correlates with organizational prosocial or citizenship-type behaviors than with traditional productivity or in-role performance."

[3] ★Jeffrey Pfeffer, *Power: Why Some People Have It and Others Don't*, Harper Collins, 2010: "One of the biggest mistakes people make is thinking that good performance—job accomplishments—is sufficient to acquire power and avoid organizational difficulties."

Read the management book by Owen,[1] it summarizes most of the popular techniques managers use to make employees be afraid of them. Remember Office Space, the movie?"[2]

"Sure, it's hilarious," he smiles.

Even though being rather primitive, it's one of my favorite films. "There is a lot of sad truth in that movie. The manager is always hard to get, always unpredictable, plays behind your back, ignores your results, spreads rumors, gives unnecessary and inconvenient tasks, requires you to work overtime, makes you look stupid, and so on. The arsenal is huge."[3]

"Sounds a lot like our team," he sighs.

> The best way to deal with unprofessional management is to treat it as a bad weather, and stay focused on project needs and requirements.

"Most teams and managers look like that, that's why the movie is so funny—we recognize ourselves there. But the root cause of this situation is not the evil nature of the managers. Instead, it's a combination of two factors: our innate desire to have a master[4] and their lack of management knowledge. On one hand, they simply don't know how to create plans, define quality standards, resolve conflicts, calculate budgets, and evaluate risks. On the other hand, we are used to being 'beaten up' and can't imagine any other alternative management format," I feel that I'm saying something that Dennis is not really ready to hear.

"What do you suggest?"

"We can't change the system, but we can change our attitude and behavior. I just told you, don't work out of guilt. Simply put,

---

[1] See footnote 3 on page 20.
[2] *Office Space* (1999) by Mike Judge.
[3] Yegor Bugayenko, *How Do You Punish Your Employees?* (blog post) https://goo.gl/AaVDN4, 2016.
[4] Alexandre Kojève, *Introduction to the Reading of Hegel*, Basic Books, 1969: "In his nascent state, man is never simply man. He is always, necessarily, and essentially, either Master or Slave."

forget the managers and how much they like you.[1] Don't work for them. Don't pay attention to their complaints. Don't worry about them being unhappy. Don't take them seriously. They are just monkeys, dispatching tasks and trying to make you feel guilty. Ignore them. Work for the project instead. You know what the project needs, what its customers need, what the technical problems are, what contribution is required from you—do exactly that. Adrian, of course, will try to correct your actions, will give you some orders, will interfere and distract you—it's annoying and inevitable. Take him as a bad weather, nothing else. As noise. Your real boss is the project, not that guy."

"I like the philosophy, dude. Want to talk to Adrian about it?" he laughs.

"Maybe next time, it's time to go home now," I smile and stand up starting to pack my laptop.

---

[1] Mark C. Bolino, *Citizenship and Impression Management: Good Soldiers or Good Actors?* Academy of Management Review, Volume 24, Number 1, 1999: "There are two reasons why impression-management motives are likely to reduce the impact citizenship behaviors have on organization/work group effectiveness. First, when individuals undertake actions based upon impression-management concerns, they are less able to devote their full attention to the task at hand. Second, when citizenship behaviors are motivated by impression-management concerns, individuals may consciously invest less effort or expend less energy in carrying out the behavior."

Software architect

Logic and plans vs emotions and power (134) – Management by force (135) – Meritocracy (136) – Employees are robots (136) – Manageable data (137) – Who is a project manager? (137) – PMBOK and Rita's book (137) – Management is important (137) – Strawberries (138) – Golf, Bentley, and prostate exams (138) – Sadness of life (138) – Fool the system! (138) – Modern slaves (139) – The architect configures the product (139) – Configuring a product (139) – The rules (140) – A strong architect is always hated (140) – Quality wall (141) – Constantly working with the rules (141) – Quality rules examples (142) – We have no architect (143) – Hysterical architects (143) – A movie director allegory (143) – Technical dictator (144) – Making enemies (145) – Meetings and white boards (145) – Firing the architect (146)

PROFESSIONAL project management is not based on feelings and emotions. Instead, it must be based on cool-headed, logical thinking and planning.[1] However, this is not what is appreciated now.[2] In most teams, managers are bad parents and employees are spoiled kids. When everybody is motivated and full of energy,

---

[1] Jeffrey Pfeffer, *Leadership BS: Fixing Workplaces and Careers One Truth at a Time*, Harper Business, 2010: "If you are a leader seeking to actually change a workplace's conditions so as to improve employee engagement, satisfaction, or productivity, or if you are an individual seeking to chart a course to a more successful career, inspiration is not what you need. What you need are facts, evidence, and ideas."

[2] Thomas Teal, *The Human Side of Management*, Harvard Business Review, November 1996: "Great managers are distinguished by something more than insight, integrity, leadership, and imagination, and that something more bears a close resemblance to heroism."

we talk about "jelled" teams[1] and "flat,"[2] authority-free organizations.[3] However, when someone gets lazy, the boss all of a sudden is the boss, with a strong voice, harsh words, and all the necessary power in his or her hands.

We've had this management-by-force paradigm dominating for ages, mostly because people were uneducated, social protection and justice mechanisms were rather primitive,[4] and we didn't have computers. Now, human kind is becoming smarter every year, using any form of coercion is becoming difficult, and work automation is taking over. It's the right moment to replace an angry boss with objective metrics. Meritocracy is the new management philosophy,[5] which basically means that everybody gets what they deserve,[6] no matter who they are and what the

---

[1] Tom DeMarco et al., *Peopleware: Productive Projects and Teams*, 3rd Edition, Addison-Wesley Professional, 2013: "Once a team begins to jell, the probability of success goes up dramatically. The team can become almost unstoppable, a juggernaut for success. Managing these juggernaut teams is a real pleasure. You spend most of your time just getting obstacles out of their way, clearing the path so that bystanders don't get trampled underfoot: 'Here they come, folks. Stand back and hold onto your hats.' They don't need to be managed in the traditional sense, and they certainly don't need to be motivated. They've got momentum."

[2] Ghiselli, Edwin E. et al., *Leadership and Managerial Success in Tall and Flat Organization Structures*, Personnel Psychology, Volume 25, Number 4, 1972.

[3] Nicolai J. Foss et al., *Why Managers Still Matter*, MIT Sloan Management Review, Fall 2014: "In today's knowledge-based economy, managerial authority is supposedly in decline. But there is still a strong need for someone to define and implement the organizational rules of the game."

[4] Michael Young, *The Rise of the Meritocracy*, Transaction Publishers, 1994: "The socialists accelerated the growth of large-scale organizations, and, unlike small businesses, these encouraged promotion by merit."

[5] Jim Highsmith, *Agile Project Management: Creating Innovative Products*, Addison-Wesley Professional, 2nd Edition, 2009: "The core value of an egalitarian meritocracy runs deep in the agile movement. It is surely not the only core value that can produce products, but it is a core value that defines how the majority of agilists view themselves."

[6] Roy T. Fielding, *Shared Leadership in the Apache Project*, Communications of the ACM, Volume 42, Number 4, 1999: "The Apache project is a meritocracy—the more work you have done, the more you are allowed to do."

excuses are.[1]

In order to put meritocracy into action, we need metrics.[2] An objective and emotion-free management needs numbers, which are explicit indicators of our performance and laziness, successes and failures. Implicit indicators, to the contrary, are our words, tears, promises, and excuses. If everything we give to our managers is implicit, we can't really hope to get anything logical and reasonable back. We act like kids, trying to please our parents, and managers act like mamas and papas, screaming to punish and giving chocolate bars to reward. Instead, if we looked like robots to them, always having personal green or red lights on top of our heads, they would be much more comfortable with telling us what to do, rewarding and punishing us.[3]

> **Meritocracy is the management paradigm of the future, when everybody will be rewarded and punished based on what they do, not who they are.**

Of course, all of us are humans and we do have feelings and emotions. We love and we hate, we have good and bad moods, we get energized and lazy—but all of this is just a noise for a manager, whose job is to filter it out and focus on our results. A good manager can filter out the noise, a bad one will let it become a distraction and a primary basis for decision-making. Same with kids: if we respond to their

---

[1] Evert Eckhardt et al., *The Merits of a Meritocracy in Open Source Software Ecosystems*, Proceedings of the 2014 European Conference on Software Architecture Workshops, 2014: "Within a true meritocracy, one would expect people to perform less than their subordinates to be succeeded by them."

[2] Norman E. Fenton et al., *Software Metrics: A Rigorous and Practical Approach, Revised*, 2nd Edition, Course Technology, 1998: "It is difficult to imagine electrical, mechanical and civil engineering without a central role for measurement. Indeed, science and engineering can be neither effective nor practical without measurement. But measurement has been considered a luxury in software engineering ... When measurements are made, they are often done infrequently, inconsistently, and incompletely."

[3] Harold Kerzner, *Project Management, a Systems Approach to Planning, Scheduling, and Controlling*, 12th Edition, Wiley, 2017: "The problem is that standard plans for merit increases and bonuses are based on individual accountability while project personnel work in teams with shared accountabilities, responsibilities, and controls. It is usually very difficult to credit project success or failure to a single individual or a small group."

misbehavior emotionally, they don't learn anything and only get worse; if we respond logically and reasonably, they respect us and learn.

Our bosses get angry and use their voice and all other punishment tricks not because of their innate evil temper, but because they simply don't know what else they can do in the absence of any manageable data about us. All they can tell about us employees is that we are either "doing the right thing," or "something is not right." How else can they coordinate us with such an absence of data?

Dennis interrupts my thinking: "You said earlier that my real boss is the project. What does it mean in a practical sense? Who does what? What is the role of a team lead?"

"It's simple, a project manager, or a team lead, as you call it, is an architect of a project," he raises eyebrows getting ready to ask, but I interrupt, "Yes, an architect. Pay attention, an architect of the project, not the product."

"I don't really see any difference."

"You need to read PMBOK[1] or, better yet, that awesome book by Rita."[2]

"I'm a programmer, not a manager. I don't need it," he smiles and says what I hear so often.

"It's a mistake you're making. If you don't know the management you will never become anyone higher than a regular programmer. You will maybe become a senior one, but will never be a head of department, or a VP, or a CTO."

> Knowing the rules of management is one of the key success factors for a technical career.

"I don't want that, I want to sell strawberries," he says absolutely seriously.

"What?"

"Dude, look at what we are doing. We are writing this code,

---

[1] Project Management Institute (PMI), *A Guide to the Project Management Body of Knowledge*, 6th Edition, 2017.
[2] See footnote 5 on page 105.

making money, buying all these MacBooks and iPhones, but we are not happy. The point of life is to be happy, isn't it?"

"I guess. Aren't you happy?"

"I would be way happier if I were selling strawberries," he sighs. "Just open a fruit shop at the corner and make people happy every day, my whole life. Can you imagine that?"

"You would be bored to death. You need action."

"Maybe you're right," he says after thinking for a few seconds. "But I do love strawberries though," he smiles.

It seems that I feel something similar, but I reply: "As long as you are not selling strawberries, you are doomed to work in this software business and it's better to be at the top of it. While you are a programmer, you are right at the bottom. You work a lot and you earn just a little. When you become a team lead or a head of department, you work way less, take bigger risks, and earn more. Then, eventually, you become a director, take much bigger risks, your hair gets gray, you take prostate exams every few months, and you make a lot. Then, if you're strong enough, you become a VP or even a CTO, stop understanding anything about software development, start playing golf, your proctologist becomes your best friend, and you buy a Bentley. You can actually climb all those stairs faster if you are risky and lucky. Also, if you pick the right startup, you win a jackpot and get to the Bentley position in just, say, six years. But that's a very rare situation, I wouldn't bet on it."

"I don't see a strawberry anywhere in your story," he smiles.

> Being rich and successful inevitably means being part of the system, with its hierarchical laws of power and subordination.

"There is none. It's a miserable life. Pay attention, I didn't even mention three wives you are going to change on your way up, multiple divorce lawyers that will scam you even better than your darlings, five kids that will hate you for so many different reasons, and all different sorts of anti-depressant pills you will be taking to stay interested in being alive."

"Lovely, so what's your point?" he doesn't smile anymore.

"You need to fool this evil system before it kills you. You have to become smart enough to take all the good parts it offers and not get caught by the bad ones."

"Which are ...?"

"Money! Money is the good part. Slavery is the bad one. By slavery, I mean exactly those wives, kids, golf, and your prostate. You need to learn how to take money and give them back nothing. In other words, don't become a slave, but earn like a good one."

"Slaves don't earn a lot, dude ..."

"Actually, they do. You picture slaves as those poor guys building pyramids. Modern slaves are different. Look at me and you. Those are some modern slaves right there: smart, intelligent, professional, politically correct, good looking, and depressed." Adrian approaches my desk and stands next to us, listening. I realize that it's time to change the subject: "Back to my point: a project manager is an architect of a project. A product and a project are two different things. A product is something we are developing, a piece of software. It's a tangible thing. On the other hand, a project is an activity, not a thing. A project is what happens when we all sit together in front of our computers and write that software. A project may produce a number of products and a product may be created by a number of projects. Make sense so far?"

"I guess," Dennis says and Adrian gets back to his desk, rotates the chair to see us, sits down, and continues listening.

I continue, "A software product has an architect, a person who makes key technical decisions and takes responsibility for them. The job of the architect is not to develop the product, but to configure it the way everybody can contribute and not break it, even if ..."

"What do you mean by 'configure,'" Adrian interrupts.

"Look, an architect is not the creator of the software,[1] even

---

[1] Martin Fowler, *Who needs an architect?* IEEE Software, Volume 20, Number 4, 2003: "An architect's value is inversely proportional to the number of decisions he or she makes."

though he can and must write some code,[1] but the one who does the scaffolding, putting borders and limits on the design, makes decisions that prevent the product from falling apart. Let's say we are supposed to create a very simple calculator software. You are a programmer and can write it in less than an hour. I'm the architect. I'm telling you that it has to be written in Java, it must not use any frameworks, and it must have a test coverage of more than 80%. That's the architectural activity right there. I don't write the code, but I instruct you how to do it, putting some limits on your work. However, if I'm doing it verbally, I'm a bad architect. A good architect would configure the development environment the way that you, as a developer, would not be able to break the rules."

> The main job of a software architect is to define technical rules, principles, and limitations, which the team must obey.

"The rules?" Adrian seems concerned.

"Yes, the rules. Look, this may sound harsh, but building a good product is always about saying, 'No.' You can't create anything decent if you keep accepting whatever your team is suggesting. You must be the bad guy, who almost always rejects what everybody else is doing and demands something better. Without it, there is no reason for your existence in a project anyway, right? If you love everybody and accept almost everything they do, you are not needed. They can survive without you. A good architect is always a bad guy who is used to being hated."

DENNIS smiles. "Dude, come on, stop this! Hated?"

"I know, it may sound weird, but think about it for a second. Quality is always about cutting off what's bad in order to give living space to what's good. And cutting off in a software project means rejected code changes, terminated tasks, discharged

---

[1] Anthony Langsworth, *Should Software Architects Write Code?* November 2012, https://goo.gl/vGN61n: "Understanding code means the architect can use his or her judgment more effectively rather than rely on which developer is more persuasive."

programmers, strict rules enforced, tight control applied, and permanent fights. In most cases, especially when the project is still young and the team is not mature enough, the bad is everywhere. The architect inevitably becomes a hated figure, if he is really good, because he has to remove the bad in order to let the good live and flourish. Of course, the bad will fight back and find ways to kick the architect out."

"Yeah, like a super hero, right?" Dennis doesn't want to take me seriously.

"Yes, dude, that's what I'm getting at," I reply seriously. "But a good architect is smarter than a super hero—he won't fight with the evil directly on a daily basis. Or maybe he is just too lazy for that, but he simply doesn't do it. Instead, he 'configures' the product so that it fights for itself. He builds a quality wall around the product, which doesn't allow the bad to get through."

"A wall?" Dennis scratches his nose.

"It's a metaphor. The architect invents rules and makes sure they are enforced by creating software that does that. The software that controls the quality is the wall. Take the calculator example again. I'm an architect and I

> A good software architect invests most of the time into building an automated quality wall around project artifacts.

want the software to have 80% test coverage always. If I just tell you, a programmer, to do that, you will agree and tomorrow will break this rule for some reason. Maybe you will be just lazy to create a new unit test, or you will be in a hurry, or I will be on vacation, or I will already be fired. It won't matter. It will happen. Just asking you to keep coverage over 80% is not enough at all. I need to find a way to enforce it. The first and the most primitive way is to be in the office every day and raise hell every time you break the rule. You will be afraid of me, will hate me, but the rules will be obeyed. This is how bad architects behave."

"How do good ones behave?" Adrian asks.

"Well, good architects make sure that it's technically impossible to break their rules," I feel good that Adrian is interested. "For example, by technically prohibiting any Git commits or merges into the main branch if the changes violate the coverage control rule. The architect just makes sure that the build breaks if the coverage is lower than 80% and makes sure nobody can commit if the build is broken. Implementing this once, the architect may rest assured that his rules will always be obeyed. Well, as long as the technical control mechanisms are in place. No need to cross the office multiple times a day checking who is doing what and how many rules are getting ready to be violated. Instead, the architect implements them once, makes sure they are enforced, and gets back to new rules. The job of the architect is to constantly work with the rules. More precisely, to review what technical risks are the most critical in the project, invent new rules to prevent them from happening, put those rules in action through software scripts and triggers, watch them being obeyed or violated by the team, and start again with new risks. This is what I call 'configuring' the project."

ADRIAN doesn't seem to be very happy with my concept: "Well, it sounds interesting, but what about helping the team, teaching junior programmers, reviewing the code, meeting with product owners? Shouldn't the architect do all that?"

"I think all of this is less important. Moreover, I would say that all those activities exist only if the architect doesn't do his job right—doesn't configure the product tightly enough."

"Tightly?" Dennis loves to catch me by the word.

"Yes, that's the right word. The tighter the rules are, the more stable and self-sufficient the project is. It will be difficult to break it or turn it into a mess."

> The job of an architect is to permanently invent and implement new quality control rules, making them as tight as possible.

"Can you give a few examples of the rules you are talking about?" Adrian stays interested.

"Sure, for example: the build must always be clean; code coverage must always be at a certain level; static analyzers must not have any complaints; each modification to the code must go through two reviewers; database changes must be versioned; all source code must be in Git; design decisions must be documented with at least two possible alternatives; deployment must be done automatically; production environment must not be accessible by the development team. I can probably come up with many others. What's important is that most of the rules can and must be put in action through software tools. The job of an architect is to configure the product in a way that it protects itself against chaos."

Everybody stays quiet for a few seconds. Dennis stands up and stretches his back. Adrian keeps rotating the chair. I take a sip out of my cup. The tea is cold. Time to make a new one. I forgot where we started from, but it looks like I gave them some information to think about. Did I forget any important rules?

The problem is that there is no such thing as a software architect in our team. This is very typical to many other teams—they just don't have architects.[1] They have programmers, testers, managers, designers, but not architects. Well, they do have that title, sometimes.[2] They give it to some people when they are ready to quit and the company doesn't have enough money to keep them with a raise. Instead of a raise, those poor coders get the "architect" title and keep writing code.

I'm actually wrong; Having the title allows them to not write code anymore. Architects discuss, talk, blame programmers for errors, patronize junior programmers, and do exactly what a bad architect would do, as I just said to Dennis: raise hell when something is not right. There are no real architects in modern teams. At least, I haven't seen any.

---

[1] Michael Keeling, *Design It!: From Programmer to Software Architect*, Pragmatic Bookshelf, 2017. "On some teams, architect is an official team role. On other teams, there is no explicit role and teammates share the architect's responsibilities. Some teams say they don't have an architect, but if you look closely, someone is fulfilling the architect's duties without realizing it ... If your team doesn't have an architect, congratulations, you've got the job!"

[2] Philippe Kruchten, *What do software architects really do?* Journal of Systems and Software, Volume 81, Number 12, 2008: "Kent Beck at an OOPSLA workshop in Vancouver in the fall of 1992: --Hmm, 'software architect' it's a new pompous title that programmers demand to have on their business cards to justify their sumptuous emoluments."

> An architect must have enough authority to make any technical decision and stay personally responsible for the consequences.

A real architect is someone similar to a movie director.[1] It's a person who is personally responsible for the product. If the movie is boring, we blame the director. If some actors don't act, we blame the director. If the camera is shaking, we blame the director. We always blame the director. On the other hand, we give a lot of credit to the director if the movie is great. The movie is the child of the director. Of course, in order to raise the kid right, the director has to have all the necessary power and authority to make any possible decision during the course of the movie's making. How else is it possible to be responsible for something if one can't make all necessary decisions about its creation, right?

A similar role a software architect should play in a software project: be a director with absolute responsibility and authority. Whatever goes wrong, it's the architect's personal fault. Anything the architect says, we quietly obey. It's a dictatorship role and that's how it should be.

Most teams nowadays play technical democracy, making decisions all together, after lengthy discussions and white boarding. This leads only to chaos, nothing else. A group of people can't create anything if it doesn't have a leader, a dictator, a chief, an author. Look at Apple at the time of Steve and look at it now. Steve was accused of being "rude"[2] by many of his co-workers, I believe, for one simple reason—he was a strong and passionate director of Apple products. He was taking full responsibility for them and wanted to have an ability to make any decision he

---

[1] Peter Eeles, *Characteristics of a Software Architect*, The Rational Edge, IBM Resource, 2006: "Using the film industry as an analogy, the project manager is the producer (making sure things get done), whereas the architect is the director (making sure things get done correctly)."

[2] Walter Isaacson, *Steve Jobs*, Simon & Schuster, 2011: "I think honestly, when he's very frustrated, and his way to achieve catharsis is to hurt somebody. And I think he feels he has a liberty and a license to do that. The normal rules of social engagement, he feels, don't apply to him. Because of how very sensitive he is, he knows exactly how to efficiently and effectively hurt someone. And he does do that."

thought would be right, no matter how much such a decision would hurt anyone around.

Good software architects make good software products and they also make a lot of enemies if they are good and passionate about what they do, not only about their salaries—just like good directors or any other professionals,

> Making enemies and being constantly hated by many is part of the job description of a software architect.

Of course, being strong and making enemies is not enough to make a high-performance web site or an Oscar-winning movie. One also has to know how programming or filming works. Of course, an architect can't know everything about the product under development. That's what the team is for, to help the architect to fill his knowledge gaps and do what he can't do, because he only has twenty four hours in a day. A smart architect knows how to use the team right so that it produces the most it can.[1] Does the word "use" sound offensive here?

MEETINGS, white boarding, emails, chats, experimenting, and many other techniques must be used in order to collect information from the team and poke their brains. An architect must organize and encourage team members, but must always be the final decision maker. There is absolutely no place for democracy in software development. It must be a dictatorship, nothing else.

A strong dictator is always better than democracy. A dictator may be wrong and will be wrong very often, but he will pay for all mistakes.[2] He knows how much. Making mistakes is an inevitable

---

[1] Yi Zhou, *Take Responsibility for Your Decisions* in ★*97 Things Every Software Architect Should Know: Collective Wisdom from the Experts* by Richard Monson-Haefel, O'Reilly Media, 2009: "Many architects wrongly assume they have to make every architectural decision. Therefore, they position themselves as know-it-all experts. In reality, there's no such thing as a universal technical genius. Architects have areas in which they are quite proficient, areas in which they are knowledgeable, and areas in which they are simply incompetent. Adept architects delegate decisions about domain problems in which they are not proficient."

[2] Simon Brown, *Are You a Software Architect?* February 2010, https://goo.gl/nSBTW6: "There's a big difference between contributing to the architecture of a software system and being responsible for defining it yourself."

part of any creative process. The question is who is making them and how much responsibility that person has. Group responsibility is not a responsibility at all. Only individual responsibility counts.

> Until the architect is fired, he must have full power to make any technical decisions, no matter what the team or the boss are saying.

A project must be ready to replace the architect when he starts making too many mistakes. Also, the project must have a punishment mechanism for the architect, which will correct his behavior before it's too late. How exactly that might work depends on the project, its compensation policy, and on how much risk it is ready to tolerate. But having no architect and relying on team's ability to make the right decision in a democratic mode is a suicidal path for a project.[1] Even the worst architect is better than no architect[2]—the project can fire him and teach others a lesson. If there is no architect, nobody will learn any lesson. The only lesson we will learn is that there is no order and we can sit here for as long as those big guys have enough money to pay our salaries. Whether this is really bad for us programmers on a payroll—is a separate question.

---

[1] Len Bass et al., *Software Architecture in Practice*, 2nd Edition, Addison-Wesley Professional, 2003: "The architecture should be the product of a single architect or a small group of architects with an identified leader."

[2] Matthew R. McBride, *The Software Architect*, Communications of the ACM, Volume 50, Number 5, 2007: "Without strong supervision from the software architect, projects and attempted solutions tend to fall apart due to the weight of unmitigated complexity. "

Losers and winners

Money is the fuel, not the goal (147) – Why is life miserable? (147) – Winner's gene (147) – "The world is mine" (148) – "Me and you are losers" (148) – Billionaires are normal people (149) – You already lost when you were born (149) – Talent and intelligence vs. success (149) – Re-distribute all money in the world (150) – Fairness vs. profitability (150) – Money is not the goal, power is (151) – Ethics (151) – "He who keeps his words doesn't deserve to be a king" (151)

D<small>ENNIS</small> takes off his headphones and turns to me in the chair: "Dude, you promised to give me a recipe of how to make a lot of money," he giggles.

"Money won't help you. To be happy you need power, not money. Money is just the gasoline in your car, not the target you are aiming for. You know what Rockefeller said[1] about that? He said that, if your goal is to become rich, you will never achieve it. I believe he meant that if you just want to have a full tank of gas, you will never win the race. The race cup is the goal, not the fuel."

"You do remember, that I want to sell strawberries, right, dude?" he laughs.

"You don't want to sell them," I stay serious, "You just keep telling this story to yourself in order to explain why your life is miserable and you have to sit in front of the computer ten hours a day developing some Java code for some capitalists. Without this strawberry story you would have probably already hanged yourself in the bathroom. Do you want to know why your life is miserable?"

> Poor people earn money, rich ones take money away from others.

"Why?" he stops smiling.

"Because you don't have the winner's gene."

"What?"

"Look, don't get offended, I will tell you something all those

---

[1] Jacob M. Braude et al., *Complete Speaker's and Toastmaster's Library*, Prentice Hall, 1992.

how-to-get-rich books[1] never mention. All people are different, from the moment they are born. Even Aristotle said[2] that some of us are born to be winners and give orders, while others are born to be losers and work for winners. Whether this quality is innate or is being developed during the first few years of our life, I don't really know. What I know is that the key difference between winners and losers is in their attitude towards money, property, power, results, success, all those things. Losers know that they have to work hard in order to obtain all that, but they never really achieve anything big. This is what the books teach us—work hard, stay focused, wake up at 6 a.m., don't drink, don't smoke, help others, save every dollar—and you will be rich eventually. The truth[3] is that rich people don't behave like that. They drink, they beat up their wives, they don't focus, they lose a lot in Vegas, they barely show up in the office, they lie to their partners and employees, they cheat, and they steal. Some of them don't even pay taxes," I hope he gets the sarcasm. "They don't do what the books say. They behave in a very opposite way and they win. Because they are not losers. Winners, unlike losers, believe that everything already belongs to them. All they need to do is take it."

He stands up and clicks his fingers: " 'The world is mine' concept, huh?" Dennis refers to Tony Montana,[4] I guess.

"Yes, man, exactly that. The world is already yours, if you have that winner's gene. Some people are born with it. Others—the majority of us—are not. Me and you, obviously, are losers. No matter how hard we work our whole life, we will never be truly rich. Because we believe that to get rich we must earn it."

"How else you are going to get the money if you don't earn it?

---

[1] Timothy Ferriss, *Tools of Titans: The Tactics, Routines, and Habits of Billionaires, Icons, and World-Class Performers*, Houghton Mifflin Harcourt, 2016.
[2] Aristotle, *Politics*, Part V, 350 B.C.E: "It is clear, then, that some men are by nature free, and others slaves, and that for these latter slavery is both expedient and right."
[3] Robert Greene, *The 48 Laws of Power*, Penguin Books, 2000.
[4] *Scarface* (1983) by Brian De Palma.

Rob a bank?"

"You don't get the point. Look at that computer business icons like Bill Gates or Larry Ellison. They are making a few thousand dollars every minute. Do you think they are a million times smarter than you and me? Not at all.

> The very belief that the resources in the world are distributed fairly make you poor.

They are normal people, if you talk to them. They are not wizards, they don't have a magic wand. They also brush their teeth every morning like me and you, they get lazy, they watch TV, they eat, they have sex, and they pee. But for some reason they make a few thousand times more cash every year than you do. What do you think the reason for that is? Pure luck? Their extraordinary brain power? Their exceptional talent? Maybe, but not at this order of magnitude. So, what do they have that you and I don't? And do you think you can catch up by just writing Java code faster and better?"

"Hm ... " he doesn't answer.

"Yeah, dude," I pause for a second, "you cannot. You already lost when you were born. You were made to work, while they were made to have. That's the difference. That's the bug in us: we believe in fairness, while they believe in power. And the world is based on power, not on fairness. You will work hard, you will learn new technologies, you will even create your own startups, you will get good salaries, but you will never be truly successful and rich. Because you believe[1] that, in order to get something, it is only fair that you have to work. Mind me, when I say 'you' I mean myself too. I'm in exactly the same position as you are, my friend," I smile sadly.

"I understand," Dennis says, "Don't worry, go on, what is the solution?"

---

[1] Stephen J. McNamee et al., *The Meritocracy Myth*, 3rd Edition, Rowman & Littlefield Publishers, 2013: "It is not enough for some simply to have more than others. For a system of inequality to be stable over the long run, those who have more must convince those who have less that the distribution of who gets what is fair, just, proper, or the natural order of things. The greater the level of inequality, the more compelling and persuasive these explanations must appear to be."

I smile, "There is no solution, dude. I would already be a millionaire if I knew the recipe. Do you think I'm less talented than Bill Gates? Not at all. I'm just a loser. Maybe a talented one," I sigh. "Talent, education, and intelligence don't help you become rich. Moreover, they usually are your blockers. The smarter you are, the more obvious it is for you that you have some gaps in your knowledge, that you need to learn something else, you need to work harder, you need to fix you drawbacks, and so on. While you're doing all this, less educated, less intelligent, less sophisticated, and less talented people just win. I would put it this way: winners see work as a hindrance between them and the prize, while losers see it as an instrument to get the prize. These are typical symptoms of a loser: they love to work, they enjoy being busy and tired, they have a lot of items in their agendas, they plan their work time."

"You're depressing me. I won't sleep tonight," he sighs.

"I feel sorry for you," I slightly smile.

> Hard work is not what leads to success, but what instead is a typical bottleneck on the way to it.

"Listen, I will tell you something else. I heard that idea a few years ago.[1] Imagine, we take all the money in the world and divide it equally between all people on this planet. Each of us will get somewhere around $10,000.[2] What will happen then is that very soon the money will get accumulated in the hands of the same very people that possess it now. It's a theory, of course, but it does make sense to me. Those rich guys will get their money back very soon, while you and me will start building business plans and making smart investments. I'm not saying business plans are not necessary, but we will lose. For some reasons. They will win, for some other reasons. The key reason, of course, will be that they are rich already and they never doubt that, while we expect the world to reward us with money if we do the right thing."

"I got it, I got it," he interrupts, "there is no solution?"

"Well, you can try to change yourself, but it most probably

---

[1] Robert Anthony, *Advanced Formula for Total Success*, Berkley, 1988.
[2] CIA, *The World Factbook*, https://goo.gl/EEY6cQ.

won't work. In your mind, doing what those guys are doing is bad. You want the world to look fair and it will always be more important for you to do something good, instead of doing something that generates profit. And I'm not talking about robbing a bank, which obviously is a bad thing in their minds too. I'm talking about our fundamental moral beliefs, which turn us into losers."

He looks at me. "To be rich I have to be bad?" I think for a second. "Not really, or maybe yes. I told you earlier that aiming for money is not going to help, because it's a false target. Winners don't really care about money, they care about power.[1] They want to be better than others, they want to be on top of others, they want to win and dominate. You want not to lose, that's why you need money. See the difference between 'to win' and 'not to lose'?"

"I guess," he seems very puzzled. "Do I have to be a bad guy to be rich? What's new in this idea, dude?"

"That's the very problem I'm talking about. Your attitude to power is negative. You believe that being on top of others and winning is an evil thing. You don't want to take participation in this game, you think you're better, you

> Being a good, honest citizen and being rich and successful are contradicting objectives.

are a good person, and all that. In fact, you are just crippled by modern morality, as Nietzsche would say.[2] Your fundamental beliefs are wrong, and I don't think it's possible to alter them fast. Thanks to your Christian upbringing,[3] you believe that those who treat others with respect and fairness are the good guys—they deserve to be the kings of the world. The reality is quite the opposite. Selfishness, egoism, cold-heartedness, greed, dishonesty, and deceitfulness are the qualities of kings. You know

---

[1] Rollo Tomassi, *The Rational Male*, Amazon, 2013: "The definition of power is not financial success, status or influence over others, but the degree to which we have control over our own lives."

[2] ★Friedrich Nietzsche, *Beyond Good and Evil*, 1886.

[3] ★Friedrich Nietzsche, *The Antichrist*, 1895.

that Machiavelli said[1] that he who keeps his word doesn't deserve to be a king?"

"First of all, I'm an atheist. Second, you're just bitter because you don't have a girlfriend," he laughs. "I have to hit the bathroom and maybe hang myself there," he stands up and walks away.

---

[1]See footnote 4 on page 101, Chapter 18, 1532: "A wise lord cannot, nor ought he to, keep faith when such observance may be turned against him, and when the reasons that caused him to pledge it exist no longer."

Hackers and designers

Modern education is flawed (153) – Algorithms vs. people (153) – The era of hackers (154) – Cheap computers vs. expensive programmers (155) – Open source dominates (155) – The population of programmers is growing (156) – Programming is easier (156) – Remote work (157) – Salaries are skyrocketing (157) – Maintainability is king (157) – Working code vs. software product (158) – Software ecosystem (158) – The era of designers (159) – Job security (159) – Replaceability is a merit (159) – We should code ahead (160)

W HEN I studied programming in college, almost nobody ever mentioned anything to me about management of software development. Well, there were some lectures about software engineering; They told us about Agile and eXtreme Programming and we practiced some group activities, but that was always secondary to algorithms,[1] boolean algebra,[2] relational theory,[3] finite automata,[4] and other things which I honestly don't even remember now. It seems to me that the majority of that information was given to me for nothing. I don't use it and I don't need it.

Moreover, who needs algorithm designers nowadays? Well, there are a few scientific organizations and Silicon Valley startups that invent some new methods of encryption or some new high-speed protocols, but how many of them are out there? The majority of those millions of programmers in the world are simply sticking together already-available open source components to make their living. They need to know how to do that assembling right, how to understand architecture and design, how

> The majority of programmers are not scientists or even engineers anymore. They are specialists, like plumbers or surgeons.

---

[1] Thomas H. Cormen et al., *Introduction to Algorithms*, 2nd Edition, The MIT Press, 2001.

[2] J. Eldon Whitesitt, *Boolean Algebra and Its Applications*, Dover Publications, 2012.

[3] C. J. Date, *An Introduction to Database Systems*, 8th Edition, Pearson, 2003.

[4] John Carroll et al., *Theory of Finite Automata With an Introduction to Formal Languages*, Prentice Hall, 1989.

to avoid anti-patterns, but, more importantly, they need to know how to work with people, not bytes and bits.

Universities and schools must teach us not just how to code, but how to do it in a way such that our results are maintainable. And not just maintainable by us, but by other programmers who come after us or work together with us. In other words, to make our code readable for people, not only computers. At the time of Knuth's first volume[1] computers were very expensive and programmers were crazy underpaid geeks. That was the era of "hacking," even though at that time this word had a negative meaning. Programmers constituted a small elite group of professionals, who were speaking their own language and taking showers once a week. Their key objective was to find out how to teach that stupid and slow computer to do what they wanted. In most cases, they were doing that for the first time ever in human history. It was the era of software and hardware discoveries. I didn't even exist back then.

IN the era of hackers,[2] computers were rare, expensive, and exotic toys, which most businesses didn't take seriously. To survive, programmers had to create software and hardware that would work fast enough—that was the key criteria of success. It was the time of languages like Algol, Fortran, C, Assembly, Perl, and others, which were rather cryptic and required serious brain power to create something decent or to understand what a fellow

---

[1] Donald E. Knuth, *The Art of Computer Programming, Volume 1: Fundamental Algorithms*, 3rd Edition, Addison-Wesley Professional, 1997.

[2] Steven Levy, *Hackers: Heroes of the Computer Revolution*, O'Reilly Media, 25th Edition, 2010: "The most productive people working on S&P called themselves 'hackers' with great pride."

programmer had created.[1] It was necessary to know exactly how the hardware worked in order to create a fast software.

Also, there were not so many open source projects at that time. Most software packages were commercial, people were working in cubicles, staying in one company for quite a long time. They knew their products rather well and were afraid to lose their jobs. The situation has been changing dramatically over the last decade.

First of all, the cost of computing power gets cheaper every year. For example, one gigabyte of computer memory cost about $1,000 in 2000. Now its price is below $5. The price dropped two hundred times in just seventeen years. The same is true about hard drives, monitors, CPUs, and all other hardware resources. Simply put, computers are getting more affordable every year.

Second, the growth of open source is huge. The majority of software is available now for free together with its source code,

---

[1] See footnote 1 on page 87: "In mature technology environments—the end of the wave, such as web programming in the mid 2000s—we benefit from a rich software development infrastructure. Late-wave environments provide numerous programming language choices, comprehensive error checking for code written in those languages, powerful debugging tools, and automatic, reliable performance optimization. The compilers are nearly bug free. The tools are well documented in vendor literature, in third party books and articles, and in extensive web resources. Tools are integrated, so you can do UI, database, reports, and business logic from within a single environment. If you do run into problems, you can readily find quirks of the tools described in FAQs. Many consultants and training classes are also available. In early-wave environments—web programming in the mid 1990s, for example—the situation is the opposite. Few programming language choices are available, and those languages tend to be buggy and poorly documented. Programmers spend significant amounts of time simply trying to figure out how the language works instead of writing new code. Programmers also spend countless hours working around bugs in the language products, underlying operating system, and other tools. Programming tools in early-wave environments tend to be primitive. Debuggers might not exist at all, and compiler optimizers are still only a gleam in some programmer's eye. Vendors revise their compiler version often, and it seems that each new version breaks significant parts of your code. Tools aren't integrated, and so you tend to work with different tools for UI, database, reports, and business logic. The tools tend not to be very compatible, and you can expend a significant amount of effort just to keep existing functionality working against the onslaught of compiler and library releases."

including operating systems, graphic processors, compilers, editors, frameworks, cryptography tools, and whatever you can imagine. Programmers don't need to write a lot of code anymore, they just need to be able to put together the components already available.[1]

Since the industry of computing is very different now than it was 30-40 years ago, it needs different types of human resources.

Third, the amount of programmers in the world keeps growing and they are still in a deficit. In some European countries, the demand for skilled IT personnel is twice as high as the supply their markets can provide.[2] Programmers are not the elite group of geeks anymore. The profession has already turned into a commodity. People become programmers just because they need some job to feed their families, while many years ago it was mostly a hobby or a science.

Fourth, programming languages are much higher-level now than they were before. They are standing much further away from the hardware than they were forty years ago. Programmers simply don't need to know how the hardware works anymore. They can code in JavaScript never even thinking about things like memory management, stacks, pointers, or CPU registers. A friend recently told me a story of a job interview he failed recently. He is a rather good front-end developer, with a lot of Ruby and JavaScript projects in his portfolio. He told me, being very angry, that at the interview they asked him to calculate 2^8. "How am I supposed to know that?" he was yelling at me. I was surprised but then realized that maybe he was not so wrong with his frustration. Do front-end programmers need to understand binary? He is

---

[1] Eric S. Raymond, *The Cathedral and the Bazaar*, Knowledge, Technology & Policy, Volume 12, Number 3, 1999: "Good programmers know what to write. Great ones know what to rewrite (and reuse)."; "An important trait of the great ones is constructive laziness. They know that you get an A not for effort but for results, and that it's almost always easier to start from a good partial solution than from nothing at all."

[2] Emily McCallum, *Gaps in Dutch labour market: ICT, tech and sales skills in demand*, Iamexpat.nl, July 2015: "There is a heavy demand for ICT workers with a technical college background. A whopping 76% of HR employees reported having difficulty finding enough candidates with this qualification."

twenty-two years old, by the way, without any formal computer science education. He doesn't know what a byte is, as you can see, but his projects work and people pay him $80 an hour or more for graphic design and Ruby coding. The summary of this story is that, to be a successful programmer nowadays, one doesn't need to know how hardware works.

Fifth, programmers now work remotely instead of in offices or cubicles. Thanks to the growth of high-speed internet, conferencing software, messaging tools, and distributed repository management systems like Git, along with many other innovations, remote work has become more comfortable than the alternative of working in the traditional office setting. Despite all the criticism and problems,[1] the percentage of people working remotely grows every year.[2]

Finally, the sixth change is the salaries of programmers, which have been sky rocketing for the last few decades. In 2000, when one gigabyte of memory cost $1,000, senior programmers were earning $80,000 in Silicon Valley. Now, in 2017, they are making three times more, while RAM is two hundred times cheaper. People are not just very expensive now, they are much more expensive than computers.

IF we put all six of these trends together, it will become obvious that the most important quality of a good software now is its maintainability. It is the era of designers coming, where it's way less important how fast or optimal the algorithm is than how easily

---

[1] Alan Felstead et al., *Assessing the growth of remote working and its consequences for effort, well-being and work-life balance*, New Technology, Work and Employment, Volume 32, Number 3, 2017: "Despite these drawbacks and some high profile employer U-turns, the evidence presented suggests that remote working is, on the whole, advantageous to employers and employees. It also suggests while we may not be witnessing a full-bodied revolution, the detachment of work from place is undeniably an important aspect of the changing nature of work in the twenty-first century."

[2] Laura Vanderkam, *Will Half Of People Be Working Remotely By 2020?* FastCompany, August 2014: "A recent survey of business leaders at the Global Leadership Summit in London found that 34% said more than half their company's full-time workforce would be working remotely by 2020."

a fellow programmer can understand it.[1] Businesses spend a lot of money on human resources, which are very expensive, while they can easily afford a few new servers or even a more powerful mobile phone, to solve performance of not-so-perfect-algorithm problems.

> The most important quality of a good programmer is the ability to create simple and maintainable solutions.

Of course, there are areas where hackers are still required. We still need some algorithms, we need to fly to space, we need to invent new robots, but it is just a small portion of all software products the world is developing. The majority of software doesn't require those skills.

However, a very different skill set is required. Programmers must be capable of producing the code that is readable, that is testable, that is documented, that not just works, but explains itself.

Moreover, programmers must be capable of keeping the environment around the code in a clean and disciplined manner. It's not just the code that matters anymore, it's also bug reports, requirements, pull requests, deployment scripts, logs and so on. The code by itself is just a small part of what we call a software product now. I believe Brooks[2] said something like that many years ago. There is a long path from a working piece of code to a software product that can be placed on the market and survive.

A software product is a living organism, an environment, an ecosystem, a territory with its laws, habitats, allies and enemies—use any metaphor you like. What is really important to realize is that the code itself is just an element of a software product. Hackers, who used to like algorithms, don't really get this concept. They don't appreciate rules and regulations and don't respect

---

[1] Yegor Bugayenko, *We are Done with 'Hacking'*, Communications of the ACM, Volume 61, Number 7, 2018: "It seems that the future of programming rests less in math and more in sociotech relationships between people."

[2] Fred Brooks, *The Mythical Man-Month*, Addison-Wesley, 1975: "A programming product costs at least three times as much as a debugged program with the same function."

managers and junior programmers. They enjoy writing something that only very serious developers can decrypt and understand, don't write automated tests, and prefer talking instead of writing documentation.

Designers, people of the future, have the exact opposite attitude. They tend to use simple coding structures that are easier to understand. They enjoy seeing their code being modified by other programmers, they write a lot of automated tests to support future developers, they welcome junior programmers and test their code by seeing how many issues a newbie spots when trying to use it, and they prefer documentation over meetings and phone calls.

> Hackers enjoy being important and own the code, while designers enjoy seeing the code being shared and themselves being replaceable.

The key difference is that hackers like to own the code, while designers understand themselves as a replaceable component of a software project that don't own anything except their laptops. For a hacker the developer is a king, while a designer understands that the code is king.

Obviously, thinking of themselves as replaceable resources seriously jeopardizes the designer's job security—they can easily be replaced if the project is so perfectly organized that it doesn't depend on any particular experts, everything is documented, regulated, and the code is readable and maintainable. It is true, this makes programming positions very shaky.

THE future of software development will have no full-time "jobs," but only projects, which developers will join when their skills are required and leave when their mission is completed. There will be no companies or body shops with programmers sitting there for years, doing whatever the business needs, just because their regular pay checks are coming.

Instead, there will be software projects (or maybe not only software ones?) that will assemble their teams on demand and reward people solely on the basis of their contribution. Making oneself replaceable will be one of the key merits of a software engineer.

The programmers of the future will know that the best favor they can do for their projects is to make themselves easily replaceable.

Hackers are an unmanageable and dangerous resource, which a project critically depends on simply because the code is complex, cryptic, non-uniform, and ... arrogant. Smart projects and project managers will try to get rid of hackers as much as they can—that will be the trend of the future. On the other hand, designers, unlike hackers, are good experts in working with people, not only with computers. They understand the importance of building good teams over writing code correctly.

Programmers must learn to think ahead about what will happen with their code when they leave the project, or someone new joins it, or a big portion of modifications will be required, or the company decides to open product sources to the public, or something else happens. Simply put, they have to "code ahead."

Chapter 3

Tony

POLITICS is what modern management is all about. It's not about numbers, plans, metrics, results, or deployment scripts. It's about people's emotions, fears, tears, and power struggles. People are chaotic, weak, unorganized, stupid, and very insecure. Most of us, at least. Some of us are stronger, more disciplined, self-confident, and aggressive. They climb on top of others, forming social hierarchies. Software companies, which are creating software products, are nothing else but social hierarchies, decorated with fancy Kanban boards, motivational speeches, equality slogans, and laptop stickers. However, the core principle remains the same—stronger animals enslave weaker ones. Is it how this should be in the era of robots and space travel?

Performance metrics

Comfort vs. metrics (162) – Paychecks as metrics (163) – Coarse grained metrics (163) – Lines of code (164) – Agile (164) – Rules of the game (165) – Can we work only through tickets? (166) – Racing horses (167) – Rationality is scary (167) – Emotions are attractive (168) – "Our work is not that discrete" (169) – Clarity, transparency and discipline (170) – Story points as a local currency (171) – Cryptocurrency (171)

W HEN I get back to my desk, Dennis and Bao are already arguing about something. Bao is standing, Dennis is sitting and Adrian is lying deep in his chair. I love office fights, they are always full of fun and help you learn something new.

"How will that work?" Adrian asks Dennis as I sit to my chair.

"I don't know exactly, but we can think something up," Dennis seems confused and frustrated. "Dude, what do you think about metrics?" he asks me.

"I love them," I reply, "if they make sense."

"Would be great if we had some performance metrics for our work, right?" Dennis says.

"Absolutely, but what for?"

> Effective management can only be based on facts, numbers, and metrics—nothing else.

"Exactly my point," Bao exclaims. "What do we need them for? How will they help? They will only distract and create unnecessary tension between all of us!"[1]

"And tension is bad?" I ask.

"Yes, it is," Bao seems puzzled. "What do you mean? Who wants to work under stress?"

"Well, some people do. Some people even find it stressful to work without any stress or pressure."

"Come on, you're joking, but I am serious. This is not a

---

[1] Carsten K. W. De Dreu et al., *Task Versus Relationship Conflict, Team Performance, and Team Member Satisfaction: A Meta-Analysis*, Journal of Applied Psychology, Volume 88, Number 4, 2003: "A little conflict stimulates information processing, but as conflict intensifies, the cognitive system shuts down, information processing is impeded, and team performance is likely to suffer."

competition and we are not racing horses here. We don't need any metrics. We need a comfortable work environment where we can be creative and productive. Metrics and all that carrot-and-stick management is for more primitive labor. Programming is a very creative process." He seems very proud of being one of those creative programmers. "Some may even say it's an art. How can you make artists draw their pictures under pressure of some metrics? One painting per month or you are fired?" Everybody laughs.

"I agree," I say when they stop laughing, "but no matter how artistic you are, there are still metrics. Even the best painters and artists have them. We have them too."

He asks, "What do you mean?" and I continue: "Look, we are getting our paychecks every two weeks, right? That's the metric right there. If I stop working or my management," I look at Adrian who is doodling with his face down, "is unhappy with my results, I will stop getting those paychecks. That is the metric. Very primitive and binary, but it is a metric: I either get the check or I don't. Artists have something very similar. They draw, they sing, they create sculptures, but someone eventually pays them for that work. And if they produce something nobody likes, the value of their metric will be negative. It's a separate question whether they will pay attention to this false value or not, but the metric is always right in front of them."

"I totally agree!" Dennis exclaims.

"Maybe so," Bao says after a few seconds of thinking, "what's your point?"

"My point is that this metric is very coarse grained. It's too primitive, simplistic, rude, and offensive. It simply doesn't help people, especially creative ones. It doesn't help any people. It turns us into slaves, since we don't work for the result, we work for the master. Instead of achieving some measurable and objective goals, we have to please the person who signs the paychecks."

> The presence of a monthly paycheck is the performance metric, but it is rough, coarse grained, and ineffective.

"Dude, stop that slavery ..." Bao gets angry.

I interrupt him, "Don't get me wrong, I'm not blaming anyone in particular. The entire system works like that. It's not Adrian or Tony who are guilty," Adrian looks at me sadly. "Not at all! They are in the very same position as we are. They also have masters. They also have to work for someone instead of towards some goals. We all are guilty because we are too lazy or too stupid to invent better, finer-grained metrics, which will make us work for projects, not for people."

"That's what I've been telling them, dude," Dennis stands up. "Let's create some metrics and see how they work."

"What metrics? Calm down," Bao exclaims. "Are you planning to count my lines of code?" I wonder whether he actually wrote any lines over the last few years.

"Why is it that every time I mention metrics, everybody thinks about lines of code? Since that Bill Gates joke,[1] I believe, everybody knows that counting lines is a false idea."

> Any metric is better than the absence of metrics, provided their formulas and results are regularly being re-assessed.

"What else are you suggesting to count?" Bao asks.

"Well, let's think of something," I look at Dennis for a second. "How about, uhh ... closed tickets per week?"

"Yes, for example," Dennis confirms.

"So if I don't close tickets, I'm a bad programmer?" Bao doesn't seem to like the idea, most probably because he doesn't really close anything, ever.

"Well, it doesn't mean exactly that, but it will tell us something. Measuring doesn't mean taking actions immediately. At first it's important to understand what the numbers are and then sit down together again and decide what to do with them. Why are you so afraid of metrics anyway?" I exclaim.

"Because they are counter productive! Read Mike Cohn[2] or any other author about Agile. They all say that making people

---

[1] The actual quote is something like this, although I could not find the source: "Measuring programming progress by lines of code is like measuring aircraft building progress by weight."

[2] Mike Cohn, *Succeeding with Agile: Software Development Using Scrum*, Addison-Wesley Professional, 2009.

responsible for their speed of delivery or any other 'numbers' is what kills their motivation," Bao says.

I pause for a second, thinking how to convince them and what to start with: "People don't like stress, like you said before. I agree with that. Nobody likes to live and work in fear. And stress produces fear if you don't know what it's coming from and when it will end. In other words, if you don't know the rules of the game, it becomes very stressful for you. On the other hand, if the rules are clear, even if you're losing, you will enjoy the game. The office life is yet another game we play. When the rules are well defined and we know exactly what needs to be done in order to win, we enjoy the game and become very productive, motivated, effective, you name it. However, if the only rule we have is 'make your boss happy or you are out,' the game turns into a nightmare because of the unpredictability and uncertainty that simple stupid rule implies.[1] Metrics and objective achievable goals clear the air, no matter how bad or ineffective they are. Even that silly counting of lines of code is better than making the boss happy. Of course, eventually programmers will start writing extra lines of code just to please the metrics counter, but that will easily be fixable by replacing the metric with something more meaningful, like Code Churn,[2] for example. But having no metrics is way worse than having silly metrics, no matter how controversial this may sound.

---

[1]See footnote 1 on page 128: "Whether interpersonal (despotic) or institutional (totalitarian) in form, authoritarianism produces a sense of solidarity and freedom (from responsibility) through a systematic suppression of indeterminacy and ambivalence. In the ideal-typical bureaucratic, rule-governed organization, employees are at least permitted to think what they like so long as they act in a technically competent manner. Bureaucratic workers may be inclined to invest their sense of reality and identity in the authority of the organization, but they are not systematically induced and rewarded for doing so. In principle, communication between employees that challenges or ironicizes bureaucratic authority is tolerated so long as the rules themselves are not overtly violated. In contrast, in organizations with a strong corporate culture, such 'disloyal' communication is at best strictly coded if it is not entirely tabooed: 'you either buy into their norms or you get out.'"

[2]Gregory A. Hall et al., *Software evolution: code delta and code churn*, Journal of Systems and Software, Volume 54, Issue 2, 2000.

To re-phrase Kasparov[1] I would say that a bad set of metrics is better than no metrics."

"I disagree," Bao interrupts, "Bad metrics will send wrong signals to developers. They will think that what those metrics show them is what the management thinks about them, which is not true."[2]

> The amount of tickets closed is the best metric a programmer may have.

"Why is this not true?"

"What do you mean?" Bao exclaims, "Do you you think we value developers by the amount of lines of code they write?"

"That's a bad example. Take some other metric. Say, the amount of tickets a programmer closes each week. The higher the amount, the more valuable that person is for the company, aren't they?"

B<small>AO</small> becomes emotional: "No! There are many other tasks and activities aside from closing tickets!"

"Does the company really need them to be done by us?"

"Yes, of course."

"Why can't we turn them into tickets?"

"How can you turn a discussion of a new server setup into a ticket?"

"The ticket will have a number, someone responsible for it, and a list of participants. When the discussion is over, the ticket is closed and everybody gets one point for it, for example."

"Hm ..." Bao shrugs, "that sounds weird. I've never seen any companies working like that."

---

[1] Garry Kasparov, *How Life Imitates Chess: Making the Right Moves, from the Board to the Boardroom*, Bloomsbury, 2010: "It is better to have a bad plan than no plan."

[2] Dragan Milosevic et al., *Standardized Project Management May Increase Development Projects Success*, International Journal of Project Management, Volume 23, Number 3, 2005: "It is wrong to assume that standardizing project management factors will automatically enhance project success. Standardizing project management may not necessarily improve project success and we cannot argue that increasing the level of standardization of project management factors will automatically lead to an increase in project success."

"Why do we have to care about other companies, dude?" Dennis asks.

"Because they are alive, they know what they are doing, they have been doing it for years. Nobody manages software development through those stupid tickets, guys!" Bao exclaims emotionally. "It is just too primitive. Programmers are not race horses, they don't like working and holding tickets on their foreheads. Moreover, how do you solve the problem of different sizes of those tickets? Some tasks are more complex, while others are very small. What if I close ten simple tasks this week and you close just two, but big ones. Who wins?"

> An effective management team knows how to transfer its goals into measurable objectives for its employees.

"Nobody wins, it's just a number. We will analyze it and investigate the situation. For example, we can assign those 'story points' to each ticket, in order to balance the output of different programmers," I try to make something up.

"I don't think this will work, guys," Adrian jumps in. "You have to bring it up to Tony and see what he says. We are not in the position to make that kind of decision."

"Let's go talk to him, why not?" Dennis says bravely.

"Well, if you want to," Adrian doesn't sound too optimistic. "To be honest, I'm on your side," he says to me. "I think such transparency of our performance could be helpful, but we have to talk to Tony."

"Shall we?"

"Sure."

WE, all four of us, go to Tony's office. He sits in a separate space, with a glass wall and a big white board behind him. I've never seen him using that board. Maybe it's something he needs to keep him very proud of what he is doing. People care way more about their emotions than about objective results they are getting.

We are much more irrational that we would expect.[1] Moreover, rationality is now equated to cold-heartedness, cynicism, and even cruelty. Clean and logical thinking is much less appreciated than emotions, feelings, and even uncontrolled behavior. Maybe it's not a recent trend, actually.[2]

We don't like to deal with strong and logical opponents—they scare us. It's much more comfortable to deal with someone who is vulnerable, soft, weak, and needs help. That person is much more manageable and controllable than someone who knows what to do and is capable of thinking straight. On top of that, there is jealousy: we get jealous when we see someone in a good mood, free from emotion, and thinking straight. We don't want to help that someone or trust them with our money.

> To be successful, one has to look emotional and weak because strong and rational people are scary and not trustworthy.

Ergo, to achieve more and climb higher on the hierarchical ladder, one must pretend to be driven by spontaneous and difficult-to-control emotions. That will trigger people's sympathy, which will immediately lead to trust and desire to help. In other words, it's an era of schizophrenics and anti-depressants.

"Tony, we have an idea," Dennis starts bravely. He doesn't have much to be afraid of, since Tony is not his direct boss. "Do you have a minute?"

"Sure, what's up?" Tony seems to be in a good mood.

"Well, it's not an idea," Adrian jumps in, with a more careful

---

[1] ★Richard H. Thaler et al., *Nudge: Improving Decisions About Health, Wealth, and Happiness*, Yale University Press, 2008: "The false assumption is that almost all people, almost all of the time, make choices that are in their best interest or at the very least are better than the choices that would be made by someone else. We claim that this assumption is false—indeed, obviously false."

[2] Jennifer S. Lerner et al., *Emotion and Decision Making*, Annual Review of Psychology, Volume 66, 2015: "Many psychological scientists now assume that emotions are the dominant driver of most meaningful decisions in life. Decisions serve as the conduit through which emotions guide everyday attempts at avoiding negative feelings (e.g., guilt, fear, regret) and increasing positive feelings (e.g., pride, happiness, love), even when we lack awareness of these processes."

start. "It's just a discussion we had, we'd like to hear your opinion."

"Sure, take a sit," and we sit. "Tell me," Tony is a nice guy. That's what the company pays him for—to be a nice guy. Not for the software he writes by our hands.

"How about we measure our performance with metrics and reward those who have the highest numbers?" Dennis explains impatiently.

"Well," Tony looks at Adrian, "what metrics?"

"That's the problem, we don't know what metrics," Bao jumps in.

"Dude, stop it!" Dennis gets angry, "We just discussed them. We know the metrics! We can count the amount of story points each programmer closes through the tickets. Each ticket will have a certain amount of story points and an assignee. When the ticket is closed, those points go to the account of the programmer. The more points I earn by the end of the month, the better programmer I am and the more money I get!" everybody laughs. "What's wrong? Did I explain it right?" Dennis asks me.

I nod. Tony seems puzzled. He smiles. He's got over fifty programmers under his management, he must be very careful, right?

Tony asks me, "Is this your idea?" Damn, now I am in trouble. I reply carefully, "Well, yes, I read it in a management book. It said that it's important to measure the performance in order to keep people motivated and all that. This sounds like a simple way to try it out, why not?" I feel that I'm in trouble.

"What do you think?" Tony asks Adrian. He is a smart manager—he collects all opinions around before making any decision or even opening his mouth.

"I don't think it's for us, to be honest," Adrian says and Dennis looks at him very surprised. "Maybe for some other companies, where work is more discrete, this may work. We have so many unknowns and uncertainties."

"But you said you liked it!" Dennis is always impatient and reacts immediately. Although, he is right, Adrian was in favor of the idea a few minutes before. It seems that Adrian, as a good "team player," smelled Tony's attitude towards this concept and immediately played along.

"I never said it," Adrian smiles, feeling safe behind Tony's back, "I said that we have to discuss it with Tony."

"Hold on guys, calm down," Tony raises his both hands, "Let's be professional. You?" he asks Bao.

> Under weak management, an ability to go along with the boss is the key professional skill.

"I hate it and I said it before, for the same reason as Adrian said—our work is not discrete enough. Programmers have too many other things to do aside from closing tickets. We can't simply turn them into ticket monkeys, that will offend them and won't help anything."

"Won't offend me!" Dennis exclaims, "What are you talking about? I'm a programmer and I close those tickets every day anyway. Why would it offend me?"

"Hold on," Tony says coldly. "Why do you like it, again?" Tony asks me and I realize that I should do what Adrian just did—surrender. Bao and Tony look at me, Adrian spins his phone in his hand.

WILL I surrender? No. Let's try to fight and see how it goes. A stupid decision, I know. "Well, I believe that technical people love to work when the rules are clear. Especially if and when they know what they are working for, how their results are measured, what is good and what is bad. Professional programmers enjoy clarity, transparency, discipline, all those things. The absence of clear performance metrics, which most companies, and our company too, have, is a big frustration for skilled programmers. Actually, it's a good situation for not-so-seasoned programmers, since they can't be caught. Also, it's good for lazy people."

"We don't have anyone lazy here," Bao interrupts.

"Shh," Tony raises his palm. "Go on," he says to me.

"Any metric will be helpful," I continue, "provided it is universal and transparent for everybody. Of course, we should not count the lines of code, since it's simply stupid, but we can count story points, which are assigned to tasks by the management or Masha or whoever is creating the tickets, and programmers agree with them when they start to work on a ticket. Later, by the end of the month or a week we can see who achieved what."

"And what next?" Bao interrupts.

"We reward the winners and kill the losers," I joke, but nobody laughs.

"But what about those other things people are busy with?" Tony asks, "Like meetings, for example."

"They will have less of them, if they don't really need them to achieve their primary goals, which are story points. Or they will ask meeting organizers to give them story points for their participation in the meetings."

> Convincing the upper management is a dangerous activity that must be avoided at all cost.

"Those story points will turn into a new local currency," Tony jokes and everybody laughs. "Let's use Bitcoins instead!" he jokes again and everybody laughs again.

"Let's mine our own cryptocurrency instead," Bao suggests and I realize that the discussion is over, Tony won't support the idea.

"Can you do that?" Tony seems interested in the cryptocurrency idea.

"Oh, sure, just need a few strong servers."

"Let's do it, you have my support, I will get the budget for it today!" Tony jokes again and we all laugh again.

"So, why can't we at least try, Tony?" Dennis is back again.

"Well, it seems like a very interesting idea," Tony starts and we all understand where he is heading. "Have you seen it done like that in other companies?" he asks me. "I mean, why don't Google or Facebook work like that?" This is the argument I can't really beat.

"I don't know. Because they are stupid, maybe?" I say it and understand that it was not the right thing to say.

"Yeah, right, Google is stupid," Bao immediately uses the opportunity.

"Maybe they don't care about performance and effectiveness. Or maybe their programmers are happy as they are, by just working in Google and driving multi-colored bicycles?" I try, but it's for nothing, I have already lost.

"Our programmers are not happy, or what?" Tony acts surprised. "I don't understand."

"We would be way happier if we would know how good or bad we are, I'm telling you!" Dennis exclaims.

"Dennis, you need to calm down," Tony looks at him.

"I'm sorry, I'm too emotional. I'd better go back to my coding," Dennis stands up and walks away.

We all sit quietly for a few seconds. Tony says to Adrian: "Please, talk to him. I don't understand what he is so frustrated about. Let's solve this issue, we don't need this negativity in the team. OK?"

Adrian nods. Tony says to me, "We will think about this idea. Let's just try not to shake the boat for no reason. You see what just happened with Dennis? Please, keep such ideas to yourself, if possible. Can you do that?"

I nod. I lost. The question is how much. We all stand up and walk away.

Experts and knowledge sharing

The "How does Google do it?" argument (173) – Structure first, fun next (174) – Stress and distress (174) – Responsibility (175) – Guilt (175) – Partial refunds (176) – Business knowledge (176) – Business rules (177) – Documentation (177) – Remote work (177) – People vs. documents (177) – Tickets (179) – Bus factor (179) – Subject matter experts (180)

Do I worry about Tony's attitude? Yes, I do. He may easily fire me. The guy is nice, but spontaneous. Like all nice guys. He just wants the process not to hit any sharp edges. He can't experiment with new ideas. He is responsible for a big group of people, including his wife and kids. His salary is too big, I guess, to risk it. So, no matter what we offer him, the answer will be "How does Google do it?" He can only copy those things, which already were adopted by the market and proven to be acceptable.[1]

It doesn't really matter how effective they are, what matters is that they are not risky. If something is brilliant, but "may not work," it's not for Tony. Is this cowardice? I guess. Is it caution? Yes, also true. C-level management is all about that: better do nothing than take any chances. And this company is not even very big. I can only imagine how difficult it would be to bring anything new up in a large enterprise. That's why I don't want to waste my time there.

"Don't worry, we'll get back to that discussion again," Adrian meets me at the coffee corner. "I've worked with Tony for over four years. He is a nice guy, but such ideas need time, you know ..."

> The paradox is that we, at the same time, hate control and the chaos caused by the lack of it.

"Yeah, I'm fine, it's always important to discuss what bothers us, no matter what the outcome is," I play along, pretending to be a good team player, who cares not only about performance or quality, but mostly about good team

---

[1] Roger Jones, *What CEOs Are Afraid Of*, Harvard Business Review, February 2015: "The biggest fear *[of a CEO]* is being found to be incompetent, also known as the 'imposter syndrome.' This fear diminishes their confidence and undermines relationships with other executives."

spirit and a comfortable work environment. People love it.

"Do you really think that our developers would enjoy working with tickets?" he takes his drink out of the machine and we stay in front of each other at the kitchen, holding hot paper cups with some dark liquid inside, which Americans call coffee. "I mean, people love to talk, they love the office atmosphere, they enjoy being part of the team, they are not here just to close tickets and go home," he smiles and I understand that he is talking about himself first of all.

"Of course they do," I say friendly, "me too. Who doesn't? We are not robots. But the work we do is the primary reason why we are here, right?"

"Yeah ..." he sips some coffee.

I try to understand whether he is really interested to know what I think or if he just wants to confirm something, and continue, "I really believe it's important to have a structure first and fun next. Look at Dennis. He is one of the best programmers and he is very loyal, no matter what he says about the company and him being unhappy. He stays in the office 'til late and works a lot. But he is not satisfied and very frustrated. Why is that?" I ask rhetorically. "Because he is stressed out. The stress is coming from his inability to see the borders of work and responsibility. He simply doesn't rest. Of course, he goes home, he sleeps, he plays his favorite shooters, he has weekends, and all that. But he always feels responsible for something big, which he actually can't control. He doesn't stop being responsible when his work day is over. Even when his task or ticket is closed. His work and his results are not determined and not discrete—that's what stresses him most of all."

"Hm ..." he keeps listening and sipping.

"You know there is stress and there is distress. Doctors say that stress is good for us, because it mobilizes our internal resources, boosts the nervous system, and basically gives us energy. What is important, though, is to make sure the stress goes away quickly and we can relax. If this doesn't happen and the stress stays with us for longer, it turns into a distress and eventually we get cancer."[1]

"Yeah, I've heard that," he smiles skeptically.

"I'm also not sure about the cancer concept, but distress is bad, that's for sure. This is what Dennis has got. He gets stressed when new tasks are coming in, he completes them, fixes the problems, but the responsibility doesn't go away. He stays responsible for the project even after his work is over. Simply because his responsibility is not only in the tickets, it's everywhere. He doesn't know what needs to be done to stop it and take a rest. If he would be less proficient, like many others on our team," we both smile, "he would just ignore most of that responsibility and would not care at all. He would just work from nine to five and turn off his phone after leaving the office. But he is not like that. He is loyal and feels pain for the project when something goes wrong. This is what causes distress and frustration. Our job, as a project, is to help him stay productive and positively stressed by drawing the borders around his tasks and his responsibility."

"Aha ..." he yawns with a closed mouth.

"We should officially allow him to rest when a task is over. We should say that you're not responsible for anything else, except the problems described in your tickets. When you close them, you are free. Not guilty anymore!"

> Lack of explicitly defined individual responsibility distresses and wears out those who honestly care.

"Guilty?" he smiles.

"Yes, it seems that responsibility and guilt, as emotions, are very close to each other. We can't keep Dennis guilty for such a long time. Not only him, but anyone. Instead of trying to solve problems and become not guilty, which is what we need him to

---

[1] Myrthala Moreno-Smith, *Impact of stress on cancer metastasis*, Future Oncology, Volume 6, Number 12, 2010: "The influence of psychosocial factors on the development and progression of cancer has been a longstanding hypothesis since ancient times. In fact, epidemiological and clinical studies over the past 30 years have provided strong evidence for links between chronic stress, depression and social isolation and cancer progression. By contrast, there is only limited evidence for the role of these behavioral factors in cancer initiation."

do, he simply burns out and loses hope. He feels like a prisoner, who will exit free only when his sentence period is over, not when he is done with the work."

"Yeah ..." he yawns again. It's time to wrap this conversation up.

"I'm sure we'll figure something out, though," I smile, "Let's go back to work. I will talk to Dennis, don't worry," I say what he wanted to hear, I believe, when he started this discussion.

"Thanks, let's go," and we go back to our desks.

Masha is here again, speaking with Dennis. "I explained it to you last week, don't you remember?" she sounds a bit nervous.

"Yeah, right," Dennis agrees. "Wait, I don't remember, can we go through it again, please?"

"Dennis, you're killing me! Look, when the order is closed and a client wants a partial refund, we must not refund the commission we already paid to the bank. However, if the commission is less than a dollar, we refund it. Remember?"

"Right, this commission is killing me."

Masha looks at me: "Your friend keeps forgetting what I'm asking him to do, and doesn't want to go an extra mile to really understand how the business works. He just programs, but doesn't remember what our business rules are."

"Come on," Dennis rolls his chair back and stands up, stretching his back. "You are not being fair."

"What's up?" I ask.

> Co-located projects are at bigger risk of chaos because the temptation to skip documentation is stronger.

"Tell me," Masha starts, "what do you think? Should a good programmer learn and understand business rules, or he should just implement what I'm telling him?" she says, obviously expecting my support.

"Not really," I reply.

"What?" she is surprised.

"See!" Dennis exclaims and laughs. "I won!"

"Dude, wait, let me explain. I believe that nobody in a project must possess any knowledge that is not available to everybody else through documentation. In other words, if you know something that Dennis can't read from project files, it's your fault, not his. Actually, not your fault either, it's a fault of the project."

"Here we go again ..." she sighs. "We can't write everything down, it's simply impossible. Requirements and business rules are changing so frequently, it's much faster and easier to explain them like that, in a quick chat. If we were living in different countries and working remotely, I would maybe understand that documentation is better, but not when we are in the same office."

"Faster, you're saying, right? But look at what is happening now. You need to explain it for the second time to this lazy guy," I look at him. "This is what takes a lot of time. If you would write it just once, you would not need to even come here to our desks, you would just email him the link to the document and that's it."

"Listen," she replies, "forget the documentation, we tried that last year, a few times. It didn't work. Nobody writes it, nobody reads it, it's just easier to have a chat and explain everything. That's why the company is renting this office in the first place, I believe—in order to make it possible for us to have these face-to-face conversations. If we only worked through documentation, we would not need an office. We would just work from our homes."

"What's wrong with that?" I ask.[1]

"Don't start it," she replies, "all companies have offices, look

---

[1] Christopher Groskopf, *For programmers, the ultimate office perk is avoiding the office entirely*, Quartz, April 12, 2017: "The number of programmers who work full-time from home has been growing at an average rate of 11.5% per year over the past decade."

at big companies.[1,2] This is just more convenient.[3] People are not robots. They don't like to work with documents, they like to work with people."

I shrug and smile. "Maybe they don't know how to work with documents and that's why they prefer to work with people?"

"I know how to work with documents, I've got master's degree in software engineering," she gets offended.

"He didn't mean you personally, Masha, stop it," Dennis attempts to calm her down.

"Look, don't get offended," I continue, "Isn't it obvious that the better our documentation is, the faster and easier programmers could implement your ideas? It will be more comfortable for you to work, if, instead of explaining multiple times, you could just write it down once. And I don't mean long multi-page documents, which nobody likes to write or read. Project documentation has multiple forms. The best form, to be honest, I believe is tickets. They resemble real chats, but they stay with us forever. We can always get back to the history, see what was said by who and avoid repetition of questions and answers."

---

[1]Stephane Kasriel, *IBM's Remote Work Reversal Is A Losing Battle Against The New Normal*, Fast Company, May 2017: "Until recently, IBM was one of the first and biggest proponents of remote work. But no longer. In March, the company began directing thousands of employees to work from set locations or else look for another job."

[2]Alice Truong, *Reddit Gives Remote Employees Until End Of Year To Relocate To San Francisco*, Fast Company, October 2014: "As it turns out, our teams (within each office) and remote workers did good work, but the separation has kept us from effectively being able to coordinate as well as we needed to on a full-company level. Big efforts that require quick action, deep understanding, and efficient coordination between people at multiple offices just don't go as well as we (and our users) needed."

[3]Kara Swisher, *"Physically Together": Here's the Internal Yahoo No-Work-From-Home Memo for Remote Workers and Maybe More*, AllThingsD, 22 February 2013: "To become the absolute best place to work, communication and collaboration will be important, so we need to be working side-by-side. That is why it is critical that we are all present in our offices. Some of the best decisions and insights come from hallway and cafeteria discussions, meeting new people, and impromptu team meetings. Speed and quality are often sacrificed when we work from home. We need to be one Yahoo!, and that starts with physically being together."

"But we already have tickets now," Masha argues.

"Yeah, we have them, but we keep a very small amount of information there. Most of the knowledge we keep in our heads. Imagine what will happen if the company, God forbid, loses you or this guy," I point to Dennis. "It will be a disaster, right? Because you know too much and this knowledge is not really documented anywhere."[1]

"It's called bus factor,"[2] Dennis says.

"Yes, something like that. But it's not only about that. The problem is not in losing someone, but more about knowledge circulation in the team. Knowledge accumulators are slowing down the team, even though they look like a very good thing to have at the first sight. However, they are not. To become more savvy and aggregate more knowledge, they inevitably have to block access to knowledge to everybody else. Not entirely, of course, but to some extent. Otherwise, if information is freely available and easy to understand, experts

| A smart team does everything to get rid of experts. They cause bottlenecks in the flow of knowledge.

---

[1] Peter C. Rigby et al., *Quantifying and Mitigating Turnover-Induced Knowledge Loss: Case Studies of Chrome and a project at Avaya*, Proceedings of the 38th International Conference on Software Engineering (ICSE'16), 2016: "Individuals who create software transfer their, often tacit knowledge, into the inner workings of the system making it difficult for others to maintain. It is, therefore important to evaluate the risk of developers leaving the project."

[2] Martin Monperrus, *Principles of Antifragile Software*, The First International Conference on the Art, Science and Engineering of Programming, Brussels, Belgium, 2017: "In software development, the 'bus factor' measures to what extent people are essential to a project. If a key developer is hit by a bus (or anything similar in effect), could it bring the whole project down? In dependability terms, such a consequence means that there is a failure propagation from a minor issue to a catastrophic effect."

will not show up.[1] We all will be experts, more or less. Instead, the knowledge must be spread out equally among all team members,[2] which, most likely, will mean that nobody knows anything and everything is in the documentation," I smile. "Thus, answering your original question, Masha, I believe that programmers should intentionally isolate themselves from business knowledge to prevent turning into experts."

MASHA holds her hands across her chest. "That's weird."

"Why?" Dennis is here to help me. "Sounds logical to me. Look, if I know too much about business, it will be easier for us to work, me and you, but the business will only suffer. Because nobody else will be able to understand what we are doing. Right, dude?"

"Yes. And there is one more thing about experts. Programmers are doing a very bad favor to themselves when they turn into subject matter experts. They are locking themselves up to a single domain and a single software solution. They are pushing

---

[1] Todd Sedano, *Sustainable Software Development through Overlapping Pair Rotation*, Proceedings of the 10th ACM/IEEE International Symposium on Empirical Software Engineering and Measurement, Ciudad Real, Spain, 2016: "Conventional wisdom says that team churn is detrimental to project success and that extensive documentation is needed to mitigate this effect. Unfortunately, documentation quickly becomes out-of-date and unreliable, undermining this approach. During a grounded theory study, we observed projects succeed despite high disruption and little documentation. This raised the following research question: 'How do the observed teams develop software effectively while overcoming team disruption?'"; "This is done by engendering a positive attitudes towards team disruption, encouraging knowledge sharing and continuity, as well as caring about high code quality."

[2] James O. Coplien, *Organizational Patterns of Agile Software Development*, Prentice Hall, 2004: "Define the truck number as being the number of people in the organization who have unique critical domain expertise. You don't want the truck number to be large, because that means that the probability is large that the loss of any given team member would mean the loss of critical expertise. The risk would be too high. Yet it's impossible to make the truck number very small (it's almost impossible to make it zero). Keep the truck number low; retain a small number of key experts with unique knowledge. Build a culture of shared knowledge that increases the breadth of knowledge over time, particularly for knowledge that easily can be codified, taught, or otherwise conveyed."

themselves out of the market. Also, they don't really grow as programmers. They stop learning frameworks, languages, and libraries because they don't need them. All they need stays inside one office space. One day, when they try to find a new job, they realize that the market is ready to offer them three times smaller salary than they were getting before. Job security does them a very bad favor."

"Our developers don't want to change jobs," Masha says.

"This is what the management likes to believe in. The reality is different. Professional and active programmers change jobs approximately once a year.[1] If they stay longer, it's most likely an indicator of a problem,[2] which is also known as 'I am an expert!' Their companies start to pay them more, out of a fear to lose those knowledge silos.[3] It's a trap for a business and for a programmer. They both lose eventually."

> Turning oneself into an expert in one particular project is a big career risk that a smart programmer must avoid.

"So you are saying that all developers should be stupid code monkeys, who don't care about the business at all, only about their code?" Masha asks.

"You just offended us both," Dennis laughs. "Coding by itself is as much fun as your business. For me, to be honest, it's much more fun."

---

[1] StackOverflow Developer Survey, https://goo.gl/CtCSyQ, 2017: "35% respondents said that they changed job during the last year."

[2] Vivian Giang, *You Should Plan On Switching Jobs Every Three Years For The Rest Of Your Life*, Fast Company, January 2016: "Changing jobs every couple of years used to look bad on a resume. It told recruiters you can't hold down a job, can't get along with colleagues, or that you're simply disloyal and can't commit. That stigma is fast becoming antiquated—especially as millennials rise in the workplace with expectations to continuously learn, develop, and advance in their careers."; "Workers who stay with a company longer than two years are said to get paid 50% less."

[3] Jamal Cromity, *Silo Persistence: It's not the Technology, it's the Culture!* New Review of Information Networking, Volume 16, Number 2, 2011: "Within any given organization, institution, or business, a silo of knowledge can be a person, a department, an application, a database, or a network that only one or a few people can access."

"Really?" Masha seems surprised.

"Yes!" he exclaims. "I would be absolutely happy if you keep me out of your business concepts and ideas and just tell me what needs to be implemented."

"You guys really don't want to know why we need what we ask you to implement?" she is really surprised.

"Absolutely not," I smile. "Do you want to know how we implement those features, what frameworks we use, what database optimization techniques, what programming languages, and all that?"

"No, leave me out of that," now she smiles.

"See?" Dennis stands up. "I don't need your details either. I'm not really interested in them at all. I just want to see you happy when I implement what you ask for, that's it. Happy, Masha!"

"Oh, that's so nice," she laughs.

Static analysis

Code formatting (183) – Underwear metaphor (184) – Good programmers (184) – Force (184) – We are greedy, selfish, and lazy (185) – XY Theory (185) – German shepherds allegory (185) – A software is just a small piece of a software product (187) – FindBugs (187) – Auto-formatting (188) – Educational aspect (188) – Industry-adopted style guide (189) – The stricter, the better (190) – Pre-flight builder (191) – Can we start in an existing project? (192) – Speed of delivery is the most important metric (192) – Boxing metaphor (192) – Motivational conflict (193)

DENNIS is mad. I don't know why, but it doesn't really matter. The dude is full of emotions all the time. I can't imagine how he can be a father of two if he always behaves like a child. "Let me show you this stupid code," he says. I go around the table and sit next to him. The code he is showing me is ugly, just like all other code I've seen here. I can't really understand what particularly bothers him now. Anyway, I have to pretend that I got the problem: "Yeah, I see."

"No, you don't! I formatted this piece the right way a month ago. Someone broke my formatting and I fixed it again last week. Now it's ugly again. What's going on?"

"Who did this?"

"Git says it's Tom."

"Let's go find and kill him."

"Dude, I'm not kidding, it's very annoying. I keep doing the same work over and over again. I guess we have to sit down and agree about the rules of formatting. Otherwise we will waste a lot of time. It's your job, let's gather a meeting."

> Lack of uniformity in the coding style causes even more frustration than functionality defects.

"Have you talked to Tom already?"

"No, but what's the point. Someone else will do the same. We need to agree—all together, the entire team. Don't you think?"

"Not really."

"Why not?" he closes the laptop, crosses his arms, and looks at me.

"We need a static analyzer and a pre-flight builder."

The assumption that programmers can and should write the code right just because they are good programmers is very popular.[1] I've heard a joke that we don't show up in our offices wearing just underwear, not because there is a written rule about that, but because that's not how we feel we should behave.[2] The same, they say, is true about our coding style and our attitude to quality. We don't write bad code just because we don't feel like it. Maybe this metaphor makes sense?

HE exclaims impatiently not even listening to what I'm saying: "No, dude! We need good programmers, who understand how to write code properly."

"Good programmers?"

"Yes, good ones. Don't you think so? You are always in favor of quality, don't you understand that the way code looks is important?"

"I do. But it's not about programmers being good or bad. All of them are good. If we talk to Tom now, he will say that you are a bad programmer and he had to re-format the code after you and re-wrote some parts of it. He will blame you. You blame him. It's very subjective. I'm, in general, strongly against these 'good vs. bad' definitions when we're talking about people. We all are good and we all are bad, depending on the circumstances. The job of the project is to make sure programmers do what the project wants and needs. Not because they are so innately good and can't live without us, but because they have no other choice. Machiavelli said that people do good only if you force them to.[3] It's silly to expect everybody do what we, as a project, think is good, like writing high-quality, properly formatted Java code.

---

[1] Robert L. Glass, *Frequently Forgotten Fundamental Facts About Software Engineering*, IEEE Software, Volume 18, Number 3, 2001: "Good programmers are up to 30 times better than mediocre programmers, according to 'individual differences' research."

[2] GeePaw Hill brought this up in Shift-M podcast episode No.27: https://goo.gl/ip1gt6.

[3] Niccolò Machiavelli, *Discorsi sopra la prima deca di Tito Livio*, 1517, Book 1, Chapter 3: "Men never do good unless necessity drives them to it."

They will write what they think is good enough if we don't force them to behave differently."

"Force? That Italian guy you keep quoting lived a hundred years ago,[1] when the world was totally different. We don't force anyone anymore, dude. Do the reality check."

"Just because they told you so doesn't mean it really is like that."

"They?"

"I mean, you believe that nobody forces anyone anymore, but in reality we are still the very same people who lived at the time of Machiavelli or even Sun Tzu. We are greedy, selfish, lazy— all that. When the business needs us to work for it, it has to invent instruments to force us. Actually, it has to invent both a carrot and a stick. And I don't mean anything negative with that. They are basically rules and discipline, which help us stay focused and synchronized. I'm just saying that everybody just doing the best they can, like Kant suggested,[2] won't really help in team work," I explain and ask myself how far away this concept is from the modern trend of self-motivated programmers, self-regulated teams, and toothless management.

> There are no good or bad programmers, there is only weak or strong management.

H<small>E</small> asks, suddenly, "Have you heard about the XY Theory?"[3]

---

[1] Niccolò Machiavelli lived in the 15th century and died on the 21st of June, 1527 (aged 58).

[2] Immanuel Kant, *Grundlegung zur Metaphysik der Sitten*, 1785: "Act only according to that maxim whereby you can, at the same time, will that it should become a universal law," which is also known as "The Categorical Imperative."

[3] Douglas McGregor, *The Human Side of Enterprise*, Adventure in Thought and Action, Proceedings of the Fifth Anniversary Convocation of the School of Industrial Management, MIT, 1957: "The philosophy of management by direction and control–regardless of whether it is hard or soft—is inadequate to motivate because the human needs on which this approach relies are today unimportant motivators of behavior."

"Yes, sure, and I don't really believe in the 'Y' part of it.[1] Of course, there are people who would try to do good all the time, but it's only because their carrots and sticks are engraved so deeply inside of them that they don't really need anything else from the outside. They were born and raised in a very moral and disciplined environment, and learned very well that even an attempt to do anything bad to other people will cause a severe punishment.[2]

> Our innate, as we see it, desire to do good is the result of taming and training many generations ago.

They learned it when they were three years old.[3] Now, they are twenty and we call them responsible and accountable. In reality, they are just perfectly trained—just like those German shepherds who don't touch a piece of meat on the ground and we take it as them being intelligent. In reality, they were shocked by high-voltage electricity a few times when they tried to eat something from the floor and the instinct has developed pretty well. They are still the same dogs, ready to eat whatever they feel suitable, but the training made them look and behave more disciplined and 'good,' as we understand it."

"Let's train programmers with electricity, then," he suggests.

"You are joking, but there is a lot of truth in this joke. We do need some sort of high-voltage electricity, which will direct us

---

[1] See footnote 1 on page 128: "Theory Y philosophy was built upon the assumption of a spontaneous consensus between individual needs and corporate objectives that had been denied and distorted by bad (theory X) theory. This assumption was naive because it took no account of deep-seated conflicts of interest within organizations that revolve around social divisions of ownership and control."

[2] Jacob Neusner et al., *Golden Rule: The Ethics of Reciprocity in World Religions*, Continuum, 2009: "The Golden Rule—'do to others as you would have them do to you'—finds a place in most religions and is universally acknowledged to form a part of the shared heritage of human wisdom."

[3] Alfie Kohn, *Unconditional Parenting: Moving from Rewards and Punishments to Love and Reason*, Atria Books, 2006: "Behaviorists assume that everything we do can be explained in terms of whether it produces some kind of reward, either one that's deliberately offered or one that occurs naturally. External forces, such as what someone has previously been rewarded (or punished) for doing, account for how we act—and how we act is the sum total of who we are."

all to the right quality of code. Without that, we are like those dogs—very energetic, but chaotic."

CREATING a piece of software that works is just a small part of the entire job.[1] It's much more difficult to create a software product which customers can use. However, we keep teaching programmers mostly algorithms, languages, boolean logic, and frameworks, paying almost no attention to everything else that turns a piece of software into a working product, including support, maintainability, documentation, requirements, planning, estimates, and so on. Coding is just a small part of our job. Dennis seems to be a perfect example of a coder who cares only about his Java statements and thinks that everything else is just way less important and could be done by somebody less intelligent.

"Static analysis," I start to explain, "is a process of checking the quality of code without executing it. There has to be a tool that goes through your Java classes and finds where they look incorrect. They may work perfectly good, though—this is what a static analyzer won't care about. What will matter is how they look. The formatting issues will immediately be spotted, and many other things too, depending on the quality of the analyzer."

"Have you used them?"

"Sure, in my open source projects."

"That's my point—you use them in open source, where the quality of programmers is low. Don't you think that | A strong static analyzer is the best teacher of programming.

if all developers are smart and senior these tools are obsolete?"

"Not really, quite the opposite, actually," I smile, "and you have a very low opinion about the open source territory. Static analyzers not only check formatting and bracket positioning, but also make a lot of recommendations for quality improvements.

---

[1] See footnote 2 on page 158.

Take FindBugs,[1] which is rather powerful and pays attention to different aspects of the quality, like security, for example. To be honest, I learned a lot about Java just by listening to it. Static analyzers are like collective wisdom of the many smart programmers who created them and contributed to them.[2] Imagine that you have a very experienced code reviewer sitting next to you all day long, pointing to the places in your code that can be improved. Would this be helpful?"

He takes a piece of gum. "I guess," he thinks for a few seconds. "Isn't it possible to automate them? I mean, instead of pointing me to the wrong code, the tool can just fix it automatically. Just like that auto-formatting feature in IDEA.[3] I just click a button and the entire class is formatted the right way. Can't we automate everything to work like that?"

"I guess we can, for the most primitive formatting issues, but I still believe that it's a wrong approach, even for the spaces-and-brackets problems. There is a very important educational factor in all that. If you format everything automatically, you will never learn anything and will keep making the same mistakes again and again. Coding is not just making computer do what you want, but also making other people understand your intention, your idea, your way of thinking. Formatting of the code, the way you name your variables, methods, and classes—is the language you

---

[1] Nathaniel Ayewah et al., *Using Static Analysis to Find Bugs*, IEEE Software, Volume 25, Number 5, 2008: "FindBugs now recognizes more than 300 programming mistakes and dubious coding idioms that can be identified using simple analysis techniques. FindBugs also includes some more sophisticated analysis techniques devised to help effectively identify certain issues, such as dereferencing of null pointers, that require such techniques and occur with enough frequency to warrant their development."

[2] Brian Chess, *Secure programming with static analysis*, Pearson Education, 2007: "Static analysis can find errors early in development, even before the program is run for the first time. Finding an error early not only reduces the cost of fixing the error, but the quick feedback cycle can help guide a programmer's work: A programmer has the opportunity to correct mistakes he or she wasn't previously aware could even happen. The attack scenarios and information about code constructs used by a static analysis tool act as a means of knowledge transfer."

[3] Dennis is talking about IntelliJ IDEA, an IDE for Java by JetBrains.

speak to your fellow programmers. I believe it's important for every programmer to feel the language and enjoy using it.[1] Not just auto-format and move on."

"You know what I think?" he asks rhetorically. "I think that most of them will complain about this analysis because each of them enjoy using their own style. Look at Tom. Just like you said, he re-formatted my code not because he was evil, but because he thought that it looked better that way. Now, you will give him the static analyzer and he will be very surprised and frustrated. He will have to forget his own style and start using your style. See the problem, dude?"

> Static analyzers enrich the project with the wisdom accumulated and adopted by the entire industry.

"Our style," I pause for a second. "It's not my style or your style, it's an industry-adopted style, which we take from the open source libraries. That's the beauty of it—it doesn't belong to anyone. If somebody were to complain about it, I can always say that it's not me who invented it. It's something the industry recommends. Instead, if we sit together and create a corporate style guide, like many other companies do, every programmer will have all the reasons to complain, because no matter how good the style guide will be, it will have problems. If it will be us against him—I'm talking about a new programmer—we may lose. If it will be the market against him, he won't have any chances," I smile.

D<small>ENNIS</small> looks into the window. "Yes, make sense ... I am sure everybody will complain about it though, dude. It will take a lot of time to clean up the code and write it absolutely perfect, just

---

[1] Caitlin Sadowski, *Lessons from Building Static Analysis Tools at Google*, Communications of the ACM, Volume 61 Issue 4, 2018: "Developer happiness is key. In our experience and in the literature, many attempts to integrate static analysis into a software-development organization fail. At Google, there is typically no mandate from management that engineers use static analysis tools. Engineers working on static analysis must demonstrate impact through hard data. For a static analysis project to succeed, developers must feel they benefit from and enjoy using it."

like those tools want. We are not robots, man, we make mistakes and it's not really a big deal. The code works, after all. Are you sure we really need such strict control?"

"Well, how do you know it's 'so strict?' These tools are very configurable: they can be very strict or rather loose. Of course, the stricter, the better. And you're absolutely right, the development will slow down for each particular task and each programmer because it won't be enough just to make the code work anymore; it will be necessary to make it clean, too, before it gets accepted by the project. How long it will take depends on the skills of each individual, but overall it will definitely be slower. However, the entire project will start moving forward faster because there will be less mess in the 'master' branch. Look at yourself now: your frustration because of the changes made by Tom, and the time you spend now to fix them—all this is time being wasted. And you're not alone. The entire team does things twice or many more times, or doesn't do them, but lives with a messy code base. Strict rules will make our life easier. And, you know what? The stricter the rules, the better. I believe that a project has to regularly invest some effort to make its rules stronger. The older the project, the more strict its rules have to be."

> A project must constantly invest into its static analyzers, to make their rules stronger and stricter.

"Interesting ... I'm sure we will have a lot of resistance and most of those guys," he points over his shoulder, "will be against these rules."

"Yes, they will."

"OK, let's do it, then!" he laughs.

"We can, but there will be bigger problems than resistance."

"Like what?"

"We can't just start using them immediately and to its full extent. Because they will find so many issues that we won't be able to fix them ever."

"We will fix them eventually, one by one."

"That's the thing—we must not do it one by one, we must either fix everything or forget the whole thing. Because the static analyzer must not be used as a informative tool. It must be a gate keeper, that rejects everything that is not good enough, protecting our 'master' branch."

"Rejects?"

THE word 'reject' seems to be the most annoying component of the quality philosophy, which most of programmers don't like to hear. They expect quality control to be nice to them. But it's not possible. "Here is how it should work,"[1] I reply. "We install the tool and run it. It reports all the problems it can find. We go through the entire code base and fix all issues. The tool says that the code is clean. Then, we prohibit anyone to commit anything directly to the 'master' branch. Instead, everybody, including you and me, will have to work in their own branches. Let's say, you fix a bug and do it in your own branch. When the branch is ready, you bring it to the pre-flight builder. It's a robot, a script. It takes your branch, merges it into the 'master,' and asks the static analyzer whether everything is clean. If it breaks any formatting rules, the robot says that your branch is not good and it doesn't get into the 'master.' If there are no violations, your branch will be merged and the code will appear in the 'master.' That will be the high-voltage electricity for you. You will always know that if you break the formatting, your code won't be merged. The rules will be the same for everybody, of course. The robot won't care where the code is coming from, either from you, Tom, me or Tony. Everybody is equal for it."

"Hm ...," he thinks, "sounds interesting, let's do it."

"I'm telling you, we can't just do it. It's easy to do when the project just starts and the code base is empty—we just configure the analyzer and the robot and start coding. In our situation we

> The static analyzer must be a gate keeper in front of the code repository, rejecting the changes that violate any rules.

can't configure the robot, since it will reject everybody, because the analyzer will report a lot of issues now. And we can't fix them all, because there are too many."

---

[1] Yegor Bugayenko, *How to Prevent SVN Conflicts in Distributed Agile PHP Projects*, php|Architect, August 2010.

"So, we're screwed?"

"Yeah, I guess so. But making a deal with Tom is not a solution either. You will agree with him about certain coding practices, but tomorrow somebody else will break your code again. All those 'coding style guides' are just words, if you ask me. I don't believe in agreements and contracts if they are not enforced and automated by mindless robots. People are good liars, robots are less capable of that—for now."

"Very soon they will learn that too," he laughs. "Look, I like your idea, let's think how we can implement it. What about starting with a small set of rules, can we? Instead of turning those tools you mentioned to their full power, can we configure them to report only a few types of problems? For example, can we just make sure that we use four spaces everywhere instead of tabs. Believe it or not, but in some parts of our code, which are rather old, there are still tabs somewhere. I don't know who did that, but I regularly fix them."

"Well, it is possible, technically, to configure just a few rules. Maybe you are right. We can try that. And we will have to create the pre-flight bot, which will merge branches in. Or we can use an existing one. Let me think about the options for the bot. In the mean time, try to investigate how some analyzer can be configured to only spot one type of problem—the tabs."

"Got it, will do."

STATIC analysis is rarely being used in these scenarios. In most projects I've seen, it is just a collection of nice graphs and reports that demonstrate how many problems the code has and sometimes some suggestions of how they can be fixed. Very rarely, or almost never, do software teams turn static analyzers into gate keepers capable of rejecting their code. It always seems more important to make the delivery fast instead of a higher quality.

The speed of delivery is the most important metric of a programmer. But this metric starts to make any sense only when there are rather strict rules and intentional obstacles, which make it rather difficult—intentionally.

This is very similar to a sport competition. Take boxing, for example. For each boxer the goal is obvious—to make as many effective hits as possible. Well, actually, to make more of them than the opponent can make, in a limited amount of time. Sounds pretty easy, keep hitting and you will win. However, there are very strict rules that prevents boxing from turning into a street fight. Without rules, it would not be a sport anymore and nobody would be interested in participating in it, since it would be very dangerous. Instead of being great athletes, boxers would be just violent and aggressive monkeys. The goal "make as many hits as possible" may and will work only if the rules are very strict. Otherwise, it will destroy the entire game.

The same is very true about software developers. They have to be motivated to deliver their code as fast as possible. There shouldn't be any other goals for them. Ideally, they have to be paid for each delivery and, the faster they happen, the more money they must be getting. However, this approach will be effective only if the project is strong enough to protect itself against poor quality. One of the best protection mechanisms and the first one that should be applied to each new piece of code is static analysis.

> Programmers must be motivated to make changes as fast as possible, while the project must reject them as aggressively as it can.

If the rules of analysis are very strict and programmers are paid to deliver as fast as possible, the quality of the project will be the highest. There always has to be the conflict between the motivation of programmers ("get rich fast") and the motivation of the project ("keep the code base clean"). If one of these motivations is not strong enough, there will be serious problems.

If programmers are aggressive and aim for money, but the project is weak and can't protect itself by static analysis, unit tests, code reviews, and automated delivery pipelines, the code base will be ruined pretty fast. On the other hand, if the project is perfectly protected and rejects anything that compromises the quality, but the programmers are not interested in pushing their code through and are simply too lazy, the development will be stuck.

Speed and quality

Humiliation of being a tester (194) – Testing is more important than coding (195) – Whose fault was it? (196) – Bug-free code is a flawed objective (196) – Delivery pipeline (197) – Sieve (198) – Weak testing (199) – Product quality is not the concern of programmers (200) – Speed first (200) – Quality first (200) – The truth in the middle (201)

JYOTI is here, talking to Adrian about something. She always sounds a bit sad and frustrated. I can understand her. It's humiliating to be a tester nowadays,[1] since companies don't really understand the true value of testing. They pay smaller salaries to test engineers than to programmers[2] and hire mostly juniors or even interns. Testing seems to be understood as a side-effect of programming.[3]

It has to be the other way around, since a software that works is just a third of a product that is ready to be used, programming is two times less important than testing. In order to turn a functioning piece of software into a product, it has to be tested thoroughly and bugs have to be reported. Without testing, the bugs will be found by its users, which will seriously affect the

---

[1] Elaine J. Weyuker et al., *Clearing a Career Path for Software Testers*, IEEE Software, Volume 17, Number 2, 2000: "As crucial as software testing is to product success, it gets little respect in most organizations."; "Because software testing is sometimes viewed as a dead-end job, the most skilled testers are typically eager to 'move up' and become programmers, analysts, or system architects."

[2] On April 26, 2018, according to PayScale, the average salary of a computer programmer in the US is $60,785. The average salary of a software tester is $55,453 (10% lower).

[3] Robert L. Glass et al., *Software Testing and Industry Needs*, IEEE Software, Volume 23, Number 4, 2006: "Test jobs are often consolation prizes for those not considered good enough to hire as software engineers, and the salary gap between developers and testers remains significant. Testers frequently complain about lack of respect, credibility, and influence. Career development is more haphazard than strategic. Most testers are self-taught, and many have never read a book on the subject. No universally agreed-on terminology and testing body of knowledge exist. University training is widely second-rate. Major test certification programs could endanger testing's future by focusing on the wrong things."

level of their satisfaction. Testing and testers drive the product forward, making it market ready. Programmers only help them fix the bugs. This may sound like a joke, and there is a lot of humor in this statement, but there is also a lot of truth.

Testing is a way more complicated and sophisticated activity than writing code.[1] Testers break the product, finding its weak spots. Programmers create it with those weak spots. The responsibility of programmers is way lower than the testers. If a tester misses something important, the plane will crash. If a programmer makes a mistake, there is still a line of testers in front of him to catch the bug.

> Despite the obvious importance of a software testing, testers are second-class citizens in most software teams.

A professional testing department is not a group of monkeys clicking the same set of buttons over and over again, all day long. Instead, they must be a team of software engineers, capable of finding weak spots, automating their finding process,[2] making reports readable and traceable,[3] and communicating issues in a way programmers can understand. Testing engineers, also known as testers, must even be paid better than programmers. Isn't it sad that the industry in most cases expects them to be cheap, junior, and quiet?

THEY talk rather aggressively and I jump in trying to understand the subject. "It's not her fault, actually," Bao says to Adrian.

---

[1] Ron Patton, *Software Testing*, Sams Publishing, 2000: "At first glance, it may appear that a software tester's job would be easier than a programmer's. Breaking code and finding bugs must surely be easier than writing the code in the first place. Surprisingly, it's not."

[2] Elfriede Dustin et al., *Automated Software Testing: Introduction, Management, and Performance*, Addison-Wesley Professional, 1999: "Much of the test effort required on a project now needs to be supported by automated test tools. Manual testing is labor-intensive and error-prone, and it does not support the same kind of quality checks that are possible with an automated test tool."

[3] Nicolas Bettenburg et al., *What Makes a Good Bug Report?* Proceedings of the 16th ACM SIGSOFT International Symposium on Foundations of Software Engineering, 2008: "Well-written bug reports are likely to get more attention among developers than poorly written ones"

"We have to test better on our side. Good programmers must be responsible for the code they write."

"Yes, I agree," she confirms.

"I know," Adrian nods, "but mistakes are inevitable."

"You can just be more careful, guys," she seems to be sad about something.

"What happened?" I jump in.

"We overcharged more than two hundred customers last night because of the bug you guys deployed yesterday," Bao explains, proudly. "Now we have to refund a lot of money," he smiles.

"Did we roll the changes back already?" I ask Adrian.

> A professional team always knows who to blame for the mistakes being made and is not afraid of openly doing so.

"Yes, half an hour ago."

"So, it's our fault?" I ask Bao.

"No, it's my fault," he smiles, sarcastically. "What kind of question is that? You guys should test better and be more serious and responsible for what you write. We are working with money, remember that. Don't blame Jyoti, she is only helping you guys make the product better, but the main responsibility is yours," he is happy about our mistake and worries very little about the damage we caused to the customers. This is understandable—each time we lose, he wins, in Tony's eyes.

"I don't think that's true," it's my turn to smile.

"What isn't true?"

"I don't think that the responsibility of a programmer is to create bug-free code. It's a very serious and fundamental mistake. Not even a mistake, but a philosophy. Thinking like that will only decrease quality and expose more bugs to the user."

"Again with your philosophical talks?" Bao gets nervous. "I have better things to do," he goes back to his cubicle. "You guys disappoint me," he throws on his way out.

"He is always like that, don't worry," Adrian says, quietly.

CALMLY, I continue, "I know, it's OK. Listen, I really mean what I just said. Expecting programmers to produce code that doesn't have bugs is a flawed idea.[1] It's not a job of a programmer to catch bugs and fix them. A programmer creates new code, thinks forward, explores new opportunities to optimize, refactor, make faster, more elegant, and all that. A programmer must never worry about the bugs the customers may see after that. A programmer must worry only about the speed of delivery. The faster the tickets are closed, the better the programmer is. Nothing else. What happened last night was a failure of our delivery pipeline."[2]

"My failure?" Jyoti looks at me, sadly.

"Well, I don't want to point fingers or offend anyone, but it was our failure, not a failure of the person... By the way, who made the mistake?"

"It was Chung," Adrian sighs. "He is still rather junior, I understand that it was my fault too that I gave him this task."

> Expecting programmers to write bug-free code is a terrible and very popular mistake.

"No! I mean yes, it was your fault, but not in giving him the task. The fault was in not configuring the delivery pipeline right."

"What is the delivery pipeline?" Jyoti asks.

"It's a full chain of procedures we perform between the moment a new piece of code is created by a programmer on his computer and the moment our customers see the new functionality online. This is called the delivery pipeline. It contains a number of steps: merging the branch, testing the code, deploying to the staging server, manual testing, deploying to the production server, and some others. The goal of this pipeline is to isolate programmers from customers as much as possible and create a tunnel of hindrances that will filter out problematic code. The pipeline should work as a sieve, which allows only the best parts of the code

---

[1] 🐙 John C. Munson, *Software Engineering Measurement*, CRC Press, 2003: "A good programmer will produce fault-free code, while a bad programmer will produce code that is fault-ridden."

[2] ★ Jez Humble et al., *Continuous Delivery: Reliable Software Releases through Build, Test, and Deployment Automation*, Addison-Wesley Professional, 2010.

to go through. Everything else must be returned for re-work.[1] When a customer complains about a bug, or many customers complain, like happened today, it's a problem with the sieve, not with programmers."

She nods and asks, "Who is responsible for the sieve?" I point to Adrian, "Well, this guy, first of all," and he smiles. He obviously knows what I'm talking about, but perfectly realizes that his boss, Tony, has no idea about the delivery pipeline and just wants the software "to work." That's why Adrian takes it like an interesting conversation, without any real consequences.

"Well, I'm not saying that Adrian is the only person who should develop the pipeline. We all have to participate. We actually have some elements of it already, like the automated build, some unit tests, and your department. There will be way more in the future, like static analysis, integration tests, maybe some automated A/B tests, performance and load tests, maybe even blue-green deployments.[2] As you see, you guys are also a very important element of the pipeline. The bug that the customers faced this morning was supposed to be caught by your testers. Pay attention that the programmers are not part of the delivery pipeline. They create the input for it. What happens after they finish creating and modifying the code is the pipeline. So, if we analyze this particular incident, it's obvious that we must not blame Chung for making the mistake, we must not blame Adrian for giving Chung the task he is not ready to work with, but we must blame Adrian for not making the pipeline strong enough and Jyoti for not being a strong enough element of it."

"So, it is my fault?" she asks again.

"Don't make it personal, it's nobody's fault," Adrian interrupts.

"Well, I would actually make it personal," I interrupt, "but

---

[1] Michael T. Nygard, *Release It!: Design and Deploy Production-Ready Software*, 2nd Edition, Pragmatic Bookshelf, 2018: "We call it a build pipeline, but it's more like a build funnel. Each stage of a build pipeline is looking for reasons to reject the build. Tests failed? Reject it. Lint complains? Reject it. Build fails integration tests in staging? Reject it. Finished archive smells funny? Reject it."

[2] Martin Fowler, *BlueGreenDeployment*, 2010, `https://goo.gl/GQsavF`

in a professional way. It's not your fault as a person. You're a good person, you care about the business we run here, you are eager to learn new things, and all that. Nobody is saying that it's a failure of you personally. What I'm trying to say is that it's a failure of our testing department. You are the head of it now, so it's a defect in your management, which is not a failure, but information for improvement. Now you know where is the defect and will be able to fix it."

"How can I fix it?"

"I don't really know right off the bat, but we can discuss later. The problem is obvious, right," I look at her and she nods. "Our testing is weak. It lets the bugs slip through and damage our customers. We have to find a way to make it stronger."

> A weak delivery pipeline is always guilty in all problems customers experience in production.

"Maybe it's better to stop making bugs?" Jyoti asks and I wonder whether she wasn't really listening or her position does make some sense. Maybe we are guilty of the bugs we make?

I have seen this mentality before and I don't think it's really possible to do anything with it. Managers used to think that "no bugs" means high quality.[1] Well, it is high quality when the user doesn't see any bugs. But there are a number of ways to achieve that. The most obvious and the worst one is to ask us to create fewer bugs.[2] What can they do to make us write the software with fewer bugs inside? They can train us, they can ask or even beg, they can threaten us, they can even replace us with other programmers who are supposed to be "better."

All of that may work. The number of bugs may be lower,

---

[1] Steve Maguire, *Writing Solid Code*, Greyden Press, 2013: "With the growing complexity of software today and the associated climb in bug rates, it's becoming increasingly necessary for programmers to produce bug-free code much earlier in the development cycle, before the code is first sent to the testing group."

[2] Raymond R. Panko, *Spreadsheets on Trial: A Survey of Research on Spreadsheet Risks*, Proceedings of the Twenty-Ninth Hawaii International Conference on System Sciences, 1996: "We do not make mistakes all the time, but we consistently make a certain number, even when we are being careful."

especially if we are scared enough. However, the speed of delivery will seriously suffer. We will care more about quality than about the speed and this process will be totally unmanageable. We will always have the excuse that the quality is too low yet to merge or release.

The management will rely on us in the area of quality and won't invest enough into the delivery pipeline. They will assume that it's our job to produce the quality code, not their job to control us and filter the bugs out.

> The most important trait of a good programmer is the ability to deliver changes fast, passing all quality checks.

The correct solution is different: We must not be responsible for the quality at all. It's not our job to care about customers or about bugs they see. Our job is to produce code. The job of the management is to organize quality assurance and quality control systems the right way and to reject broken elements and accept only those that work.

The only valid metric a programmer should have is the speed of delivery. The more tickets I close per day, the better programmer I am. Of course, closing a ticket means passing all possible quality checks. My job is not to write something of a high quality, but to write code that is capable of passing those checks. How many managers are out there who are capable of facing the reality and enforcing this philosophy?

O``BVIOUSLY``, each company and each project have their own, unique quality standards. Some projects may care only about the speed, since their goal is to create a prototype, raise venture capital and re-write the entire product from scratch. In such a project why should I produce anything of high quality, if the project doesn't have any checks in the delivery pipeline? Not because it's bad, but because this is their business case. For such a project I would just deliver as fast as possible.

To the contrary, another project may have a very strict quality control system with a very-hard-to-fool delivery pipeline, which will reject almost everything, unless it really satisfies all possible quality checks. Such a project may exist in healthcare industry, where any bug may cost someone their lives. In such a project I would also try to deliver as fast as possible, making all possible bugs, but the code will be rejected and I will be required to re-work, polish, improve, etc.

In other words, there has to be a constant permanent conflict between speed and quality. We must be motivated to deliver faster, while the company must be motivated by its business situation. The truth will be somewhere in the middle.

When we see too many bugs in production, or they are too critical, it's a clear signal for us that it's time to make our quality control system stronger. If the pipeline is too weak, it passes too many bad elements through. We must not blame programmers or replace them. This won't help. We must add new filters to the pipeline.

> The balance between speed and quality must be determined by the business case, not by programmers.

The only reason to replace a programmer is when he is slow. All other reasons are just excuses management is using when being unable to admit its own failures. Just like in this morning incident: neither Adrian nor Jyoti is ready to say that it was their fault. They want to blame Chung, because it is easier. Isn't it obvious that the real trouble makers are them?

Delivery pipeline

Blame is counter effective (202) – Fear (202) – Eustress and distress (203) – Depression (203) – Individualism (205) – Feature branches (207) – $20 for a merged branch (208) – Money doesn't motivate (208) – Money does motivate (209) – The best motivator is clear rules of the game (209) – ABC players (211) – Git flow and release branch (212) – Unlimited number of bugs (213) – Test to break (213) – Down merging (214) – Stabilizing the product (214) – Abandoned branches (215) – Obstacles (216) – Acceptable vs. perfect quality (216)

ADRIAN looks at me and smiles, "Jyoti does have a point. We might pay more attention to our code. Look, this particular bug, it was obvious. Let me show you the code," he opens the laptop. Jyoti looks at me.

"No need, dude, I'll look at it later. You seem to be missing the point," I try to stay calm. "We should not blame Chung, this is not effective. Moreover, it's dangerous. It will be a wrong message to all of us. Everybody will just get scared, but the real problem won't be fixed."

"Which is?" he closes the laptop.

| Making programmers responsible for bugs only creates fear and slows down the development.

"Our weak delivery pipeline!" I try to stress the "weak" part. "By scaring programmers, we will only slow down the development.[1] People will be stressed without really having any instruments to release from the stress. Just asking everybody to 'write better code' doesn't really help, because they never know where the next trouble will be, who will cause it, or how much money will it cost. It's like walking on a minefield: a permanent stress—they never know which part of the code will explode next. We just shift the responsibility for the quality to the shoulders of programmers and tell them: 'there are mines over there, walk carefully!' Imagine what they feel."

---

[1] Julia Evans, *Fear makes you a worse programmer*, https://goo.gl/MeLGxN, 2014: "If you're scared of making changes, you can't make something dramatically better, or do that big code cleanup. Maybe you can't even deploy the code that you already wrote and tested, because it feels too scary. You just want to stick what's sort-of-working, even if it's not great."

"You are exaggerating," Adrian smiles.

"Well, maybe a bit. We need productive and effective people, who are capable of writing a lot of code and never get tired. By giving them ambiguous rules of the game we are killing their motivation and distress them.[1] They will not write better code, they will quit."

JYOTI asks: "What is distress?" I respond: "Well, there is a theory[2] that says that there are two types of stress: eustress and distress. The former, even though it's uncomfortable, leads to personal growth, while the latter has negative implications. Eustress comes and goes, staying with us only temporarily. It challenges us.[3] However, a persistent stress that is not resolved through coping or adaptation is known as distress, may lead to anxiety, withdrawal, and depressive behavior."[4]

"Interesting. I didn't know that stress could be positive," she smiles.

"It is. Without stress there would be no progress, no growth,

---

[1] Jeremy Stranks, *Stress at Work: Management and Prevention*, Elsevier, 2005: "Positive stress is one of the outcomes of competent management and mature leadership where everyone works together and their efforts are valued and supported. It enhances well-being and can be harnessed to improve overall performance and fuel achievement. It is the negative stress, or distress, such as that arising from having to meet set deadlines or delegate responsibility, commonly leading to ill health, that needs to be considered by employers as part of a stress management strategy."

[2] Hans Selye, *Confusion and controversy in the stress field*, Journal of Human Stress, Volume 1, Number 2, 1975.

[3] Debra L. Nelson et al., *Health psychology and work stress: A more positive approach*, Handbook of occupational health psychology, Volume 2, 2003: "Eustressed workers are engaged, meaning that they are enthusiastically involved in and pleasurably occupied by the demands of the work at hand. Workers can be engaged and perceive positive benefits even when confronted with extremely demanding stressors."

[4] James Campbell Quick, *Preventive stress management in organizations*, 2nd Edition, American Psychological Association, 2013: "The stress response is highly functional when properly managed, leading to eustress and elevated performance. However, there is also a downside to the stress response, for individuals and for organizations, which is called distress. Distress occurs when the stress response is not well managed or when it goes awry."

and no motivation.[1] We definitely need stress in order to achieve something.[2] However, the stress must go away the moment the goal is achieved. When I see a new task or a bug in the morning, I get stressed out: something is not working, someone needs me to create something new for them, I'm uncertain about the result, I'm scared to break the code that already works, and so on. I start working with the task in order to get out of the stress zone. Now, imagine, I finish working, my code goes to production, and I don't know whether it's the end of the story or, the next morning, Bao will show up in the office with a smiley face, saying that a few hundred customers just lost their credit card numbers because of me. See?" I take a short pause. "The end of the task will not take me out of the stress zone. I will stay there at night, while being at home, and in the morning, while driving to the office. I will literally live in the stress zone. My stress will become a distress, which may even lead to some serious health issues, like depression."[3]

"I agree!" she exclaims.

> To avoid distress, responsibility must be defined individually and explicitly.

"Of course you do," I smile, "This problem is relevant to all of us. We all are distressed, and the more group responsibility we have on our shoulders, the less productive we become and the more depressed. Being responsible for everything means being responsible for nothing and, at the same time, permanently being

---

[1] ★Gary P. Latham, *Work motivation: History, theory, research, and practice* Sage Publications, 2007.

[2] Matthew Blake Hargrove et al., *Generating eustress by challenging employees: Helping people savor their work*, Organizational Dynamics, Volume 42, 2013: "We suggest that managers generate healthy stress among their employees."

[3] C. H. Hansen et al., *Screening medical patients for distress and depression: does measurement in the clinic prior to the consultation overestimate distress measured at home?*, Psychological Medicine, Volume 43, Number 10, 2013.

ready to be blamed.[1] It's a position of a slave, excuse me for saying this. Instead, the right formula is when everybody is responsible strictly for their tasks and areas of control. I must not care at all about what happens after my task is finished. My code is merged to the 'master'? I'm done. This is the only possible and valid definition of done: If you accepted my code, don't blame me for any mistakes afterwards," I smile and wonder how bad my words may sound to someone who is used to the pro-communistic "group responsibility and accountability" mindset. Isn't it close to what Marx expected to happen in the society of the future?

ADRIAN says sarcastically: "Sounds like an extreme individualism[2] to me."

"Yes, it is. Of course, the team will not work effectively and will not even exist, if there is no glue between the selfish and greedy individuals."[3]

---

[1] Susan Michie, *Causes and management of stress at work*, Occupational and Environmental Medicine, Volume 59, Number 1, 2002: "Situations that are likely to cause stress are those that are unpredictable or uncontrollable, uncertain, ambiguous or unfamiliar, or involving conflict, loss or performance expectations."; "If stress persists, there are changes in neuroendocrine, cardiovascular, autonomic and immunological functioning, leading to mental and physical ill health."

[2] Harry C. Triandis, *Individualism-Collectivism and Personality*, Journal of Personality, Volume 69, Number 6, 2001: "In individualist societies people are autonomous and independent form their in-groups; the give priority to their personal goals over the goals of their in-groups, they behave primarily on the basis of their attitudes rather than the norms of their in-groups, and exchange theory adequately predicts their social behavior."; "The more complex the culture, the more individualist It is likely to be."

[3] Harry C. Triandis et al., *Allocentric versus idiocentric tendencies: Convergent and discriminant validation*, Journal of Research in Personality, Volume 19, Issue 4, 1985: "Those who are allocentric (*they center their attention and actions on other people rather than themselves*) are more likely to emphasize the values of cooperation, equality, and honesty, and those who are idiocentric (*they tend to focus more on their own goals and needs rather than in-group ones*) to emphasize the values of comfortable life, competition, pleasure, and social recognition. Those who were allocentric reported receiving more social support and a better quality of social support; those who were idiocentric were higher in achievement motivation, alienation, anomie, and reported greater loneliness."

"Come on, we're not selfish and greedy," Jyoti smiles.

"Unfortunately we are not," I reply seriously. "We used to work because of stress, not because of greed or interest. And I don't mean us here, in our team only. I mean the entire industry. Look at this situation with Chung. A few minutes ago you were planning to go find the poor dude and blame him for all the money we lost this morning. That would be a lot of guilt on his young shoulders. He would be super stressed for the next few weeks. And he would become very manageable. He would do anything we tell him. This is the easiest way for any boss to manage and control his people: stressing them out and making them guilty. They will constantly try to get out of the stress zone and will never succeed. It will work, for quite a lot of time, until they burn out and quit. Then, they take a rest for a few months, relax, and find a new boss, who will start developing a new wave of guilt in them. The key success factor," I show the quote marks with both hands, "in this model is the group responsibility. Just make us responsible for the overall result of the project and we will be distressed forever."

> Attributing bugs to their authors doesn't make them more responsible, only more scared.

"How can you imagine it any other way? People wouldn't be responsible for anything? What kind of team would it be? I don't get it," Jyoti says and I feel that she still wants me to admit that this morning bug was our failure.

"I didn't say they won't be responsible for anything, don't get me wrong. I want us to be responsible for our individual tasks and our personal mistakes. Let's take a look at this mistake Chung made yesterday. Let me show you how I would like to see the situation and you tell me what's wrong with it. First, Adrian asks Chung to implement that feature or fix the bug, I don't know what it was ..."

"He was fixing Dennis's bug, actually," Adrian interrupts.

"See, you're calling mistakes by the names of the people who made them, which is absolutely wrong!" I exclaim. "That's exactly the point I'm trying to make: we must not blame programmers for their bugs. They belong to them only until the code is merged to the repository. After that, all bugs are ours!" I exclaim and think to myself: Would it be too dangerous to release programmers from their personal responsibility for mistakes? What will they be left with if the management doesn't catch up and fill the gap with a better management system? Wouldn't we create a bigger problem than we have now?

JYOTI smiles, "OK, OK, please continue your story." I continue: "So, Adrian asks Chung to fix our bug," I emphasize 'our' and they both smile. "Chung creates a branch[1] and starts working with it. He is a junior developer. Let's say he has no idea what is right and what is wrong in this repository. So, he inevitably makes mistakes. Many of them. Some of them are very serious. But he doesn't care, because he knows that our delivery pipeline is super strong and won't let any serious problems slip through to production. In a few hours or days, he finishes his work and runs all unit tests. Some of them are red, because he made some mistakes. He fixes the mistakes, if he can. If he can't, he goes around the office, asking for help. I don't know what he would be doing, actually. Maybe he would ask on StackOverflow, maybe demand help through project documentation, doesn't matter. What matters is that at this stage all problems belong to him. Anything that goes wrong, it's his fault. If unit tests are red, it's his fault. If the build is not clean, it's his fault. He may ask for help, but we don't owe him anything here. He is entirely on his own."

"Sounds harsh," Adrian comments.

"Well, yes, it is harsh. It is a very stressful time for him. He has to fix the bug, but he doesn't really know how. In order to put an end to the stress, he has to see his branch being merged to the repository. It's similar to what athletes feel when they run for a hundred meters. They need to get to the finish line and it's

---

[1] Len Bass, *DevOps: A Software Architect's Perspective*, Pearson Education, 2015: "The problem with doing all of the development on one trunk is that a developer may be working on several different tasks within the same module simultaneously. When one task is finished, the module cannot be committed until the other tasks are completed. To do so would introduce incomplete and untested code for the new feature into the deployment pipeline."

a very stressful activity. However, they know for sure where that goddamn line is and they know that, right after it, the stress will completely go away."

"You like metaphors, don't you?" Jyoti smiles.

> What motivates us best of all is isolated problems with definitive solutions at their ends.

"They help us understand the point better, don't they? So, back to the Chung's story. He has a branch and he makes all the necessary changes there. He knows that in order to accept his branch our delivery pipeline has to make sure it doesn't violate our quality rules and doesn't lower our quality bar. He knows the rules: the build must be clean, all unit and integration tests must be green, there should be no static analysis violations, and, of course, a few code reviews must raise no serious concerns. He makes all the necessary efforts to get his code through these barriers. He knows that right after the finish line is crossed and the branch is in the repository, he is free. So, eventually, it happens. We accept his branch, merge it in and let him go. We even celebrate this event somehow. Maybe even give him some monetary reward, say, $20," they both smile.

J YOTI says, "Money is not everything people work for, you know? There were some studies[1] confirming that the association between salary and job satisfaction is very weak. Moreover, some say[2] that, when rewards are tangible and foreseeable, intrinsic motivation decreases. In other words, people simply don't enjoy working for

---

[1] Timothy A. Judge et al., *The relationship between pay and job satisfaction: A meta-analysis of the literature*, Journal of Vocational Behavior, Volume 77, 2010: "Earnings are only weakly satisfying to individuals even when they confine their satisfaction to an evaluation to their pay."

[2] Edward L. Deci, *A Meta-Analytic Review of Experiments Examining the Effects of Extrinsic Rewards on Intrinsic Motivation*, Psychological Bulletin, Volume 125, Number 6, 1999: "Careful consideration of reward effects reported in 128 experiments leads to the conclusion that tangible rewards tend to have a substantially negative effect on intrinsic motivation, with the limiting conditions we have specified. Even when tangible rewards are offered as indicators of good performance, they typically decrease intrinsic motivation for interesting activities."

money nowadays, especially programmers.[1] And if they do, the benefits of extrinsic rewards tend to decay over time."[2]

"I have heard that, yes, but I believe most of those studies[3] do not contradict to the good old carrot-and-stick philosophy. Some of them actually confirm[4] that what motivates us most of all is being in control of our own successes and failures. Some dispute[5] the claim that extrinsic rewards always damage intrinsic motivation, and so on. Look at sport competitions, which seem to be one of the most stressful activities humans do. Athletes seem to have a lot of motivation and manage to achieve excellent results having very strict rules of the game, and a very obvious explicit package of carrots and sticks. If we have something very similar for programmers, they will be grateful."

> The best motivator is a set of obvious and fair rules with decent rewards.

"Why give Chung twenty dollars, then?" she smiles.

"The best motivator, in my opinion, is clear rules of the game, in which nobody can cheat, in combination with a strong com-

---

[1]Sarah Beecham et al., *Motivation in Software Engineering: A systematic literature review*, Information and Software Technology, Volume 50, Issues 9–10, 2008: "A good salary can be motivating in unstable environments and early in an engineer's career, although salary is usually considered a hygiene factor."

[2]D. J. Stipek, *Motivation and instruction*, Handbook of educational psychology, Macmillan, 1996.

[3]Emily R. Lai, *Motivation: A literature review*, Person Research's Report, 2011: "Tangible rewards can be especially damaging to intrinsic motivation, as can negative performance feedback and positive feedback when it is administered controllingly."

[4]Jacquelynne S. Eccles et al., *Motivational beliefs, values, and goals*, Annual Review of Psychology, Volume 53, 2002: "Not knowing the cause of one's successes and failures undermines one's motivation to work on the associated tasks."

[5]Suzanne Hidi et al., *Motivating the academically unmotivated: A critical issue for the 21st century*, Review of Educational Research, Volume 70, Number 2, 2000: "Although we acknowledge the positive effects of individual interest, intrinsic motivation, and the adoption of mastery goals, we urge educators and researchers to recognize the potential additional benefits of externally triggered situational interest, extrinsic motivation, and performance goals."

petition.[1] As those psychologists would say: an ability to be in control of our own successes and failures. Money, as a reward, can only be used where the rules are absolutely transparent and unambiguous. The money by itself is not the goal,[2] the rules are."

"If this is so obvious, as you say, why is it most other software teams don't practice this approach? At least, I haven't seen any companies where such strict rules of motivation and delivery are

---

[1] Morton Deutsch, *Cooperation and Competition* in *The Handbook of Conflict Resolution: Theory and Practice*, Jossey-Bass, 2006: "Competition can vary from destructive to constructive: unfair, unregulated competition at the destructive end; fair, regulated competition in between; and constructive competition at the positive end. In constructive competition, the losers as well as the winners gain. Thus, in a tennis match that takes the form of constructive competition, the winner suggests how the loser can improve, offers an opportunity for the loser to learn and practice skills, and makes the match an enjoyable or worthwhile experience for the loser. In constructive competition, winners see to it that losers are better off, or at least not worse off than they were before the competition."

[2] A. L. LeDuc Jr, *Motivation of Programmers*, SIGMIS Database, Volume 11, Number 4, 1980: "Money as an external motivator is an endlessly fascinating subject. If there is a successful external motivator, it would seem that money should be it; it is tangible, quantifiable and can be traded as an individual desires. For many years in the programming business, it was clear that money was a strong motivator—it drove people into the profession, in Gold Rush fashion. It moved them from job to job and it 'rewarded' them for heroically long hours. And yet, things have changed. Nowadays the young DP student is more likely to come to programming because it is fun or because it offers job possibilities and future security, not because it offers riches. For most people, money is a singularly poor external motivator, as many authorities now believe. Even if money is a motivator, it loses its power with repetition. It may be useful, in that case, only as an attention getter."

in place. Why is that?"[1]

"It's a good question. I believe that even though strict and transparent rules are beneficial for self-motivated and ambitious programmers, who enjoy being challenged and grow—'A' players, as Jack Welch calls them[2]—they make up only 20% of any team, in compliance with the famous Pareto principle. The rest of the team consists of 'B' players (70%), who work adequately and 'C' players (10%) who don't work at all. Add weak and incompetent management to the mix and you get the picture: discipline is not appreciated. The majority doesn't like to be challenged and faced by the quality rules and requirements. Instead, they wants to do as little as possible, be paid, and go home to watch TV. The management is too weak to fight with the majority and enforce the rules. The result is obvious: programmers manage their bosses, not the other way around," I look at them and think maybe it's only me who thinks that it's bad? Maybe most software teams and programmers find it perfect that they are not managed by anyone?

JYOTI sighs, "I don't think I fully agree with you, but let's get back to Chung's story and the pipeline. I'm really interested. What should have happened next?"

"When his branch is merged and he got his twenty bucks, he is free to go and pick the next task or a bug to fix. It's not his code

---

[1] Paul S. Licker, *The Japanese Approach: A Better Way to Manage Programmers?*, Communications of the ACM, Volume 26, Number 9, 1983: "Instead of a concern with the total person and his relationship to the organization, management offers tit-for-tat paychecks, narrow specialization, and early obsolescence. With a holistic approach, managers would take a broad view of the work environment rather than focus on specialized tasks such as producing code or debugging. In a holistic environment, a programmer would be responsible for completing programs; the manager, for assuring the programmer does this. But most programmers work in an environment that is not holistic. And those programmers who don't become obsolescent early may opt for the obsolescence of programmer supervision. Still others move into systems analysis. The remainder, suggests Kraft, become a faceless, unpromotable mass of second-class programmers whose sole motivation to work is money."

[2] Jack Welch et al., *Jack: Straight from the Gut*, Business Plus, 2003: "Business has to be fun. For too many people, it's 'just a job.'"

anymore, we will never get back to him with any issues related to the piece he just added or modified," I look her right in the eye. "Never!"

"OK," she laughs, "I got it, never!"

She seems to understand me, but I decide to re-iterate anyway: "We accepted the code, our quality checks said 'all right' and there is absolutely no reason for us to call it Chung's code anymore. We are done with this guy. The first step of the delivery pipeline has been successfully passed."

"What's next?" she asks.

"There are many possible scenarios,[1] but I prefer this one: At some point, your team branches out of 'master' and calls it a 'release branch.' You deploy the code from this branch to a staging web environment. It has to be very similar to the production one.[2] Then, you start testing and breaking it."

"Breaking?" she smiles.

"Yes, as we discussed before, remember? The point of testing is to break the product under tests. Your objective is to find as many bugs as possible and report them. The more you find, the better. But you have to have certain numbers in mind. Say, you should test and break, until you find ten critical defects or the amount of all defects found per day drops below five. Something like that. I'm not sure about the exact numbers, but there should be some measurable exit criteria. We need to know exactly when you will stop testing and the product will be ready for delivery."

"Can't I just tell you when it doesn't have any bugs and that's

---

[1] Lorna Mitchell, *Git Branching Strategies*, **net**, Issue 267, 2015.

[2] Gerald D. Everett, *Software Testing: Testing Across the Entire Software Development Life Cycle*, John Wiley & Sons, 2007: "The goal of a testing environment is to cause the application under test to exhibit true production behavior while being observed and measured outside of its production environment. Achieving this goal can be just as challenging as designing and executing the tests themselves."; "The next kind of testing environment you may find is called a 'staging' environment or a 'migration' environment or a 'deployment' environment. The developers see this environment as the next place their programs go prior to 'going live.' It represents the collection point over time of all finished programming. It also represents an excellent testing environment for the finished programming both as the finished components become available and as the application itself becomes complete."

it? That's what we are doing now—testing it to confirm that it's bug-free," I realize that everything I told her before wasn't really helpful, or maybe she is trolling me.

"That is a very wrong approach! Any product has bugs. Any, Jyoti, any!" I say and she smiles. I guess she thinks that I'm a bit crazy. "It's very wrong to say or assume that a software has no bugs. It does have bugs, a lot of them. The only question is when and who will discover them. Our job, as a team, is to discover and remove them before our customers do. Thus, having a goal of confirming that the software is bug-free is against our primary goal. We need bugs, not an absence of them. The absence of them while the product is in our hands means only one thing—their presence when it shows up in front of a customer. See my point?"

"I guess ..." she says, mostly to calm me down, I feel.

"OK, then your goal is to test, break, and report bugs. Your primary motivation is bugs, nothing else. Moreover, the number of them. The more you find, the better. I would even suggest to pay you and your guys for them."

"Twenty dollars!" Adrian jumps in.

"You guys seem to be very skeptical about money, but I'm telling you, it may really work if the management system is properly designed. Anyway, forget the twenty dollars. My point is that Jyoti has to be motivated to find bugs and the number of them should matter most. We should incentivize her and her department to show us big numbers. At some point in time, it will become more and more difficult for them to find bugs in the new release. We all know that they are still there, the bugs, but the cost of finding each of them gets higher every day. At some moment, when the numbers are big enough, we make a decision that the release is ready to go."

> The product is ready for release when testers can't find any more bugs, despite being explicitly motivated for that.

Even though I have never seen this product release concept being verbalized and preached by the management of software teams, they do work according to it. They release when the manager, or the entire team, if they don't emphasize the manager's role, feel that it's the right time to do it. They don't collect metrics, don't know how many bugs were found and reported, they very often don't even track them. But their feeling is based on metrics, even though they're grounded by numbers. They feel that the product is ready when the stream of bugs "doesn't look scary anymore." Maybe this "gut feeling" is good enough and we don't need metrics?

A<small>DRIAN</small> asks, "Wait, what about fixing the bugs?" and I reply: "Right, I forgot. So, all bugs Jyoti finds she reports to us, where each bug has a property, pointing it to the release number, which is equal to the Git branch name. Bugs are assigned to programmers and they have the highest priority, comparing to all other tickets. Well, this priority question is not so binary. Maybe some of them will be minor and will not be fixed urgently or never. It's a decision management should make for each particular bug. I mean you, Adrian, it's your decision. The job of Jyoti is to find bugs, our job is to fix them. Every fix should be merged to the release branch and also down-merged to the 'master' branch."

"You mean back-porting?"[1]

"Well, it's forward-porting in this case. The changes merged into the release branch must show up in the 'master' as well. Thus, the entire release branch has to be merged 'down' to the 'master.' There will be some technical issues, of course, but we will discuss them later, when the time comes. What is important is that the release branch must not diverge from the 'master' or we will have big issues later. It must be the place for fixing bugs in an isolated way. The point of having this branch is to stabilize the product under test. If we were to test the 'master,' we would never finish, because it is under very aggressive development. We would simply test forever because the speed of finding bugs will never decrease. Programmers will introduce new ones every day and Jyoti will discover them. They will fix, she will discover new ones. It's a

---

[1] Yi Li et al., *Semantic Slicing of Software Version Histories*, IEEE Transactions on Software Engineering, Volume 44, Number 2, 2018: "Occasionally, developers need to migrate a specific functionality—e.g., a feature or a bug fix—from one branch to another. Back-porting is one example of such a migration, when changes made in a newer version of software are ported to an earlier one in order to provide the updated functionality to all users."

never ending process. In order to reach some more or less stable point, we need to isolate developers and testers."

"What if that point in time never happens?" she asks. "Or just takes too long."

"This may happen. We may create a release branch, start testing and breaking it, report bugs, and wait for the metric to reach a desirable number. But it will not happen because ... I don't really know because of what," I pause | A release attempt may be abandoned if testing has too much success in finding bugs.

and think. "OK, for example, one of the features we branched was not fully implemented in 'master'—we basically branched a very unstable and incomplete piece of code. We try to stabilize it, but it doesn't happen. In the mean time, more changes are already added to 'master' and the code is more stable there. What do we do? We just drop the release branch, delete it and start from scratch. We may call it an 'abandoned release attempt,' which is a perfectly normal situation. Of course, we should try to avoid them, but they may happen. We won't lose anything except time."

"Which is a very important thing," Adrian smiles.

"Of course, it is, but quality is more important, isn't it? Well, depends on the project, of course. In our case, when our customer base is rather big and market reputation is important, quality matters most. Am I wrong?"

"You are right," Jyoti confirms. "What's next?"

"When the release branch is ready, we deploy it to production. That's it. There is no more magic, just three steps in the delivery pipeline: merging Chung's branch into 'master,' stabilizing the release branch, and deploying the release branch to production. The first step rejects all the bad parts from programmers, the second step tries to break the product in all possible ways, and the third one just delivers the result to customers. That's why it's called 'delivery' pipeline—because the overall goal of all this is to deliver our product to our customers."

A<small>DRIAN</small> asks, "But you said that there should be many obstacles in the way. Now there are only three steps. Where are the obstacles?"

"There must be many of them. First, we must do everything we can to reject Chung's branch. We must put tools, validators, checkers, testers, automated tests, and manual reviews in its way. It must be very difficult to merge anything except the absolutely highest quality. Second, we must make your testing very complicated and powerful, to break the product in all possible ways, including performance, stress, load, usability, and A/B testing.[1] Your department should be the strongest in the company," I look at Jyoti. "You must have programmers, engineers, designers, and architects, who are capable of creating automated obstacles and using existing tools and instruments. Since you will be motivated to find as many bugs as possible, it will be in your primary interest to not drop the speed of bug discovery in every next release."

"So, we will never release, then?" Jyoti asks.

"We will, since management doesn't really need perfect quality. Some quality at some point will be considered as acceptable and we will release."

"We should not reveal this strategy to our customers," she smiles.

"You are right, they must not know that the product they see still has a strong flow of bugs and a long backlog of already found but not yet fixed ones. But this is the reality, which a software team either embraces and manages, or is afraid of.[2] I vote for the

---

[1] Rex Black et al., *Foundations of Software Testing ISTQB Certification*, Cengage Learning EMEA, 3rd Edition, 2012.

[2] Barry W. Boehm et al., *Software Risk Management*, IEEE Software, Volume 14, Number 3, 1997: "Software managers would be more inclined to acknowledge and manage their risks if they were more aware of comparable organizations that had already chosen to move in that direction. Although there is evidence that software risk management is beginning to affect many companies and government agencies, published word of that experience remains minimal. There is a reason why this has been and will probably continue to be true: Doing software risk management makes good sense, but talking about it can expose you to legal liabilities. If a software product fails, the existence of a formal risk plan that acknowledges the possibility of such a failure could complicate and even compromise the producer's legal position. There is reason to suspect that most risk management practitioners have adopted a 'don't ask, don't tell' attitude toward publication of their successes"

first option. You?"

"I don't know, it all sounds new and a bit weird," she smiles peacefully.

"Let's have lunch, then," and we all stand up.

The conflict between testers and programmers, even though it may sound logical on paper, is rarely possible in real life. Mostly because they are people and stay close to each other in one office and in one project environment.

> Quality is a product of a conflict between programmers and testers.

They tend to avoid confrontation, both at the interpersonal and professional levels. Testers feel bad when they find bugs and programmers feel bad when they make them. Ideally, this must not happen. Instead, testers must be rewarded when they find bugs and programmers must be rewarded when they fix them. Bugs are the fuel of a software project. As any fuel is toxic and dangerous, bugs seem to scare us too. Is it possible for a software team to achieve such a high level of mastery when bugs are welcome and everybody celebrates them?

Epilogue

In the next volume, Jyoti will develop a new testing policy and present it to Tony for approval; Dennis will add static analysis to the automated build cycle; they will try to start counting bugs coming from manual testers; performance indicators for programmers will be introduced as an experiment; continuous integration will be discussed in detail and its pitfalls will be analyzed; independent technical reviews will be introduced and Tony will try to hire a remote consultant for that; and Tony will hire an outsourcing team to increase the speed of development.

USA, Ukraine, Russia
2017–2018
Designed in LaTeX

Index

ABC players, 211
accident, 76
accountability, 29, 39, 127, 205
achievements, 147
action, 138
Adams, J. Stacy, 22
Adams, Scott, 63
Adkins, Lyssa, 31
Adzic, Gojko, 90
agenda, 52, 149
aggression, 193
Agile, 31, 49, 67, 164
Aiello, Bob, 73
Alexander, 40
algorithms, 100, 153, 157
allies, 158
Allott, Robin, 53
Altman, Sam, 57
altruism, 95, 97–99
amateurs, 28
Ammann, Paul, 119
Andreoni, James, 81
Andriole, Stephen J., 90
Androutsellis-Theotokis, Stephanos, 46
animals, 43
Anthes, Gary H., 30
Anthony, Robert, 150
anti-depressants, 138, 168
anxiety, 203

API, 59
   RESTful, 103
Apple, 144
appreciation, 100
aquarium, 21
architect, 16, 35, 37, 38, 68, 106–109, 137, 139, **140**, 140, 141, 143, 145, 146
architecture, 16, 105, 153
Aristotle, 148
arrogance, 35
art, 24, 42, 100, 162, 163
Assembly, 154
atheism, 128, 152
athletes, 207, 209
attitude, 129, 147, 159
attractiveness, 168
Atwood, Jeff, 93
authority, 39, 42, 106, 107, **143**, 144
auto-formatting, 188
automated build, 198
autonomy, 37
Axelrod, Saul, 81
Ayewah, Nathaniel, 188

Babula, Michael, 98
Bacchelli, Alberto, 73
Bach, James, 31

221

back-porting, 214
backlog, 216
bank, 148, 150, 176
Barker, Richard, 29
Bass, Bernard M., 94, 100
Bass, Len, 146, 207
Bateman, Thomas S., 81
battles, 40
Baumeister, Roy F., 51
Beck, Kent, 71, 72, 74, 143
Beecham, Sarah, 209
beer, 34
behavior, 167
Beizer, Boris, 113, 114
benefits, 95
Bentley, 138
Bercovitch, Jacob, 105
Berkel, Laura Van, 39
Bertolino, Antonia, 112
best practices, 46
betrayal, 17, 58
Bettenburg, Nicolas, 195
Bhatt, Pankaj, 78
Bible, 22
bicycles, 171
billionaires, 149
binary, 156
birthday, 20
Bitcoin, 171
Black, Rex, 113, 123, 216
blackmail, 41
blame, 60, 86, 88, 108, 143, 196,
    201, 202, 205, 206
body, 18
Boehm, Barry W., 216
Boehm, Christopher, 39
Bohns, Vanessa K., 52
Bolino, Mark C., 133
Bolton, Patrick, 40
Bonnera, Sarah E., 82
Booch, Grady, 107
books, 147

boolean algebra, 153
boss, 19, 24, 40, 41, 101, 108,
    126, 130, 131, 135,
    137, 144, 168, 206
bottlenecks, 61, 179
boxing, 192
brackets, 187, 188
brains, 149
branches, 72, 74, 190, 211
    abandoned, 215
    feature, 207
Braude, Jacob M., 147
Brooks, Fred, 158
Brown, Simon, 145
budget, 89, 97
bug tracking, 63
bugs, 33, 63, 71, 111, 113, 118,
    122, 196, 197,
    199–202, 206, 212–214
    pay for, 123, 124
    unlimited amount, 213
    unlimited amount of, 118
build, 72, 78
    pre-flight, 72
bullying, 57, 61
Burgess, Heidi, 105
Burkeman, Oliver, 59
bus factor, 179
business, 70, 86, 100, 157
bytes and bits, 153

C, 154
cables, 76
cages, 21, 22
calculator, 139
California, 36, 70
camera, 143
cancer, 174, 175
capitalists, 147
car, 147
career, 33, 34, 137, 138, 181
Carpenter, Arthur L., 78

222

carriers, 21, 23, 43, 44
Carroll, John, 153
carrot and stick, 100, 129, 185, 209
cars, 56, 137
Chacon, Scott, 74
changes, 193, **200**
chaos, 64, 65, 102, 142, 144, 173, 176, 186
Charette, Robert N., 29
charisma, 93
chats, 145, 178
Chaudhry, Abdul Qayyum, 95
Chauhan, Naresh, 113
checkers, 216
Chess, Brian, 188
Chevrolet, 19
chief, 144
children, 53, 54, 84, 138, 173
Christianity, 127
Chulani, Sunita, 122
CIA, 150
citizens, 195
　good, 150, 151
clarity, 170
Cloke, Kenneth, 104
Cochran, Craig, 116
Cockburn, Alistair, 30, 31
code, 91
　ahead, 160
　formatting, 183
　monkeys, 181
　reviews, 73, 79, 80, 86, 142, 216
　style, 183, 189
　throw away, 90
Code Churn, 165
Coelho, Jailton, 46
coercion, 58, 126, 131, 135
coffee, 24, 174
　machine, 20
Cohen, Cynthia F., 116

Cohen, Jason, 79
Cohn, Mike, 30, 164
cold-heartedness, 167
college, 153
comfort, 162
commanders, 40
commission, 176
commitment, 25
communism, 100
community, 27, 47
companies
　big vs. small, 20
compassion, 127
compensation, 146
competition, 209
competitors, 19
compilers, 46, 155
complaints, 132, 197
complexity, 99
components, 155
compromise, 105
computer science, 156
concurrency, 62
conflict, 103, 104, 107, 132, 193, 217
　between speed and quality, **201**
　resolution technique, 105
　　lose-lose, 105
　　win-lose, 105
　　win-win, 106
Conger, Jay A., 94
Conner, Shawn, 41
consensus, 105
consequences, 129
continuous delivery, 26
contract, 42
contribution, 159
control, 28, 38, 40, 54, 130, 140, 173, 191, 206, 209, 210
Converse, Sharolyn, 108
Coplien, James O., 180

Cormen, Thomas H., 153
corporate values, 127
country, 32
cowardice, 173
CPUs, 155
Craigslist, 17, 33
credentials, 33
Cromity, Jamal, 181
cruelty, 167
cryptocurrency, 171
CTO, 137, 138
cubicles, 157
customers, 70, 80, 187, **197**, 199, 204, 215, 216
cynicism, 167

Dagenais, Barthélémy, 46
danger, 96, 202
data, 103, 137
database, 49, 142
Date, C. J., 153
dating, 18, 28
Davis, Harold, 79
Davis, James H., 95
De Dreu, Carsten K. W., 162
De Palma, Brian, 148
deadline, 127
death, 53
Deci, Edward L., 83, 208
decision making process, 108
decisions, 24, 109, 139
decomposition
 of complexity, 99
dedication, 25
defects, 118, 183
 in management, 96, 97
definition of done, 87, 88
deliverables, 29
delivery pipeline, 193, 196–200, 202, 208, 215
Delumeau, Jean, 53
demands, 131

DeMarco, Tom, 135
democracy, 21, 107, 109, 144, 145
deployment, 33, 142
 blue-green, 198
depression, 130, 139, **203**, 204
design, 106, 142, 153
designers, 143, 153, 157, 159, 160
 the era of, 159
Desor, Didier, 21
despise, 41
Deutsch, Morton, 210
DevOps, 19
dictators, 32, 144, 145
disaster, 179
discharging, 173
discipline, 32, 40, 41, 108, 158, 170, 185, 186
discoveries, 154
distress, 174, 175, 203, 204
division of labor, 22
doctor, 113, 174
documentation, 108, 158, **176**, 177, 178, 187, 207
documents, **178**, 178
dogs, 185, 186
domination, 24, 43
drinking, 147
Durkheim, Emile, 22
Dustin, Elfriede, 80, 118, 195

Eccles, Jacquelynne S., 209
Eckhardt, Evert, 136
ecosystem, 158
editors, 155
education, 126, 149, 153, 156
Eeles, Peter, 144
effectiveness, 171, 173
egoism, 95, 98–100, 151
Ehrenreich, Barbara, 58
electricity, 186

elite, 154, 156
Ellison, Larry, 149
emails, 145
embarrassment, 33
emotions, 51, 56, 92, 136, 167, 168, 172
empathy, 51, 53, 56, 127
empire, 57
employee, 18
employers, 18, 24, 34
employment, 17
encryption, 153
enemies, 41, 46, 145, 158
Engels, Friedrich, 43
enslavement, 127
environment, 142, 158
equity, 22
equity theory, 22, 95
errors, 143
ethics, 44
Europe, 156
eustress, 203
Evans, Julia, 202
Everett, Gerald D., 212
evil, 151, 189
excuses, 135, 136
executives, 27
exit criteria
    of task, 88
Exodus, 22
expectations, 118
experiments, 88
experts, 62, 64, 66, **179**, 179
    subject matter, 180

face-to-face, 177
Facebook, 16, 23, 60, 171
facts, 162
fail fast, 96, 97
fail safe, 97
failures, 18, 97, 197, 201, 209
fairness, 43, 86, 93, 149, 150

fantasies, 19
Farrell-Vinay, Peter, 117
father, 136
fault, 26, 144, 176, 196–198, 207
    personal, 198
fear, 41, 51, 57, 65, 131, 196, 199, 202, 206
Feathers, Michael C., 71
features, 80, 86, 88
feelings, 136, 167
Felstead, Alan, 157
Fenton, Norman E., 136
Ferriss, Timothy, 129, 148
Fielding, Roy T., 135
fight, 102, 106, 108
files, 176
film, 132
film making, 143
filters, 201
FindBugs, 187
finger, 126
finite automata, 153
fire, 126
fire-fighting, 95
firing, 33
flattery, 25, 33
Fogel, Karl, 45
force, 32, 103, 105, 126, 184
forefathers, 129
formalities, 65
formulas, 164
Fortran, 154
Foss, Nicolai J., 135
Fowler, Martin, 139, 198
Frakes, William B., 46
frameworks, 27, 45, 60, 155, 180, 182
freedom, 28, 41, 57, 126, 130
friendship, 56
frustration, 47, 61, 76, 98, 175, 194

fun, 45, 162, 181
Furuyama, Tsuneo, 29
future, 159

game, 31, 165, 192, 203, 209
gasoline, 147
gate keeper, 192
Gates, William, 149, 164
geeks, 154, 156
Gelperin, David, 112
Gert, Bernard, 43
Ghiselli, Edwin E., 135
Giang, Vivian, 181
Giardino, Carmine, 20
Gilb, Tom, 79
Gilbert, Dennis L., 23
Gillies, Alan, 115
girlfriend, 152
girls, 28
Git, 60, 74, 142, 157, 183, 205
Git flow, 212
GitHub, 16, 27
Glass, Robert L., 184, 194
glue, 51
goal, 210
God, 22, 43
golf, 138
good boy, 126
Google, 60, 171, 173
Gousios, Georgios, 73
greed, 99, 100, 130, 151, 185, 205, 206
Green, David G., 57
Greene, Robert, 148
Groskopf, Christopher, 177
growth, 203
guilt, 29, 51–54, 129, 130, 132, 175, 206
    for task failure, 86
    instincts, 131

habitats, 158
habits, 46

hackers, 159, 160
    the era of, 154
hacking, 154
Hall, Gregory A., 165
Hansen, C. H., 204
happiness, 137, 138
happy
    product owner, 86
hard drives, 155
hardware, 154–156
Hargrove, Matthew Blake, 204
Hars, Alexander, 34
Harvey, Steve, 18
hate, 140
health, 204
health assurance, 115
healthcare industry, 200
Hegel, Georg Wilhelm Friedrich, 105
help, 47
Henriques, Gregg, 56
heroism, **31**, 31
Herzberg, Frederick, 85
Hetzel, Bill, 118
Hidi, Suzanne, 209
hierarchy, 21, 22, 39, 61, 168
Highsmith, Jim, 30, 135
Hill, GeePaw, 184
hindrances, 149, 197
Hirschi, Travis, 43
hobby, 156
Hoffman, Martin L., 51
holacracy, 21
Homès, Bernard, 115
honesty, 33, 175
Howe, David, 53
Hughes, Geoffrey, 57
human resources, 24, 156, 157
humans, 136
Humble, Jez, 197
humiliation, 194
humor, 194

Humphrey, Watts S., 111
Hunt, Andy, 71
husband, 34
Hutcheson, Marnie L., 116

ideas, 67, 90, 168, 173
IEEE, 118
IEEE 610, 118
IEEE 830, 89
illusion, 36
independence, 28
individualism, 205
industry, 156
infants, 53
influencers, 24
information, 50, 64, 179
information flow, 65
Inozemtseva, Laura, 76
instinct
    survival, 52
instructions, 39
intelligence, 149
IntelliJ IDEA, 60, 188
interview, 17, 18, 33, 35
investments, 150
investors, 16, 19, 41
iPhone, 137
irrationality, 167
Isaacson, Walter, 144
ISO 9000, 115
ISO 9001, 115
isolation, 197
issues, 190
ISTQB, 75

jackpot, 138
Janzen, David, 71
Java, 18, 23, 44, 50, 54, 62, 75, 96, 147, 149, 184
JavaScript, 23, 156
jeans, 49
Jie Lu, 108
JIRA, 64

job, 16, 155, 181
    full-time, 159
    interview, 156
    market, 180
    satisfaction, 208
    security, 64, 65, 78, 159, 180
    title, 37, 116
Jobs, Steve, 144
Johnson, James, 90
joke, 57, 184, 186
Jones, Capers, 29, 125
Jones, Roger, 173
Joyce, Richard, 44
JSON, 103, 126
Judge, Mike, 132
Judge, Timothy A., 208
justice, 126

Kan, Stephen H., 120
Kaner, Cem, 115, 125
Kant, Immanuel, 185
Karyagina, Tatiana, 53
Kasparov, Garry, 166
Kasriel, Stephane, 178
Kay, Alan, 3
Keeling, Michael, 143
Kelly, Fred C., 92
Kerr, Steven, 101
Kerzner, Harold, 136
Kimball, Roger, 57
kings, 151
kitchen, 174
Kitchenham, Barbara, 117
Knafo, Ariel, 53
knowledge, 64, 176
    accumulators, 179
    gaps, 145
    sharing, 61, 179
    silos, 181
Knuth, Donald E., 154
Kohn, Alfie, 186

Kojève, Alexandre, 132
Kotter, John P., 127
Kruchten, Philippe, 143

labor, 162
Lai, Emily R., 209
Lakhani, Karim R., 47
Langsworth, Anthony, 140
languages, 27, 180, 182
laptops, 159
Larman, Craig, 30
Las Vegas, 147
Latham, Gary P., 204
laws, 32, 138, 158
Lawson, Nolan, 45
lawyers, 138
laziness, 90, 92, 95, 99, 128, 130, 136, 141, 170, 185
leader, 144
leadership
    charismatic, 93
    laissez-faire, 93
    transactional, 93
    transformational, 93
lectures, 153
LeDuc Jr, A. L., 210
Lee, Amanda, 47
legacy code, 76
Lenssen, Philipp, 92
Lerner, Jennifer S., 168
Lessing, Doris, 57
lessons learned, 146
Levine, John M., 104
Levy, Steven, 154
Lewis, William E., 119
Li, Yi, 214
liars, 192
libraries, 45, 180
Licker, Paul S., 211
lie, 126
Lieberman, Henry, 124
life, 137
    miserable, 147
limitations, 140
lines of code, 164, 166
logic, 83, 134
losers, 147–150
love, 16, 32, 33, 36, 56, 64, 97
loyalty, 17, 19, 30, 31, 50, 58
luck, 149

MacBook, 137
Machiavelli, Niccolò, 101, 152, 184, 185
magic, 215
magic wand, 149
Maguire, Steve, 199
Maier, Corinne, 23
maintainability, 157, 158, 187
maintenance, 28
majority, 42, 44, 211
management, 21, 28, 63, 102, 132, 173, 200
    by force, 134
    incompetent, 211
    is stupid, 131
    lack of, 103
    mistakes, 116
    strong, 58
    stupid, 96
    weak, 31, 33, 49, 96, 170
managers, 22, 32, 50, 54, 67, 102, 132, 136, 143, 158
    are monkeys, 132
    are noise, 131
market, 19, 34, 194
marriage, 97
Marx, Karl, 43
masters, 132, 163
Mayer, Bernard, 104
McBride, Matthew R., 146
McClelland, David C., 32
McConnell, Steve, 50, 85, 87, 121

McGregor, Douglas, 185
McGregor, John D., 117
McNamee, Stephen J., 149
Medinilla, Ángel, 101
meetings, 65, 103, 107, 109,
    144, 145, 159, 171, 183
  stand up, 49
memory, 155, 157
mentality, 199
mentoring, 142
Mercedes-Benz, 19
merge, 72, 208
  down, 214
meritocracy, 135, 136
merits, 159
metaphor, 184, 208
metrics, 136, 162–164, 166, 169,
    170, 213
Michie, Susan, 205
microservice, 108
millionaires, 38, 149
Milosevic, Dragan, 166
minefield, 202
minority, 42
mission, 25, 159
mistakes, 34, 35, 51, 145,
    195–197, 206, 207
Mitchell, Lorna, 212
money, 16, 19, 21, 33, 38, 41,
    44, 56, 58, 82, 93, 97,
    137, 139, 147, 148,
    150, 151, 168, 193,
    196, 202, **208**,
    208–210
monitors, 155
monkeys, 195
Monperrus, Martin, 179
Monson-Haefel, Richard, 145
mood, 168
Moore, George Edward, 44
Moore, Jr., Barrington, 32
Moorman, Robert H., 98

morality, 43, 185
Moreno-Smith, Myrthala, 175
Morris, Langdon, 31
Moses, 22
mother, 53, 54, 126, 136
  figure, 54
motivation, 54, 74, 78, 83, 86,
    105, 130, 164, 169,
    193, 203, **208**, 208,
    210, 211, 213
  by punishment, 86
mountain, 39
Mountain View, 38
movie, 143, 145
mug, 20
Mulcahy, Rita, 105
Munson, John C., 197
Myatt, Mike, 38
Myers, Glenford J., 63
mystery, 19
myth, 29

Naik, Kshirasagar, 117
Nelson, Debra L., 203
Neusner, Jacob, 186
nice guy, 173
Nietzsche, Friedrich, 43, 128,
    151
non-carriers, 21, 23, 43
Novembre, Giovanni, 52
numbers, 162
Nye, Francis Ivan, 54
Nygard, Michael T., 198

obeyance, 40, 144
obligations, 42
obstacles, 216
Odumeru, James A., 93
Oettingen, Gabriele, 59
offense, 57, 87
office, 16, 18, 34, 42, 49, 157,
    165, 177
  atmosphere, 174

fights, 162
Office Space, 132
open source, 27, 28, 33, 34, 45,
    47, 153, 155, 187
operating systems, 155
orders, 41, 131
Organ, Dennis W., 128, 131
organization
    flat, 134
Oscar, 145
overtime, 130, 132
Owen, Jo, 20

pain, 175
painting, 42
Panko, Raymond R., 199
paradox, 28, 40
parents, 52, 53
Pareto principle, 211
passion, 145
Patton, Ron, 195
paychecks, 17, 19, 64, 123, 159, 163
payroll, 28, 78, 146
peace, 105
penalties, 81
people, 102, 157
    good vs. bad, 27
performance, 49, 81, 136, 167, 171, 173, 216
Perl, 154
personnel, 156
Pfeffer, Jeffrey, 131, 134
philosophy, 30, 76, 196, 200
phone, 24
phone calls, 159
physics, 89
Piketty, Thomas, 21
Pink, Daniel H., 100
plans, 29, 52, 132, 134
playboys, 34
plumbers, 153

PMBOK, 137
PMI, 137
poker, 36
politeness, 24
political correctness, 56, 57
politics, 20, 65
Pollock, Jackson, 42
population, 156
positive thinking, 58
power, 25, 32, 38, 62, 65, 106, 107, 134, 138, 147, 149, 151
Powers, Paul, 18
Prause, Christian R., 75
pre-flight build, 191
pressure, 162
price, 155
pride, 36
principles, 32, 46, 78, 140
priority, 63
prison, 175
prize, 149
problems, 70
process, 31, 103
proctologist, 138
product, 16, 137, 139, 158, 194
product owner, 88
profit, 91, 95, 130, 150
programmers
    good, 130
    of the future, 160
programming
    languages, 154, 156
progress, 104, 203
project, 91, 130, 139, 159
    boring, 16
    co-located, 176
    is your boss, 131
project manager, 137, 139
promises, 136
proof of concept, 92, 107
prostate, 138

protection, 193
protocols, 153
prototype, 90
punishment, 80, 81, 83, 85, 86,
    96, 100, 108, 128, 132,
    136, 137, 185
    corporal, 127
pyramids, 139

qualification, 33
quality, 26, 31, 74, 79, 110, 121,
    140, 141, 184, 187,
    192, 195, 196, 199,
    200, 202, 217
    acceptable, 216
    assurance, 111, 114, 115,
        200
    checking gate, 87
    control, 141, 142, 200
    of code, 60, 186
    wall, 141
Quick, James Campbell, 203

race car, 147
racing horses, 167
racism, 56
rank pulling, 66
Rasmusson, Jonathan, 29
rationality, 167
rats, 21, 44
Raymond, Eric S., 90, 156
re-work, 197, 200
readability, 158
receptionist, 16
recipe, 147
recognition, 100
refactoring, 196
refunds, 176
regulations, 32
rejection, 51
relational theory, 153
relax, 174
release, 117, **212**, 213–215

attempt, 215
reliability, 126
remarks, 131
remote work, 157, 177
Renatus, Flavius Vegetius, 40
replaceability, 159
report, 38, 40
reporting, 38
reputation, 26
requirements, 52, 62, 92, 103,
    177
    refinement, 89
    specification, 89
resistance, 99, 190
resources, 52, 89, 90, 159, 160
respect, 35, 36
responsibility, 26, 28, 31, 42, 83,
    88, 106, 107, 127, **143**,
    144, 173–175, 195,
    196, 200, 202, 204, 205
    for scope borders, 87
    individual, 26, **175**
    individual vs. group, 145
rest, 175
results, 89, 93, 111, 130, 131,
    147, 164
resume, 16, 33
rewards, 80, 83, 85, 93, 100,
    108, 128, 136, 171,
    208–210
    extrinsic, 209
rich, 138, 147, 148, 150, 151
Ries, Eric, 96
Rigby, Peter C., 179
Rind, Bruce, 57
risks, 46, 132, 173, 181
rituals, 51
road, 31
robots, 136, 158, 174, 189, 191,
    192
Rockefeller, John, 147
role, 107

roll back, 196
Romano, Nicholas C., 104
Rome, 127
Roth-Hanania, Ronit, 53
Rothman, Johanna, 120
Rubin, Kenneth S., 88
Ruby, 156
rules, 31, 46, 65, 67, 78, 83,
       139–142, 165, 177,
       184, 185, 190, 192,
       203, 209, 211
    of business, 176
    tight, 142
rumors, 132

Sadowski, Caitlin, 189
safety net, 76
Saiedian, Hossein, 88
salary, 19, 38, 95, 130, 143, 145,
       146, 157, 194
San Francisco, 56
San Jose, 56
Sandred, Jan, 45
satisfaction, 194
scandal, 108
scapegoat, 59, 65
scare, 202
Scarface, 148
Scheff, Thomas J., 51
Schermerhorn Jr., John R., 127
schizophrenia, 168
schools, 154
Schulz-Hardt, Stefan, 104
Schweiger, David M., 105
science, 156
scientists, 153
scope, 86, 87
    of work, 174
screen, 44
Scrum, 49
security, 187
Sedano, Todd, 180

self-obsession, 62
selfishness, 54, 151, 185, 205
Selye, Hans, 203
sense of humor, 60
servers, 17, 26, 103, 197
service provider, 103
Sethi, Vikram, 84
severity, 63
Sewell, Nick, 112
sex, 149
Shafer, Joy, 79
Shahid, Muhammad, 75
shaming, 57
Shepard, Terry, 71
Shepherds, 185
shooters, 174
Shore, Jim, 96
sieve, 198
signals, 166
Silicon Valley, 38, 56, 153, 157
sin, 22
sincerity, 56
skepticism, 90
skills, 158, 190
Skogstad, Anders, 94
slavery, 126, 127, 139, 163
slaves, 126–130, 134, 139, 163,
       205
slogan, 26
smoking, 147
social justice, 135
social protection, 135
socialism, 127
society, 53
sofa, 34
softness, 168
software
    packages, 155
soldiers, 40, 41
solid thinking, 31
soul, 18
space, 158

spaces, 188
specialists, 153
specification
    by example, 90
speculation, 63
speed, 177, **192**, 193, 196, 199, 200
Spinellis, Diomidis, 78
StackOverflow, 181
startup, 16, 17, 27, 138, 149
static analysis, 142, 183, 185, 187, 189, 190, **191**, 192, 198
stealing, 22
Steinmacher, Igor, 47
Stendhal, 99
stick, 127
Stipek, D. J., 209
story points, 167
Stranks, Jeremy, 203
strategies, 25
strawberries, 137, 138, 147
strength, 25, 168
stress, 82, 162, 174, 175, 202, 203, **204**, 206, 207
structure, 174
stupidness, 25
subordination, 40, 138
success, 31, 40, 138, 147, 209
super hero, 141
surgeons, 153
surrender, 102
survival, 20, 41
Sutherland, Jeff, 49
SWEBOK, 75
Swisher, Kara, 178
synchronization, 62
syphilis, 113

t-shirt, 16, 49
talents, 24, 98, 149
taming, 186

Tangney, June P., 52
tasks, 29, 89, 140, 205
    borders of, 87
    tracking, 67
taxes, 147
TDD, 71
tea, 24
teachers, 52, 53, 187
teaching, 142
Teal, Thomas, 134
team, 20, 140, 159, 195
    jelled, 134
    lead, 137
    player, 169, 173
    spirit, 127, 173
temper, 137
Ten Commandments, 22
tension, 162
Ternary Software Inc., 21
testers, 110, 113, 116, 118, 119, 143, 194, **195**, 217
testing, 110, 113, 194, 195, 212, 214
    A/B, 216
    automated, 122
    deliverables, 122
    exit criteria, 212
    goal of, 111, 114
    integration, 198
    is not discrete, 118
    metrics, 119, 124
    motivation, 119
    performance, 216
    stress, 216
    success of, 121
    usability, 216
    weak, 199
tests, 72, 75, 79, 86, 159
    A/B, 198
    automated, 70, 158
    coverage, 74, 75, 141, 142
    scripts, 111

unit, 47, 70, 78, 198, 207
Thaler, Richard H., 168
the right thing, 128
The Ten Commandments, 22
theft, 22, 24, 43
thievery, 43
threat, 64
tickets, 52, 63, 66, 67, 81, 91,
    101, 164, 166, 170,
    174, 175, 178, 196
time, 50
time machine, 89
Timur, 40
Tomassi, Rollo, 151
Toner, Jerry, 128
tools, 88, 91, 187, 216
Torah, 22
toys, 154
Tozzi, Christopher, 45
traffic, 56
training, 186
transaction, 93
transparency, 63, 167, 170
trap, 181
trauma, 102
Trevino, Linda Klebe, 108
Triandis, Harry C., 205
trolling, 212
Trotsky, Leon, 101
trust, 168
tunnel, 197
TV, 34
twenty dollars, 209, 213
Tzu, Sun, 40

UML, 60
uncertainty, 165
underwear, 184
uniformity, 183
Universe, 43
universities, 154
unknowns, 86, 169

unpredictability, 165
usefulness, 128

vacation, 108
vagueness
    of requirements, 86, 89, 99
values, 22, 29
    intangible, 93
venture capitalists, 19
villages, 56
violations, 191
violence, 126, 127
vision, 25
Von Bergen, C. W., 82
voting, 107
Votta Jr., Lawrence G., 109
Vroom, Victor Harold, 83
vulnerability, 168

wages, 22
war, 105
water, 24
Watkins, John, 112
weakness, 25, 105, 168
weather, 132
web design, 156
weekend, 174
Welch, Jack, 211
West, David, 118
West, Joel, 45
Weyuker, Elaine J., 194
whip, 81
white boards, 144, 145
Whitesitt, J. Eldon, 153
Whittaker, James A., 112
Wiegers, Karl E., 79, 86, 88
wife, 97, 138, 173
Williams, Eric, 127
Williams, Laurie, 72
Willmott, Hugh, 128
Windows, 47
winner's gene, 147
winners, 147, 151

wisdom, 187
witch-hunt, 57
wives, 147
wizards, 149
work, 149
work environment, 173

XML, 49, 50
xUnit frameworks, 114
XY Theory, 185

yawning, 176
Young, Michael, 135
Yourdon, Edward, 131
Yukl, Gary, 94

Zhang, Xihui, 121
Zhou, Minghui, 47
Zhou, Yi, 145
Zitek, Emily, 39

Made in the USA
Coppell, TX
12 December 2020